Financial Markets Management

Class XII

by

Harsha Jarani

Financial Markets Management
Class XII
by Harsha Jarani

Copyright © 2024

All Rights reserved.

ISBN: 978-93-69078-60-8

Published by

DOUBLE 9 BOOKS

2/13-B, Ansari Road
Daryaganj, New Delhi – 110002
info@double9books.com
www.double9books.com
Tel. 011-40042856

ABOUT THE AUTHOR

I am highly elated to pen down this book with the aim to foster and imbibe current directional methodological approach that can be fulfilling the recent demands of acquiring the knowledge related Financial Markets Management. Future Perspective of this subject are highly in demand to meet the existing market competition. This book has been systematically crafted to provide crystal clear analytical understanding of the facts and figures associated with the subject and to be students friendly . I'm having keen interest in this subject therefore, it interests me to put forth 180-degree crystal clear information, interpretation, comprehension, analysis and understanding based contents that may fulfil the demand of youngsters of 21st century. I am highly elated with the publication of the First edition of this book. I am sure that it will be able to meet the current demands of aspiring students. I am Ms. Harsha Jarani, has written this book (Financial Markets management) for STD XII CBSE Board. I have been striving hard to bring easy solutions with the publication of this reference book looking at the least number of resources available for the subject in the market.

CONTENTS

Acknowledgment

"I would like to express my heartfelt gratitude to the following individuals for their invaluable support and contributions to this book:

My Husband (Anil Jarani) My son (Manan Jarani) for their unwavering encouragement and guidance throughout my academic and professional journey.

My colleagues and peer, for their valuable insights and feedback on the manuscript.

The financial market regulators and professionals, for their contributions to the development of the financial market ecosystem.

And lastly, to all the readers, for their interest in financial market management and their trust in this book as a valuable resource.

This book is a testament to the power of collaboration and the pursuit of knowledge. I hope it serves as a valuable resource for students, professionals, and anyone interested in financial market management."

Preface

"*Welcome to the world of financial markets! As a Class XII student, you are about to embark on a fascinating journey into the <u>realm of finance, where markets, instruments, and institutions </u> intersect. This book is designed to be your guide and companion as you explore the exciting and dynamic field of financial market management.*

In the following pages, we will delve into the fundamental concepts, theories, and practices that underpin financial markets. From the basics <u>of financial instruments to the intricacies of market regulation, we will cover a wide range of topics that will equip you with a deep understanding of how financial markets work.</u>

Through real-world examples, case studies, and interactive exercises, this book aims to make complex concepts accessible and engaging. Whether you aspire to become a financial analyst, investment banker, or simply a savvy investor, this book will provide you with the essential tools and knowledge to navigate the financial markets with confidence.

Unit 1
Introduction to Securities Market and Trading membership

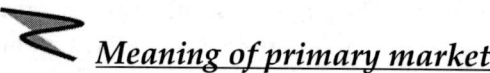 *Meaning of primary market*

Primary Market provides an opportunity to The issuers of securities, <u>both Government and corporations, to raise resources to meet their requirements of investment.</u>

Securities, <u>*in the form of equity or debt,*</u> can be issued in <u>*domestic/ international markets*</u> at *face value, discount or premium.*

The primary market issuance is done either through public issues or private placement. Under Companies Act, 1956, an issue is referred to as public if it results in allotment of securities <u>*to 50 investors or more.*</u>

However, when the issuer makes an issue of securities <u>*to a select group of persons not exceeding 49 and*</u> which is neither a rights issue nor a public issue it is called a private Placement.

Types of primary markets

The primary market comprises two main segments: the equity market and the debt market.

1) Equity market

In this segment, companies issue shares to the public for the first time. This is usually done through an IPO, where a company offers a portion of its ownership to investors in exchange for capital. The equity market allows companies to raise funds for expansion, research and development, debt repayment, or other business activities.

2) Debt market

In the debt market, entities issue bonds or debentures to raise capital. These are essentially loans taken from the public, and in return, the issuer pays periodic interest to the bondholders. The debt market is a crucial avenue for the government and corporations to meet their financial obligations by borrowing from investors.

Functions of primary market

The primary market serves several important functions:

1) Capital formation

The primary function of the primary market is to facilitate the raising of capital by companies and government entities. This capital is essential for financing various projects, expansion plans, and meeting operational needs.

2) Price discovery

The initial sale of securities in the primary market helps in determining their fair market value. The pricing is influenced by factors such as the company's financial health, industry trends, and overall market conditions.

3) Investor participation

The primary market provides an opportunity for individual and institutional investors to become stakeholders in companies or creditors to government entities.

This broadens the investor base and contributes to a more inclusive financial market.

4) Facilitates economic growth

By enabling companies to raise funds for expansion and development, the primary market contributes to overall economic growth. It encourages entrepreneurship, job creation, and innovation.

Advantages

1) Capital infusion

The primary stock market allows companies and governments to raise capital for various purposes, fostering economic growth and development.

2) Investor profit potential

Investors participating in the primary stock market, especially during an IPO, have the potential to benefit from capital appreciation if the value of the securities increases in the secondary market.

3) Transparent pricing

The primary market contributes to price discovery, ensuring that securities are initially priced based on market demand, financial performance, and other relevant factors.

(Note: Price discovery is the process of determining the price of an asset in a marketplace through the interactions of buyers and sellers.)

Disadvantages

1) *Market risks*

The primary market is not immune to market risks. Factors such as economic downturns, industry-specific challenges, and geopolitical events can impact the performance of newly issued securities.

2) *Lack of liquidity*

Unlike the secondary market, where securities can be bought and sold easily, the primary market involves a lock-in period for initial investors. This lack of liquidity can be a disadvantage for those who may need to liquidate their investments quickly.

3) *Information asymmetry*

Investors may face challenges in obtaining accurate and comprehensive information about a company during an IPO. This information asymmetry can pose risks for investors who rely on incomplete or inaccurate data.

4) *Volatile initial performance*

The performance of securities in the secondary market can be highly volatile initially. This volatility may lead to unpredictable outcomes for investors, both positive and negative.

What is a Secondary Market

Secondary Market refers to a market where securities are traded after being offered to the public in the primary market or listed on the Stock Exchange.

Secondary market *comprises of equity, derivatives and the debt markets.* The secondary market is operated through two mediums, namely, the Over-the-Counter (OTC) market and the Exchange-Traded market.

OTC markets are informal markets where trades are negotiated.

The main advantages of secondary markets are as follows:

- Investors can get the cash they need, by selling their shares in a secondary market. Buyers are always present to purchase these valuable *securities*, which are perfect for investors who may be tight on liquidity.

- The secondary market is a **valuable indicator** of what **the current fair valuation** for any company might be.

- The secondary stock market is heavily regulated to keep investor's funds safe. The regulations are rigid as the market provides liquidity and capital formation, for both investors and companies.

- With the power of securities, **investors can mobilise their savings more quickly and easily.** Securities are an important investment vehicle that allows for the quicker mobilisation of funds without compromising on safety or risk-taking.

➤ What are the Limitations of the Secondary Market?

- The prices of securities in a secondary market are subject *to high volatility.* Price fluctuations may *lead to sudden or unpredictable*
- *losses* for investors.
- Buying and selling in a secondary market can be *time consuming.* Investors have to deal with the *tedious paperwork involved before completing final transactions.*
- Investors must be careful with their brokerage commissions because they are taxed every time the trade is made. *Commissions can have a huge impact on investors and may even decrease your profit margin if you're not paying attention.*
- Multiple external factors *influence the investments in a secondary capital market* thereby subjecting them to high risk. These may lead investors' existing valuations to change rapidly within seconds.

💲 *Market Capitalisation*

Market capitalization is defined *as the value of all listed shares of the country's exchanges.* It is computed *on a daily basis.*

Market capitalization of a particular company can be computed as a product of the number of shares outstanding and the closing price of the shares. **Here the number of outstanding shares refers to issue size of the stock**

Here's the formula for calculating market capitalization:

Market capitalisation = number of outstanding shares × price per share

For example, a company with 20 million shares selling at Rs.50 a share would have a market cap of Rs.1 billion.

➤ What is Market Capitalization Ratio?

The Market Capitalization Ratio is defined as market capitalization of stocks divided by GDP. It is used as a measure of stock market size.

💲 *What is Turnover?*

Turnover for a share is computed by multiplying the traded quantity with the price at which the trade takes place. Similarly, to compute the turnover of the companies listed at the Exchange we aggregate the traded value of all the companies traded on the Exchange.

Turnover in the National Stock Exchange (NSE) refers to the total value of sales for delivery-based transactions where stocks are purchased and held for more than one day before being sold. For example, if 100 Reliance shares are bought at Rs 800 and sold at Rs 820, the selling value of Rs 82,000 (820 x 100) can be considered as turnover.

➤ ### *What is the Turnover Ratio?*

The Turnover Ratio is defined as the total value of shares traded on a country's stock Exchange for a particular period divided by marketcapitalization at the end of the period. It is used as a measure of trading activity or liquidity in the stock markets.

Turnover Ratio = Turnover at Exchange / Market Capitalisation at Exchange

Share turnover is a ratio that indicates how easily stocks can be liquidated against cash. It is calculated by dividing the total number of shares traded over a particular period by the number of shares outstanding during that period. A high share turnover indicates a good time to trade stocks, while a low share turnover indicates a bad time to trade stocks

 ## *What are the products?*

The financial products dealt in security market are i) share, bonds, any other scripts of any securities like nature are dealt in the market ii) government securities iii) derivative securities iv) units of collective instrument scheme v) interest and rights in security or any other instrument so declared by the central government Security is normally of three types

    a) Equities

    b) Debt security

    c) Derivative security

Who are participants?

In security market generally there are three types of participant namely

    a) Investor

    b) the issuer

    c) intermediaries

All these participant are regulated by security exchange board of india (SEBI), Reserve Bank of india, ministry of corporate affairs (MCA), Department of Economic affairs (DEA) and Ministry of finance

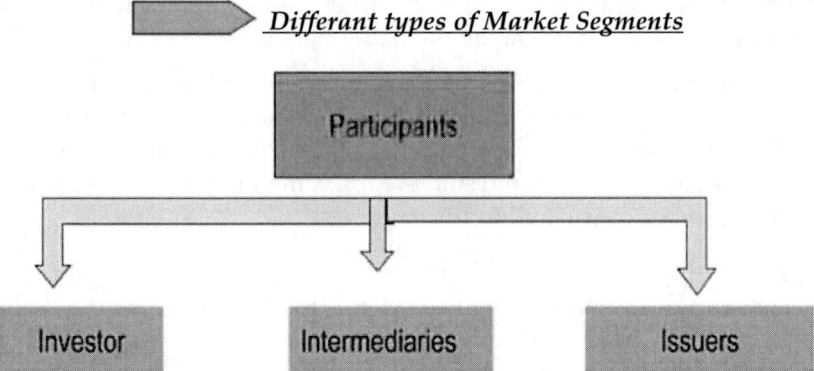

Different types of Market Segments

Participants

Investor   Intermediaries   Issuers

1) _Wholesale debt market_

The wholesale debt market (WDM) segment _is a formal trading platform for trading a wide range of debt securities._ This platform is a fully automated screen based system, which enables members across the country to trade simultaneously with ease and efficiency This segment at NSE commence its operation _in June 1994._

Dealing in a wide range of securities like _central and state government securities, commercial papers, certificate of deposit etc._

Difference between wholesale debt market and retail debt market

Retail debt market is when you and I take a loan and that company sells a part of their loan book to a financial institution. Wholesale debt is when government raises huge amounts of money by issuing Bonds, mostly to banks.

2) _Capital market segment_

The Capital Market segment of the National Stock Exchange of India (NSE) is a trading platform for securities, including equity, preference, debentures, exchange-traded funds, and retail government securities.

The NSE began trading in the Capital Market segment _on November 3, 1994_ and within a year became the largest stock exchange in India in terms of volumes transacted. The trading system of the Capital Market segment is also known as the National Exchange for Automated Trading - Capital Market (NEAT- CM).

A capital market is a financial market where long-term securities are bought and sold. These securities include equity-backed securities and debt instruments that are over a year. Capital markets trade mostly in long-term securities, such as stocks and bonds

3) *Future and option market*

Futures and options are the major types *of stock derivatives trading in a share market.* These are contracts signed by *two parties for trading a stock asset at a predetermined price on a later date.* Such contracts try to hedge market risks involved in stock market trading by locking in the price beforehand.

This segment commence its operation *in june 2000*

Products dealt in the market are *index option, stock option, warrants, debentures etc.*

Futures and options (F&O) are derivative products in the stock market. Since they derive their values from an underlying asset, like shares or commodities, they are called derivatives. Two parties enter a derivative contract where they agree to buy or sell the underlying asset at an agreed price on a fixed date Derivative are trade in capital market also

4) *Currency derivative market segment*

This segment at NSE commenced its operations on August 29, 2008,in a currency derivative contract, an investor buys or sells a specific amount of a currency pair on a predetermined date and rate. The agreed-upon future date is also called the delivery or maturity date for the contract. Currency derivatives can help protect against currency fluctuations and contain volatility risk in foreign currency exchange rates.

➤ *Eligibility Criteria for Membership at NSE*

The standards for admission of members are laid down by the Exchange in terms of corporate structure (shareholding pattern), capital adequacy (Paid up capital), net worth, Interest Free Security Deposit (IFSD), Collateral Security Deposit (CSD), track record, education, experience etc. This is done to ensure quality broking services so as to build and sustain confidence among investors in the Exchange's operation

- The shareholders holding the majority of shares have a dominant role in the affairs of the company.
- In case of any default by the broking entity, the Exchange takes action against the persons who are behind the company.
- The Exchange, therefore, needs to know the background, financial soundness and integrity of the shareholders holding such controlling interest. (DPG)

The Dominant Promoter Group (DPG) is a set of individuals or entities that hold a controlling interest in a corporate trading member of the National Stock Exchange of India (NSE). The DPG can include individuals or entities that jointly or severally hold at least 51% of the member entity's paid up equity capital, either directly or indirectly. In the case of a partnership firm or Limited Liability Partnership (LLP), the term "dominant promoter" can be replaced with "dominant partner"

Hence, during the admission process the dominant shareholders are called for an interview with the Membership Recommendation Committee (MRC).

The DPG can also include the following entities:

- An unlisted company with a net worth of at least Rs. 50 crores and that has been in existence for at least three years
- A listed company
- Central or state government-owned financial or development institutions with a net worth of at least Rs. 50 crores
- Scheduled banks or financial institutions

Unlisted corporate trading member

There are three conditions which makes them to become eligible dominant promoter group

- If a person holds 51 % share in corporate on his own or with his
  - o His relatives
  - o Person falling under the definition of control
  - o Strategic investor

Control : Control is the ability to make the major corporate decisions for a company. While a board of directors might sometimes look like they hold this ability, it ultimately lies with majority shareholders – in other words, any individual or group holding at least a 51% stake.

Strategic investor:- Strategic investors mean the corporates or individual investors that add value to investments they make through industry and personal ties that can assist companies in raising additional capital)

- *Listed corporate trading member*
  If any member declared as promoter in
  - o Any document or
  - o Any offer document for securities to
  - o Public
  - o Existing shareholders
  - o In the shareholding pattern (Whichever is later)

Will be eligible to constitute dominant promoter group

3) _Corporate shareholder to be identified as dominant shareholder:-_

Corporate shareholder is allowed to be identified as dominant shareholders (Dominant Promoter Group - DPG) of a corporate trading member provided

a) Corporate shareholder identifies any person or persons as their dominant promoter group as per the aforesaid norms applicable to the corporate trading member.

b) In case the dominant promoter group consists of more than one corporate shareholder, the dominant promoter group should be identified separately for each such corporate shareholder

4) _Foreign entity_

a) Any foreign entity through their own indian subsidiary company can get the trading membership in the exchange, subject to the following compliance

→ promoting foreign entity should be either bank or insurance organisation and regulated by central bank or any authority of that country

OR

→ The promoting entity should be
   ◆ Brokering house or participant in securities market
   ◆ Should be regulated by relevant authority
   ◆ Such relevant authority should be member of IOSCO

OR

→ The promoting foreign entity is one whose domestic or subsidiary is registered withSEBI

b) The promoting foreign entity shall hold, not less than 51 % of the controlling stake in the applicant company to take trading membership

c) The net worth of the promoting foreign entity should be at least Rs. 50 Crores.

5) _Others :_

The following entities are allowed to be identified as dominant shareholder(s) provided they have a networth of at least Rs.50 crores:

a) Scheduled Banks;

b) Central or State Government owned Finance and/or Development Institutions;

c) Any financial institution registered and regulated RBI, or SEBI, or IRDA;

d) Any other entity that is recognised as a dominant shareholder in the opinion of relevant authority.

A foreign entity can become the part of dominant promoter group (DPG) with the existing trading member by following the prescribed norms specified by RBI, SEBI from time to time

Important points

1) Corporate trading members will also be allowed to change their shareholding pattern so long as such change is within the above norms and the existing Dominant Promoter Group (DPG) continues to hold controlling interest and prior approval from the Exchange is obtained.

2) In case of any change in the DPG, the trading member is required to seek fresh approval of the Exchange

3) Inter-se transfer of shareholding among the dominant promoters, however will be exempt from the formalities

4) Any changes in the shareholding require prior approval from the Exchange, except in case of shareholding changes related to public shareholding in a listed company.

Failure to maintain the required level of shareholding by DPG is treated as a breach of the continuing membership.

This is because the existing DPG would no longer hold controlling interest in the trading member corporation.

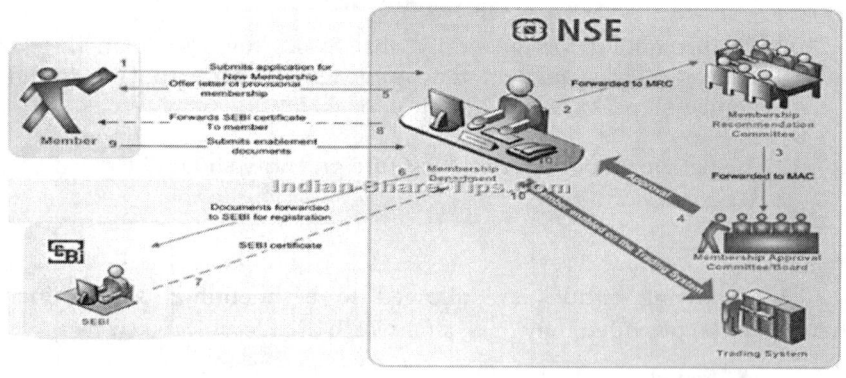

The admission procedure for new membership depicted in above figure is explained below:

1) Applicants are required to submit application form, in the prescribed format along with other relevant documents to the Exchange.

2) The application for new membership is then forwarded to Membership Recommendation Committee(MRC).

3) *The MRC conducts interviews of the applicants for trading membership.*

- In case of corporates, the dominant shareholder and designated directors;
- In case of individuals, the individual himself and
- In case of partnership firms – two designated partners have to appear for the interview)

4) The MRC recommends the names for admission of trading members to the Membership Selection Committee (Sub-committee of board of directors)/Board of directors of the Exchange.

5) Membership Selection Committee (MSC) after taking into consideration the recommendations of the MRC either approves or rejects the applications.

6) On getting approval from MSC (NSEIL/NSCCL), an admission on a provisional basis is provided to the applicant subject to certain conditions like registration with SEBI, submission of relevant fees/ deposits and documents.

7) The documents of the member are then forwarded to SEBI for registration. After satisfying all the prescribed norms, SEBI grants a Registration Certificate in the name of the applicant.

8) The applicant then has to remit the prescribed membership deposits along within the time frame prescribed in the demand advice attached to the offer letter

9) After obtaining SEBI Registration, the trading member completes all the formalities and requirements such as payment of fees/deposits and submission of relevant documents.

The dealers on CM segment are required to clear the *Capital Market (Dealers) Module of NCFM;*

The dealers on Futures & Options Segment are required to clear the Derivatives Market (Dealers) Module

Dealers in the Currency Derivatives segment are required to clear the National Institute of Securities Market (NISM) Series I- Currency Derivatives Certification Examination.

This is a prerequisite without which user-ids are not issued. After compiling with all the formalities the SEBI will issue the id and enable the NEAT system for trading member

Reforms In IndIan Securities Markets Over a period

The Indian securities market has undergone remarkable changes and grown exponentially, particularly in terms of resource mobilisation, intermediaries, the number of listed stocks, market capitalisation, turnover and investor population. The following paragraphs list the principal reform measures undertaken since 1992.

1) Creation of Market Regulator:

Securities and Exchange Board of India (SEBI), the securities market regulator in India, was established under SEBI Act 1992, with the main objective 16 and responsibility for

    a) protecting the interests of investors in securities,

    b) promoting the development of the securities market, and

    c) regulating the securities market.

2) Screen Based Trading:

Prior to the setting up of NSE, the trading on stock exchanges in India was based on an open outcry system. The system was inefficient and time consuming because of its inability to provide immediate matching or recording of trades. In order to provide efficiency, liquidity and transparency, NSE introduced a nation-wide on-line fully automated screen based trading system (SBTS) on the CM segment on November 3, 1994.

3) Reduction of Trading Cycle:

Earlier, the trading cycle for stocks, based on type of securities, used to vary between 14 days to 30 days and the settlement involved another fortnight. The Exchanges, however, continued tohave different weekly trading cycles, which enabled shifting of positions from one Exchange to another. It was made mandatory for all Exchanges to follow a uniform weekly trading cycle in respect of scrips not under rolling settlement. In December 2001, all scripts were moved to rolling settlement and the settlement period was reduced progressively from T+5 to T+3 days. From April 2003 onwards, T+2 days settlement cycle has been followed.

4) *Derivatives Trading:*

In order to assist market participants in managing risks better through hedging, speculation and arbitrage, SC(R) A was amended in 1995 to lift the ban on options in securities. Trading in derivatives, however, took off in 2000 with index futures after a suitable legal and regulatory framework was put in place. The market presently offers index futures, index options, single stock futures and single stock options.

5) *Demutualisation:*

Historically, stock exchanges were owned, controlled and managed by the brokers. In case of disputes, integrity of the stock exchange suffered. NSE, however, was set up with a pure demutualised governance structure, having ownership, management and trading with three different sets of people. Currently, all the stock exchanges in India have a demutualised set up.

6) *Dematerialisation:*

As discussed before, the old settlement system was inefficient due to

      a) the time lag for settlement and

      b) the physical movement of paper-based securities.

To obviate these problems, the Depositories Act, 1996 was passed to provide for the establishment of depositories in securities with the objective of ensuring free transferability of securities with speed and accuracy.

There are two depositories in India, viz. NSDL and CDSL. They have been set up to provide instantaneous electronic transfer of securities. Demat (Dematerialised) settlement has eliminated the bad deliveries and associated problems.

To prevent physical certificates from sneaking into circulation, it has been made mandatory for all newly issued securities to be compulsorily traded in dematerialised form. Now, the public listed companies making IPO of any security for Rs.10 crore or more have to make the IPO only in dematerialised form.

7) *Clearing Corporation:*

The anonymous electronic order book ushered in by the NSE did not permit members to assess credit risk of the counter-party and thus necessitated some innovation in this area. To address this concern, NSE had set up the first clearing corporation, viz. National Securities Clearing Corporation Ltd. (NSCCL), which commenced its operations in April 1996.

8) *Investor Protection:*

In order to protect the interest of the investors and promote awareness, the Central Government (Ministry of Corporate Affairs1) established the Investor Education and Protection Fund (IEPF) in October 2001. With similar objectives, the Exchanges and SEBI also maintain investor protection funds to take care of investor claims. SEBI and the stock exchanges have also set up investor grievance / service cells for redress of investor grievances. All these agencies and investor associations also organise investor education and awareness programmes.

9) *Globalisation:*

Indian companies have been permitted to raise resources overseas through the issuance of ADRs, GDRs, FCCBs and ECBs. Further, FIIs have been permitted to invest in all types of securities, including government securities and tap the domestic market. The investments by FIIs enjoy full capital account convertibility. They can invest in a company under portfolio investment route up-to 24% of the paid up capital of the company. This can be increased as applicable to the Indian companies concerned, by passing a resolution of its Board of Directors followed by a special resolution to that effect by its general body.

The trading platform of Indian exchanges is now accessible through the Internet from anywhere in the world.

10) *Launch of India VIX2 2:*

Volatility index is a measure of the market's expectation of volatility over the near term. It measures the amount by which an underlying Index is expected to fluctuate in the near term, based on the order book of the underlying index options. India's first volatility index, India VIX (based on the Nifty 50 Index Option prices) was launched by NSE in April 2008.

11) *Direct Market Access:*

In April 2008, SEBI allowed the direct market access (DMA) facility to the institutional investors. DMA allows brokers to offer their respective clients direct access to the Exchange trading system through the broker's infrastructure without manual intervention by the broker.

12) _Launch of Securities Lending & Borrowing Scheme:_

In April 2008, the Securities Lending & Borrowing mechanism was allowed. It allows market participants to take short positions effectively with less cost.

13) _Launch of Currency Futures:_

On August 29, 2008, NSE launched trading in currency futures contracts in the USD-INR pair for the first time in India. Trading in other currency pairs like Euro – INR, Pound Sterling – INR and Japanese Yen was further made available for trading in March 2010.

14) _ASBA:_

Application Supported by Blocked Amount (ASBA) is a major primary market reform. It enables investors to apply for IPOs / FPOs and rights issues without making a payment. Instead, the amount is blocked in investors' own account and only an amount proportionate to the shares allotted goes out when allotment is finalised.

15) _Launch of Interest Rate Futures:_

On August 31, 2009, futures on interest rates were launched on the National Stock Exchange. Issue of Capital and Disclosure Requirements (ICDR) Regulations 2009: In August 2009, the SEBI issued Issue of Capital and Disclosure Requirements (ICDR) Regulations 2009, replacing the Disclosure and Investor Protection (DIP) Guidelines 2000. ICDR Regulations 2009 would govern all disclosure norms regarding issue of securities.

Who can become member of NSE

Trading members of the National Stock Exchange of India (NSE) have access to a nationwide trading facility for equities, derivatives, debt, andhybrid instruments and products. They can also provide a fair, efficient, and transparent securities market to investors.

Other benefits of NSE membership include:

- Electronic trading
- Wide range of securities
- High liquidity
- Stringent regulations
- Transparency
- Innovation
- Security
- User-friendly interface

To be eligible for NSE membership, you must meet the following criteria:

- Minimum net worth of ₹ 500 crores
- Minimum CRAR of 10 per cent
- Net NPA should not exceed 3 per cent
- Made net profit for last 3 years

NSE offers four membership categories: Trading member, Trading cum clearing member, Trading cum self-clearing member, and Professional Clearing member

 ### Who can become member of the NSE

Individuals, partnerships, corporate entities, and limited liabilitypartnerships can become members of the National Stock Exchange (NSE) if they meet the eligibility criteria laid down by SEBI and NSE.

(The directors of the company shouldn't have been disqualified for being members of a stock exchange and should not have held the offices of the directors in any company which had been a member of the stock exchange and had been declared defaulter or expelled by the stock exchange)

Such other persons or entities as may be permitted from time to time by RBI/SEBI under the Securities Contracts (Regulations) Rules, 1957.

a) Any individual

	CRITERIA
Status	Indian Citizen
Age	Minimum age : 21 years
Education	At least HSC or equivalent qualification
Experience	Applicants should have an experience for not less than two years as a partner with, or an authorised assistant or authorised clerk or remisier or apprentice to, a member.

b) Partnership firm registered under the partnership Act 1932

Eligibility criteria

Where the applicant is a partnership firm, the applicant shall identify a Dominant Promoter Group as per the norms of the Exchange at the time of making the application. Any change in the shareholding of the partnership firm including that of the said Dominant Promoter Group or their sharing interest shall be effected only with the prior permission of NSE/SEBI.

	CRITERIA
Status	Registered Partnership firm under Indian Partnership Act, 1932
Designated Partners	Identify at least two partners as designated partners who would be taking care of the day to day management of the partnership
Age	Minimum age of designated partner(s) : 21 years
Designated Partners Education	Designated Partners should be at least HSC or equivalent qualification
Designated Partners Experience	Should have a minimum of 2 years experience in an activity related to dealing in securities or as portfolio manager or as investment consultant or as a merchant banker or in financial services or treasury, broker, sub broker, authorised agent or authorised clerk or authorised representative or remisier or apprentice to a member of a recognised stock exchange, dealer, jobber, market maker, or in any other manner in dealing in securities or clearing and settlement thereof.
Dominant Promoter Norms	Identify partner's sharing interest as per Exchange DPG norms

A Limited Liability Partnership as defined in the Limited Liability Partnership Act, 2008 (6 of 2009),

Eligibility criteria

Status	Registered Limited Liability Partnership under Limited Liability Partnership Act, 2008
Designated Partners	Identify at least two partners as designated partners who would be taking care of the day to day management of the limited liability partnership
Age	Minimum age of designated partner(s) : 21 years
Designated Partners Education	Designated Partners should be at least HSC or equivalent qualification

Designated Partners Experience	Should have a minimum of 2 years? experience in an activity related to dealing in securities or as portfolio managers or as investment consultants

Corporations, Companies or Institutions or subsidiaries of such Corporations, Companies or Institutions set up for providing financial services;

Eligibility criteria

Status	Corporate registered under The Companies Act, 1956 (Indian)
Minimum Paid up Equity Capital	₹ 30 lakhs
Designated Directors	Identification of at least two directors as designated directors who would be managing the day to day trading operations
Age	Minimum age of designated director(s) : 21 years
Education	Each of the Designated Directors should be at least HSC or equivalent qualification
Designated Directors Experience	Should have a minimum of 2 years experience in an activity related to dealing in securities or as portfolio manager or as investment consultant or as a merchant banker or in financial services or treasury, broker, sub broker.

Two types of Membership in NSE

a) Normal

b) Alpha

Two types of memberships are offered :

Normal - Unrestricted business expansion

Alpha - For focused proprietary trading with limited clientele

➡️ *Following Categories are available under Normal Membership:*

CATEGORIES OF MEMBERSHIP	CASH SEGMENT	EQUITY DERIVATIVES SEGMENT	CURRENCY DERIVATIVES SEGMENT	DEBT SEGMENT	COMMODITY DERIVATIVES SEGMENT
Trading Member	Yes	Yes	Yes	Yes	Yes

Trading Cum Self Clearing Member	Yes	Yes	Yes	Yes	Yes
Trading Cum Clearing Member	-	Yes	Yes	Yes	Yes
Professional Clearing Member	-	Yes	Yes	Yes	Yes

Membership can be taken in combination with any of the above segments except for Futures & Options segment which has to be taken in combination with Cash segment.

Following categories are available under Alpha Membership:

CATEGORIES OF MEMBERSHIP	CASH SEGME NT	EQUITY DERIVATIVES SEGMENT	CURRENCY DERIVATIVES SEGMENT	DEBT SEGME NT	COMMODITY DERIVATIVES SEGMENT
Trading Member	Yes	Yes	Yes	Yes	Yes
Trading Cum Self Clearing Member		Yes	Yes	Yes	Yes
Trading Cum Clearing Member	-	Yes	Yes	Yes	Yes

The National Stock Exchange of India (NSE) offers two types of membership: normal and alpha. Normal membership is for unrestricted business expansion, while alpha membership is for focused proprietary trading with limited clientele. Alpha membership is designed for firms that don't handle client accounts, and it offers quick, easy, and cost-efficient access to the trading platform.

Trading MEMBER	This category of membership entitles a member to execute trades on his own account as well as on account of his clients but, clearing and settlement of trades executed through the Trading Member would have to be done through a Trading-cum Clearing Member or Professional Clearing Member of the Exchange

TRADING CUM SELF CLEARING MEMBER	This category of membership entitles a member to execute trades and to clear and settle the trades executed on his own account as well as on account of his clients.
TRADING CUM CLEARING MEMBER	This category of membership entitles a member to execute trades on his own account as well as on account of his clients and to clear and settle trades executed by themselves as well as by other trading members who choose to use clearing services of the member.
PROFESSIONAL CLEARING MEMBER	This category of membership entitles a member to clear and settle trades of such members of the Exchange who choose to clear and settle their trades through this member.

➤ Who is the stock broker

A stockbroker, also known as a broker, is a financial expert who buys and sells stocks and other securities for retail and institutional clients. **_They are registered with a recognisedstock exchange, such as the Bombay Stock Exchange (BSE), and can work individually or for a brokerage firm._**

Stockbrokers are individuals who buy and sell stocks and other securities for retail and institutional clients, through a stock exchange or over the counter, in return for a fee or a commission. Institutional stockbrokers work with fund managers and other financial institutions, but there are also retail investors.

Stockbrokers perform a variety of functions, including:

a) Managing an investor's portfolio

b) Buying and Selling securities

c) Analysing Financial reports

d) Providing Investment advice

e) Suggesting Investment opportunities.

Most stockbrokers work for brokerage firms and handle trading for individual clients and institutions. Most sales people are compensated by credit, which can vary from business to business.

You can buy and sell orders through online discount brokers, which reduces fees. Wealthy individuals and institutions continue to use full-service brokers who offer advice, portfolio management services, and complete transactions.

SEBI grants the certificate to stock broker based on the following conditions

a) Holds the membership of any stock exchange;

b) Should abide by the rules, regulations and bye-laws of the stock exchange or stock exchanges of which he is a member;

c) Should obtain prior permission of SEBI to continue to buy, sell or deal in securities in any

d) stock exchange in case of any change in the status and constitution;

e) Should pay the amount of fees for registration in the prescribed manner; and

f) should take adequate steps for redress of grievances of the investors within one month of the date of the receipt of the complaint and keep SEBI informed about the number, nature and other particulars of the complaints.

While considering the application of an entity for the grant of registration as a stock broker, SEBI checks out if the applicant:

a) is eligible to be admitted as a member of a stock exchange;

b) has the necessary infrastructure like adequate office space, equipment and manpower to effectively discharge his activities;

c) has any past experience in the business of buying, selling or dealing in securities;

d) is subjected to any disciplinary proceedings under the rules, regulations and bye-laws of a stock exchange with respect to his business as a stock-broker involving either himself or any of his partners, directors or employees.

Registration process of Sub-broker

Sub-broker is required to obtain the certificate of registration from the SEBI as per SEBI regulation act 1992

Without that certificate he will not be allowed to operate buying and selling securities in the stock exchange.

SEBI will grant the certification until and unless

a) He had paid the prescribed fees

b) He should sort out the complaints under the grievance cell of their investor within the period of one month

c) If their is any change in his status and its constituents he need to take prior permission of SEBI to continue in buying and selling of the securities

d) Stock broker should authorised him in writing to buy and sell the securities in market

The sub-broker needs to submit the required document to SEBI as per the recommendation of the trading member.

After verifying all the documents the SEBI will forward his application for registration.

SEBI will reject the application if it finds that applicant sub broker is involved in any kind of forged, cancelled, forfeited etc securities in the market.

 ## Surrender of Trading membership

1) Surrender of trading membership is when a trading member submits a *written request to the exchange* to relinquish their membership. The exchange may permit the request if the member meets certain conditions, such as:

a) *Clearing dues*

Paying all dues to the exchange and NSCCL

b) *No pending investigations*

Declaring that no investigation, inquiry, or disciplinary action is pending against the member or any of their shareholders or directors.

c) *submitting documents*

Providing original SEBI registration certificates, proof of payment of SEBI turnover fees, and details of directors and shareholders.

d) *Requesting equipment dismantling*

Requesting the exchange to dismantle and recover any leased lines, VSATs, or other equipment provided at the member's dealing offices.

The exchange will cancel the member's registration once SEBI accepts the surrender, but the exchange will not release the member's security deposit until SEBI issues a No Dues Certificate.

2) No trading member, who has surrendered its trading membership, their partners (in case of partnership firm) and/ or dominant shareholders (in case of corporates) is eligible to be readmitted _to the trading membership of the Exchange in any form for a period of one year from the date of cessation_ of trading membership (i.e. from the date of approval of surrender).

3) The application of surrender of trading membership is subject to fulfilment of certain conditions, such as submission of original SEBI registration certificate(s) on all segments on which the trading member is registered; submission of sub-broker registration certificate(s) of all the sub-brokers associated with the trading member for onward transmission to the SEBI for cancellation etc.

4) The trading member should request the Exchange through their surrender application to _dismantle and recover all the leased line(s)/ VSAT(s) and other equipment given to them at their dealing offices._

5) A notice to public by way of a public notification in newspapers should be made by the Exchange and certain time (from the date of public notification) is given to investors, public, etc. to lodge claims against the surrendering trading member.

6) A letter is also sent to SEBI seeking pending dues, if any, from member. On the expiry of period for receipt of investor claims and on receipt of intimation of dues amount, if any, from SEBI, the total amount payable by the member should be appropriated against trading member's deposits available with the Exchange / NSCCL and the trading member will be intimated accordingly. In case the amount payable exceeds the deposits, the trading Member would be intimated to bring in the requisite amount within 21 days of intimation. Upon the failure of the member to do so within 21 days of intimation, the case shall be referred to the relevant authority for further action.

➡ Basis of Suspension of Membership

a) *MISCONDUCT*

1) *Fraud:*

If it is convicted of a criminal offence or commits fraud or a fraudulent act which in the opinion of the relevant authority renders it unfit to be a Trading Member;

2) *Violation:*

If it has violated provisions of any statute governing the activities, business and operations of the Exchange, Trading Members and securities business in general;

3) *Improper Conduct:*

If in the opinion of the relevant authority it is guilty of dishonourable or disgraceful or disorderly or improper conduct on the Exchange or of willfully obstructing the business of the Exchange;

4) *Breach of Rules, Bye Laws and Regulations:*

If it shields or assists or omits to report any Trading Member whom it has known to have committed a breach or evasion of any Rule, Bye-law and Regulation of the Exchange or of any resolution, order, notice or direction there under of the relevant authority or of any committee or officer or the Exchange authorised in that behalf;

5) *Failure to Comply with Resolutions:*

If it contravenes or refuses or fails to comply with or abide by any resolution, order, notice, direction, decision or ruling of the relevant authority or of any committee or officer of the Exchange or other person authorised in that behalf under the Bye Laws, Rules and Regulations of the Exchange;

6) *Failure to Submit to or Abide by Arbitration:*

If it neglects or fails or refuses to submit to arbitration or to abide by or carry out any award, decision or order of the relevant authority or the Arbitration Committee or the arbitrators made in connection with a reference under the Bye Laws, Rules and Regulations of the Exchange;

7) *Failure to Testify or Give Information:*

If it neglects or fails or refuses to submit to the relevant authority or to a committee or an officer of the Exchange authorised in that behalf, such books, correspondence, documents and papers or any part thereof as may be required to be produced or to appeal and testify before or cause any of its partners, attorneys, agents, authorised representatives or employees to appear and testify before the relevant authority or such committee or officer of the Exchange or other person authorised in that behalf;

8) *Failure to Submit Special Returns:*

If it neglects or fails or refuses to submit to the relevant authority, within the time notified in that behalf, special returns in such form as the relevant authority may from time to time prescribe together with such other information as the relevant authority may require whenever circumstances arise which in the opinion of the relevant authority make it desirable that such special returns or information should be furnished by any or all the Trading Members;

9) Failure to submit Audited Accounts:

If it neglects or fails or refuses to submit its audited accounts to the Exchange within such time as may be prescribed by the relevant authority from time to time.

10) *Failure to Compare or Submit Accounts with Defaulter:*

If it neglects or fails to compare its accounts with the Defaulters' Committee or to submit to it a statement of its accounts with a defaulter or a certificate that it has no such account or if it makes a false or misleading statement therein

11) *False or Misleading Returns:*

If it neglects or fails or refuses to submit or makes any false or misleading statement in its clearing forms or returns required to be submitted to the Exchange under the Bye Laws, Rules and Regulations

12) *Vexatious Complaints:*

If it or its agent brings before the relevant authority or committee or an officer of the Exchange or other person authorised in that behalf a charge, complaint or suit which in the opinion of the relevant authority is frivolous, vexatious or malicious

13) *Failure to Pay Dues and Fees:*

If it fails to pay its subscription, fees, arbitration charges or any other money which may be due from it or any fine or penalty imposed on it.

b) *UNPROFESSIONAL CONDUCT*

1) *Business in Securities in which Dealings not Permitted:*

If it enters into dealings in securities in which dealings are not permitted

2) *Business for Defaulting Constituent:*

If it deals or transacts business directly or indirectly or executes an order for a constituent who has within its knowledge failed to carry out engagements relating to securities and is in default to another Trading Member, unless such constituent shall have made a satisfactory arrangement with the Trading Member who is its creditor

3) *Business for Insolvent:*

If without first obtaining the consent of the relevant authority, it directly or indirectly is interested in or associated in business with or transacts any business with or for any individual who has been bankrupt or insolvent even though such individual shall have obtained his final discharge from an Insolvency Court.

4) *Business without Permission when under Suspension:*

If without the permission of the relevant authority, it does business on its own account or on account of a principal with or through a Trading Member during the period it is required by the relevant authority to suspend business on the Exchange.

5) *Business for or with Suspended, Expelled and Defaulter Trading Members:*

If without the special permission of the relevant authority, it shares brokerage with or carries on business or makes any deal for or with any Trading Member who has been suspended, expelled or declared a defaulter

6) *Business for Employees of other Trading Members:*

If it transacts business, directly or indirectly, for or with or executes an order for a authorised representative or employee of another Trading Member without the written consent of such employing Trading Member

7) Business for Exchange Employees:

If it makes a speculative transaction in which an employee of the Exchange is directly or indirectly interested.

8) *Advertisement:*

If it advertises for business purposes or issues regular circulars or other business communications to persons other than its own constituents, Trading Members of the Exchange, Banks and Joint Stock Companies or publishes pamphlets, circular or any other literature or report or information relating to the stock markets with its name attached.

c) *UN-BUSINESS LIKE CONDUCT*

1) *Fictitious Names:* If it transacts its own business or the business of its constituent in fictitious names or if he carries on business in more than one trading segment of the Exchange under fictitious names;

2) *Fictitious Dealings*: If it makes a fictitious transaction or gives an order for the purchase or sale of securities the execution of which would involve no change of ownership or executes such an order with knowledge of its character

3) *Circulation of Rumours:* If it, in any manner, circulates or causes to be circulated any rumours

4) *Prejudicial Business:* If it makes or assists in making or with such knowledge is a party to or assists in carrying out any plan or scheme for the making of any purchases or sales or offers of purchase or sale of securities for the purpose of upsetting the equilibrium of the market or bringing about a condition in which prices will not fairly reflect market values

5) _**Market Manipulation and Rigging:**_ If it directly or indirectly, alone or with other persons, effects series of transactions in any security to create actual or apparent active trading in such security or raising or depressing the prices of such security for the purpose of inducing purchase or sale of such security by others

6) _**Unwarrantable Business:**_ If it engages in reckless or unwarrantable or un-businesslike dealings in the market or effects purchases or sales for its constituent's account or for any account in which it is directly or indirectly interested such that the purchases or sales are excessive in view of its constituents or his own means and financial resources or in view of the market for such security

7) _**Compromise:**_ If it connives at a private failure of a Trading Member or accepts less than a full and bona fide money payment in settlement of a debt due by a Trading Member arising out of a transaction in securities

8) _**Dishonoured Cheque:**_ If it issues to any other Trading Member or to its constituents acheque which is dishonoured on presentation for whatever reasons.

9) _**Failure to Carry out Transactions with Constituents:**_ If it fails, in the opinion of the relevant authority, to carry out its committed transactions with its constituents

d) _Trading member's responsibility for partners, agents and employees:_

A trading member is fully responsible for the acts and omissions of its partners, authorised officials, attorneys, agents, authorised representatives and employees. If any such act which is against the relevant rules and regulations is committed or omitted by them then the trading member is liable to the same penalty to the same extent has that act or omission been done or omitted by itself.

e) _Suspension on failure to provide margin deposit and/or capital adequacy requirements:_

The Exchange can suspend the business of a trading member when it fails to provide the margin deposit and/or meets capital adequacy norms as provided in the Bye Laws, Rules and Regulations. The trading member shall remain suspended until he furnishes the necessary margin deposit or meet the capital adequacy requirements.

➤ Consequences of Suspension

1) Suspension of Membership Rights:

The suspended Trading Member shall, during the terms of its suspension, be deprived of and excluded from all the rights and privileges of membership including the right to attend or vote at any meeting of the general body of Trading Members of the relevant segment.

2) Rights of Creditors Unimpaired:

The suspension shall not affect the rights of the Trading Members who are creditors of the suspended Trading Member

3) Fulfilment of Contracts:

The suspended Trading Member shall be bound to fulfil contracts outstanding at the time of its suspension

4) Further Business Prohibited:

The suspended Trading Member shall not during the terms of its suspension make any trade or transact any business with or through a Trading Member, provided that it may, with the permission of the relevant authority, close with or through a Trading Member, the transactions outstanding at the time of its suspension

5) Trading Members Not to Deal:

No Trading Member shall transact business for or with or share brokerage with a suspended Trading Member during the terms of its suspension except with the previous permission of the relevant authority.

➤ Sub-Broker

Sub broker is an important intermediary between stock broker and client in the capital market segment. The trading members of the Exchange may appoint sub-brokers to act as agents of the concerned trading member for assisting the investors in buying, selling or dealing in securities.

The sub-brokers are affiliated to the trading members and are required to be registered with SEBI. A sub-broker is allowed to be associated with only one trading member of the Exchange. Trading members desirous of appointing sub-brokers are required to submit the following documents to the Membership Department of the Exchange:

   a) Copy of sub-broker - broker agreement duly certified by the trading members

   b) Application form for registration as a sub-broker with Securities and Exchange Board 36 of India (Form B)

FORM B
SECURITIES AND EXCHANGE BOARD OF INDIA
(Stock Brokers and Sub-Brokers) Regulations 1992

(Regulation 11)

APPLICATION FORM FOR REGISTRATION AS A SUB-BROKER WITH SECURITIES AND EXCHANGE BOARD OF INDIA

1. Name of applicant sub-broker :

2. Trader name of sub-broker :

3. Form of organisation :

4. Educational qualifications :

   Name :

   Status :

   Qualification :

5. Name of the member-broker and the

   Stock Exchange to which applicant Affiliated :

6. Date of acquiring sub-broker ship :

7. Infrastructural arrangements

   Office Address :

   Phone No :

8. Number of branch offices :

I certify that the information given in this application form is true to the best of my/our knowledge and belief.

Recommendation letter from the stock broker to whom I/we am/are affiliated and two references, including one from the banker as required are enclosed.

Signature : _____

Date:

Recommendation of the Stock Exchange

This is to certify that (NAME) is a recognised sub-broker affiliated to Max Stock Broking Pvt. Ltd. member - broker of this Exchange. The application is recommended/not recommended for registration by the Board.

AUTHORISED SIGNATORY

Signature

National Stock Exchange.

c) Recommendation letter to be given by the trading member with whom the sub-broker is affiliated (Form C)

d) Reference Letter from the applicant's Banker

e) Reference letter from any other Third Party (Such as CA/CS/ Lawyer/Notary or other Stock Broker

f) Declaration from Sub-Broker about Non-Conviction or presently not under trial for any offence (On the letterhead of the sub broker)

 ### *Eligibility criteria of Sub-broker*

The National Stock Exchange (NSE) defines a sub broker as someone who acts as an agent on behalf of a trading member to help investors trade securities through that member. To become a sub broker, you must meet the following eligibility criteria:

- *Be at least 21 years old*
- *Have completed secondary education (10+2)*
- *Have basic knowledge of the financial market, including trading accounts, Demat accounts, and the buying and selling process of stocks*
- *Have technical knowledge of computers and basic software like Excel*
- *Have good communication skills*
- *Have a clean financial record*
- *Have knowledge of equity, mutual funds, and more*
- *Have knowledge of the functioning of the Indian and international markets*

Once you meet the eligibility criteria, you can gather the necessary documents and submit them to the stockbroking house. These documents typically include:

- Sub-broker registration application form
- Signed agreement between the stockbroking house and the sub-broker
- Proof of address, like a passport, electricity bill, ration card, or telephone bill
- Proof of experience certificate, if applicable
- Pay processing fee of Rs. 2,000 plus GST

➤ Registration Process of Sub-Broker

No sub-broker is allowed to buy, sell or deal in securities, unless he or she holds a certificate of registration granted by SEBI.. SEBI may grant a certificate to a sub-broker, subject to the conditions that:

(a) he should *pay the fees* in the prescribed manner;

(b) he should take adequate steps for *redress of grievances of the investors within one month of the date of the receipt of the complaint* and keep SEBI informed about the number, nature and other particulars of the complaints received;

(c) In case of any *change in the status* and constitution, the sub-broker should obtain *prior permission of SEBI* to continue to buy, sell or deal in securities in any stock exchange; and

(d) He should be authorised in writing, by a stock-broker being a member of a stock exchange for affiliating himself in buying, selling or dealing in securities.

The applicant sub-broker should submit the required documents to the stock exchange with the *recommendation of a trading member.*

After verifying the documents, the stock exchange may forward the documents of the applicant sub-broker to SEBI for registration.

A sub-broker can trade in that capacity after getting himself registered with SEBI. The Exchange may *not forward the application of the sub-broker to SEBI for registration if the applicant dealt with fake, forged, stolen, counterfeit etc. shares and securities in the market.*

➤ Cancellation of registration of sub-broker

To cancel a sub-broker registration with the National Stock Exchange of India (NSE), you need to submit the following documents:

1) Board resolution or letter of authority

This document should contain approval from the partnership firm, LLP, or corporate authorised person for the cancellation.

2) Request letter

This letter should be on the authorised person's letterhead and signed by the proprietor, partner, director, or authorised signatory.

3) Public notification

If disciplinary action is pending against the authorised person, you need to submit a copy of a public notification in a local newspaper and an English daily newspaper with wide circulation. The notification should inform investors and the general public of the cancellation.

4) SEBI registration certificate

You need to submit the original SEBI registration certificate for the sub-broker. If the certificate is lost or misplaced, the main member and sub-broker must each provide an affidavit on 100 rupee stamp paper stating that it was lost or misplaced

➡️ **_Unique client code_**

A Unique Client Code (UCC) is a unique identification number assigned to each client by a stockbroker or Depository Participant (DP) to identify them in the securities market. The UCC is an alphanumeric number that brokers must maintain to maintain privacy in record keeping for their clients. The code also helps increase traceability in the markets by identifying the parties that are performing the transactions

The UCC provides comprehensive details about the clients, allowing members to have a better understanding of their needs and preferences. It is an essential tool in the world of finance, as it enables members to make informed decisions and cater to their clients' specific requirements. The capital markets regulator, SEBI, established a system for stock exchanges and depositories to link a customer's UCC to their demat account.

➡️ **_Investor service cell (ISC) and Arbitration_**

Empowerment of investors through education and protection of interest of investors is one of the primary objectives of NSE. To cater to the needs of investors Nse has established the investor service cell.

The complaints are forwarded to the trading members for resolution and seeking clarifications. The ISC follows-up with the trading members and makes efforts to resolve the complaint expeditiously.

**Investor Services Cell of the Exchange deals with the complaints of investors against the Trading Members of the Exchange or against the listed companies.**

In certain cases, on account of conflicting claims made by the investor and the trading member, _when it is not possible to administratively resolve the complaint, investors are advised to take recourse to the arbitration mechanism prescribed by the Exchange._

The Arbitration mechanism available at Exchange, helps provide for resolution towards disputes arising between the Trading member and

Constituents, out of or in relation to dealings, contracts and transactions made subject to the Bye-Laws, Rules and, Regulations of the Exchange

➤ *Why is the seperate account needed for clients and brokers?*

The National Stock Exchange of India (NSE) requires brokers to have a separate account for client demat accounts at a bank in the broker's name, with "clients" in the title. The broker must also disclose these client bank accounts to the NSE, which are displayed on the NSE website

You can have multiple Demat and trading accounts, but you can only have one with each stockbroker. Each broker has access to trading platforms, which can be confusing to navigate. You should also consider the charges of each brokerage, as some may be more expensive than others. If your Demat account is inactive for a long time, your broker may freeze it, but you should be able to recover your stocks

➤ *Code of advertisement:*

According to the NSE, trading members must submit a copy of their advertisements to the exchange for prior approval before publication in the media. The code of advertisement for trading members should include the following:

- The member's name, registered office address, SEBI registration number, logo, trade name, and CIN, if applicable
- Information that is accurate, true, fair, clear, complete, unambiguous, and concise
- A standard warning in legible font (minimum font size 10) that states "Investment in the securities market are subject to market risks. Read all the related documents carefully before investing"
- The standard warning should be audible in a clear and understandable manner in visual and accompanying voice over reiteration in audio-visual media based advertisements

➤ *Other guidelines for advertising include:*

- Advertisements should not contain statements that directly or by implication or by omission may mislead the investor
- Advertisements should not carry any slogan that is exaggerated or unwarranted or any slogan that is inconsistent with or unrelated to the nature or the risk and return profile of the product.

The National Stock Exchange of India (NSE) has a code of advertisement for trading members that requires a copy of an advertisement to be submitted to the exchange for prior approval before publication.

The revised code of advertisement, which was issued on February 2, 2023, states that advertisements *must include all communication issued by or on behalf of a stockbroker in publicly available media that may influence investment decisions*.

This includes internal communication to registered clients and forms of communication, such as written, audio, or visual, including social media.

1) Advertisement shall include all forms of communication issued by or on behalf of or in relation to Stockbroker in publicly available media that may influence investment/trading decisions of any investor/prospective investors. It also includes internal communication to registered clients that may influence investment/trading decisions.

2) Forms of communications shall include but shall not be limited to all written or audio or visual form including social media forms including use of workshops and the like.

3) Trading Members of the Exchange while issuing advertisements in the media have to comply with the Code for Advertisements prescribed by the Exchange. In pursuance of that, a copy of an advertisement has to be submitted to the Exchange to get a prior approval before its issue to publication/media.

The code of advertisement also states that:

- Advertisements should include accurate, complete, and unambiguous information
- Standard warning should be audible in a clear and understandable manner in visual and accompanying voice over reiteration
- A copy of an advertisement should be submitted to the exchange to get prior approval before its issue in publication or media
- Members should disown any advertisement issued on any platform without their consent and take appropriate legal action against the entity.

Multiple choice questions

1.	In order to provide efficiency, liquidity & transparency, NSE introduced a nation-wide on-line fully automated _____ _____ **a) Screen based trading system** b) State based ticketing system c) Small based ticketing system d) Screen based fast system	1

2.	Neat system supports an order driven market, wherein orders match on the basis of _____ & _____ priority a) Size, bid **b) price, Time** c) Quality, quantity d) Bid, lot size	1
3.	The odd lot market facility is used for _____ a) Normal market b) Retail debt market **c) Odd lot market** d) Auction market	1
4.	The branch manager receives end of day reports for all the ____ _____ under that branch **a) Dealers** b) Corporate manager c) Clients d) NCFM certificate holders	1
5.	The corporate manager is a term assigned to a user placed at the a) Lowest level **b) Highest level** c) Middle level d) Junior level	1
6.	After login to the NEAT system & before the market opens for trading; a trading member can set up _____ _____ & _____ **a) Market watch, viewing inquiry screen** b) Security descriptor, Market by price c) Previous trade, outstanding orders d) Activity log, order status	1

7.	Which of the following statements are true? i) During the open phase order entry is allowed ii) During the phase, orders are matched on a continuous basis iii) Trading all the instruments is allowed unless they are specifically prohibited by the exchange iv) The activities that are allowed at this stage are inquiry, order entry order modification, order cancellation and order matching. a) Only i b) Only ii c) Only i ii and iii **d) All of the above**	1
8.	The temporary sign off is automatically activated when the user is inactive for a period of_____. Hi **a) 5 minutes** b) 15 minutes c) 20 minutes d) 25 minutes	1
9.	Name the period after market close during which, the users have inquiry access only? **a) SURCON** b) Open phase c) Market close d) None of the above	1
10.	The NEAT system provides an order driven market, wherein orders match on the basis of _____. a) First come bases b) Highest price bases **c) Time price priority basis** d) None of the above	1
11.	IF client buy shares worth buy 225000 and sells it 175000 what should be the maximum brokerage **a) 10000** b) 20000 c) 24000 d) 14000	1

12.	Which clearing corporation commenced its operation in April 1996? a) Central clearing corporation b) International security clearing corporation **c) National stock clearing corporation** d) All of the above	1
13.	Which market segment was initially introduced in National Stock exchange a) Retail debt market **b) Wholesale debt market** c) Currency derivative market d) Over the counter market	1
14.	Who among the following is the principal regulator in the securities market **a) SEBI** b) RBI c) MCA d) DEA	1
15.	Investor protection fund was set up in _____ a) 1955 b) 1950 c) 2000 **d) 1960**	1
16.	_____ segment at NSE commenced its operation in November 1994 a) Wholesale debt market **b) Capital market segment** c) Future and option market d) Currency derivative market	1
17.	In april 2008 SEBI allowed the direct market access facility to _____ a) Bank b) Financial institutions c) Investors **d) Institutional investors**	1

18.	_____ is a n intermediary who arranges to buy and sell on behalf of clients **a) Stock broker** b) Investor c) Trading member d) Sub-broker	1
19.	Which of the following is not the consequences of suspension a) Fulfilment of contracts b) Further business prohibited c) Rights of creditors impaired **d) Office vacated**	1
20.	From the following which is not the feature of contract note a) Contract note need to issued to client within 24 hours b) It should be in proper format c) All statutory levis are separately shown in contract note **d) No need to be stamped as signed by trading member**	1
21.	Brokers usually identifies the document with respect to _____ _____ a) Contract note **b) UCC** c) Client registration form d) None of thee above	1
22.	What is the duration of payment of delivery of securities to the client **a) One working day** b) Two working days c) T+2 settlement day d) None of the above	1
23.	The authorised person are allowed to issue contract note a) True **b) False**	1

24.	A trading member deemed guilty of _____ _____ for any of the dealing in fictitious name a) Misconduct **b) Un-business like conduct** c) Unprofessional like conduct d) All of the above	1
25.	DPG stands for _____ **a) Dominant promoters group** b) Dominant permitted group c) Dominant promotion group d) None of the above	1
26.	A broker can have maximum of _____ clients a) 50 b) 100 c) 150 d) Unlimited	1
27.	In which segment group one can apply a) Individual b) Partner c) Corporate **d) Any of the above**	1
28.	MRC consist of _____ a) Four person from any discipline and a managing director from stock exchange b) Six person from any discipline and a managing director from stock exchange **c) Seven person from any discipline and a managing director from stock exchange** d) None of the above	1

29.	Which of the following statement is true about arbitration	1
	a) The reference of arbitration is need to filled within six months from the date when dispute arise along with the list of arbitrator	
	b) The arbitration received from the applicant is forwarded to respondent	
	c) The respondent is being called to fill his reply along with arbitrator within the specified time	
	d) All the statement are true	
30.	Contract note is signed by _____	1
	a) Dealer	
	b) Authorised signatory	
	c) Dominant promoters	
	d) Directors	
31.	A copy of advertisement is need to submitted by trading member to NSE	1
	a) For information	
	b) For record	
	c) After being issued to media/ public	
	d) Prior before it is issued in publication/ advertisement	
32.	Minimum net worth of for CM F&O and WDM is _____ _____	1
	a) 200	
	b) 300	
	c) 100	
	d) None	
33.	_____ is used to give information of price fluctuation, commodity or any other market	1
	a) An index	
	b) Primary market	
	c) Secondary market	
	d) None of the above	
34.	Market capitalisation ratio refers to market capitalisation divided by GDP used to measure _____	1
	a) Stock market size	
	b) Market behaviour	
	c) Market position limit	
	d) None of the above	

35.	RBI premitted _____ which means that investor holding ADR and GDR can cancel with the depository and sell the underlying assets a) Non- fungibility **b) Two-way fungibility** c) Partial fungibility d) Any	1
36.	Client registration form is filled by _____ a) Client delivers spurious shares b) Client files FIR against client **c) Client enrol himself with broker** d) Client defaults in making payments	1
37.	A stock broker means member of _____ a) SEBI **b) Recognised stock exchange** c) Any stock exchange d) RBI	1
38.	An application for arbitration need to filled with registrar within **a) 6 months** b) 5 months c) 30 days d) 1 year	1
39.	Failure to submit audited accounts comes under _____ _____ type of conduct **a) Misconduct** b) Un-businesslike conduct c) Un-professional like conduct d) Unknown conduct	1
40.	Members should have a prudent system of risk management to protect themselves from client default. _____ _____ is an important element of such a system. a) NSCCL **b) Margin** c) Capital d) Unique Client Code	1

41.	In _____ market the warrants are issued	1
	a) Currency derivative market	
	b) Future and option market	
	c) Wholesale debt market	
	d) Retail debt market	
42.	The collected margin is kept separately in which account	1
	a) SEBI	
	b) RBI	
	c) Client bank account	
	d) Agent bank account	

Define the following

a) Primary market

b) Secondary market

c) Index

d) Market capitalisation

e) Market capitalisation ratio

f) Turnover

g) Turnover ratio

h) Stock broker

i) Sub-broker

j) UCC

k) Contract note

l) Investor service cell

Answer the following questions in 20 – 30 words each

1) Write the difference between primary and secondary market?

2) What are the means of products dealt in the security market?

3) Who are the participants?

4) Who can become a member of NSE?

5) What is the suspension of business

6) What is the removal of suspension

7) What is brokerage?

8) Why is the separate bank needed for client and broker?

9) What is meant by surrender of trading membership ?

10) What is the basis of suspension ?

Answer the following questions in 30– 50 words each (3 x 2 = 6 marks)

1) What is the registration process of a sub-broker?

2) What is the admission process of registration for membership?

3) How can the trading member be declared a defaulter?

4) What are the consequences of expulsion?

5) What are the consequences of suspension?

6) What are the features of the code of advertisements?

7) What are the margins from the clients?

8) What are the characteristics of agreements between the sub-broker and client?

9) What are the different market segments ?

10) What is the role of an investor service cell ?

Unit 2
Trading

In the past, the trading on stock exchanges in India was based on open outcry system.

Under the system, brokers assemble at a central location usually the exchange trading ring, and trade with each other. This was time consuming, inefficient and imposed limits on trading volumes and trading hours. In order to provide efficiency, liquidity and transparency, NSE introduced a nation-wide on-line, fully-automated screen based trading system (SBTS). Under this system a trading member can punch into the computer, the number of securities and the prices at which he would like to transact.

𝓣𝓡 Advantages of screen based system

Screen-based trading systems, also known as electronic trading, have several advantages over traditional trading methods, including:

- *Transparency:* Participants can see the prices of securities in the market in real-time
- *Efficiency:* Information is passed on efficiently, which helps to fix prices
- *Cost, time, and risk reduction:* Increased efficiency reduces time, cost, and risk of error
- *Improved liquidity:* The high speed with which trades are executed and the large number of participants who can trade simultaneously allows faster incorporation of price-sensitive information into prevailing prices
- *Anonymity:* It provides full anonymity by accepting orders, big or small, from members without revealing their identity, thus providing equal access to everybody.

₹ Types of market

a) Normal market
  - All orders traded are of regular lot size or in multiple thereof in the normal market
  - Securities are compulsory trades in dematerialised form
  - This market consist of regular lot orders, special term orders and Negotiated Trade orders and stop loss order

b) Odd lot market
- All order less than regular lot size are traded in odd lot market
- These order is not having special terms attached to it
- In this market price and quantity, both will be considered for watching the trade Recently it is being used in limited physical market

c) Auction market
- There are 3 participants in this market
- Initiator: the party who initiated the auction process is called initiator
- Competitor: the party who enters the order on the same side of the initiator
- Solicitor: the party who enters orders on the opposite side as of the initiator

Trading system in nse

- An investor informs a broker to place an order on his behalf.
- The broker enters the order through his personal computer and sends signal to the Satellite via VSAT/leased line/modem.
- The signal is directed to a mainframe computer at NSE via VSAT at NSE's office.
- A message relating to the order activity is broadcast to the respective member.
- The order confirmation message is immediately displayed on the PC of the broker.
- This order matches with the existing passive order(s), otherwise it waits for the active orders to enter the system. On order matching, a message is broadcast to the respective member the one that came in early gets priority over the later one.

Orders are matched automatically by the computer keeping the system transparent, objective and fair.

Where an order does not find a match, it remains in the system and is displayed to the whole market, till a fresh order comes in or the earlier order is cancelled or modified.

The trading system provides tremendous flexibility to the users in terms of kinds of orders that can be placed on the system.

Several time-related (immediate or cancel), price-related (buy/sell limit and stop loss orders) or volume related (disclosed quantity) conditions can be easily built into an order.

The trading system also provides complete market information on-line. The market screen at any point of time provides complete information on total order depth in a security, *the five best buys and sells available in the market, the quantity traded during the day in that security,* the high and the low, the last traded price, etc. Investors can also know the fate of the orders almost as soon as they are placed with the trading members.

Thus, the National Exchange for Automated Trading (NEAT) system provides an Open Electronic Consolidated Limit Order Book (OECLOB).

Limit orders are orders to buy or sell shares at a stated quantity and price.

If the price quantity conditions do not match, the limit order will not be executed.

The term _limit order book' refers to the fact that only limit orders are stored in the book and all market orders are crossed against the limit orders sitting in the book.

Since the order book is visible to all market participants, it is termed as an _Open Book'

NSE is the first exchange in the world to use satellite communication technology for trading. Its trading system, called National Exchange for Automated Trading (NEAT), is a state-of-the-theart client server based application.

At the server end all trading information is stored in an in memory database to achieve minimum response time and maximum system availability for users. It has uptime record of 99.7%.

For all trades entered into NEAT system, there is uniform *response time of less than one* second.

The NEAT system supports an order driven market, wherein orders match on the basis of time and price priority.

Hierarchy of trading system

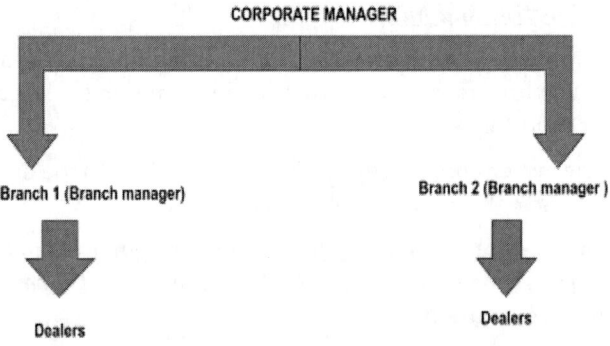

CORPORATE MANAGER

Branch 1 (Branch manager)

Branch 2 (Branch manager)

Dealers

Dealers

Corporate Manager

The Corporate Manager is the user placed at the highest level. Such a user can perform all offer-related activities and receive the reports for all branches of the trading member. Additionally, the Corporate Manager can define the offer value limits for the branches and individual dealers of his firm. This facility is available only to the Corporate Manager. The Corporate Manager can modify his own offer or offers of all dealers and branch managers of his trading member firm.

Branch Manager

The Branch Manager is the user who is placed under the Corporate Manager. Such user can perform and view Bid related activities for all dealers under that branch. The Branch Manager can modify his own offer or offers of any dealer under his branch.

Dealer

Dealers are users at the lower most level of hierarchy. A Dealer can perform and view offer related activities and information only for oneself and does not have access to information on other dealers under either, the same branch or other branches. A Dealer can modify only the Offers entered by him

 _MARKET PHASES_

Trading on the equities segment takes place on all days of the week (except Saturdays and Sundays and holidays declared by the Exchange in advance). The market timings of the equities segment are:

A) _Pre-open session_

Order entry & modification Open: 09:00 hrs

Order entry & modification Close: 09:08 hrs*

- Opening: The trading member can carry out the following activities after login to the NEAT system and before the market opens for trading: (a) Set up Market Watch (the securities which the user would like to view on the screen)

- *With random closure in last one minute. Pre-open order matching starts immediately after close of pre-open order entry._

Order matching period starts immediately after completion of order collection period. Orders are matched at a single (equilibrium) price which will be open price. The order matching happens in the following sequence: • Eligible limit orders are matched with eligible limit orders • Residual eligible limit orders are matched with market orders • Market orders are matched with market orders.

Share Price	Order Buy	Book Sell	Demand/Supply schedule		Maximum tradable Quantity
			Demand	Supply	
100	13500	11500	50500	11500	11500
104	9500	9500	37000	21300	21300
105	12000	15000	27500	36300	27500
106	6500	12000	15500	48300	15500
107	5000	12500	9000	60800	9000
108	4000	8500	4000	69300	4000

- During order matching period, order modification, order cancellation, trade modification and trade cancellation is not allowed.

- The trade confirmations are disseminated to respective members on their trading terminals before the start of normal market. After completion of order matching there is a silent period to facilitate the transition from pre-open session to the normal market.

- Limit orders are at limit price and market orders are at the discovered equilibrium price.

- In a situation where no equilibrium price is discovered in the pre-open session, all market orders will be dealt in the previous day's closing price or adjusted close price.

- Accordingly, Normal Market and Odd lot Market opens for trading after closure of pre-open session i.e. 9:15 am. Block Trading sessions are available for the next 35 minutes from the opening of Normal Market.

The opening price is determined based on the principle of demand supply mechanism. The equilibrium price is the price at which the maximum volume is executable.

In case more than one price meets the said criteria, the equilibrium price is the price at which there is minimum unmatched order quantity.

In case more than one price has same minimum order unmatched quantity, the equilibrium price is the price closest to the previous day's closing price.

In case the previous day's closing price is the mid-value of pair of prices which are closest to it, then the previous day's closing price itself will be taken as the equilibrium price.

In case of corporate action, previous day's closing price is adjusted to the closing price or the base price. Both limit and market orders are taken for computation of equilibrium price. The equilibrium price determined in pre-open session is considered as open price for the day.

In case if only market orders exist both in the buy and sell side, then the order is matched at previous days close price or adjusted close price / base price. Previous day's close or adjusted close price / base price is the opening price. In case if no price is discovered in pre-open session, the price of first trade in the normal market is the open price.

B) Regular trading session

Normal / Limited Physical Market Open: 09:15 hrs

- Pre-open: The pre-open session is for a duration of 15 minutes i.e. from 9:00 am to 9:15 am.

- The pre-open session consists of Order collection period and order matching period.

- The order collection period of 8* minutes shall be provided for order entry, modification and cancellation. During this period orders can be entered, modified and cancelled.

- The information like Indicative equilibrium / opening price of scrip, total buy and sell quantity of the scrip is disseminated on the NEAT Terminal to the members on a real time basis.

- Normal / Limited Physical Market Close: 15:30 hrs

Order matching period starts immediately after completion of order collection period. Orders are matched at a single (equilibrium) price which will be open price.

- The order matching happens in the following sequence:
  o Eligible limit orders are matched with eligible limit orders
  o Residual eligible limit orders are matched with market orders
  o Market orders are matched with market orders

C) Closing Session

The Closing Session is held between 15.40 hrs and 16.00 hrs

D) Block Deal Session Timings:

Morning Window: This window shall operate between 08:45 AM to 09:00 AM.

Afternoon Window: This window shall operate between 02:05 PM to 2:20 PM. Ok

Normal Market Open Phase:

1) The open period indicates the commencement of trading activity. *To signify the start of trading, a message is sent to all the trader workstations.*

2) The market open time for different markets is notified by the Exchange to all the trading members. *Order entry is allowed when all the securities have been opened.*

3) During this phase, *orders are matched on a continuous basis.*

4) Trading in *all the instruments is allowed unless they are specifically prohibited by the Exchange.*

5) The activities that are allowed at this stage are Inquiry, Order Entry, Order Modification, Order Cancellation (including quick order cancellation), Order Matching and Trade Cancellation

Market Close:

When the market closes, trading in all instruments for that market comes to an end. A message to this effect is sent to all trading members.

No further orders are accepted, but the user is *permitted to perform activities like inquiries and trade cancellation.*

Post-Close Market:

This closing session is available only in the Normal Market Segment. Its timings are from 3.40 PM to 4.00 PM. Only market price orders are allowed. Special Terms, Stop Loss and Disclosed Quantity Orders, Index Orders are not allowed.

The securities which are not allowed in normal market cannot be accepted

SURCON: (SURveillance and CONtrol)

Under this period after market close during which, the users have inquiry access only. After the end of the SURCON period, the system processes the data for the next trading day. When the system starts processing data, the interactive connection with the NEAT system is lost and the message to that effect is displayed at the trader workstation.

NEAT Screen

The trading on the National Stock Exchange is done through a software known as NEAT.

The NEAT screen consists of various functions to make trading a pleasant experience. These functions help us in performing various tasks like placing a buy order, placing a sell order, modifying the orders already placed, keeping a watch on the market movement, finding market depth, checking the status of an order which had been placed earlier and other various supplementary functions. Since, NEAT being a practical topic, it has been dealt beautifully in the practical manual too.

Let us now have a look at the NEAT screen first and understand the various available functions on the same.

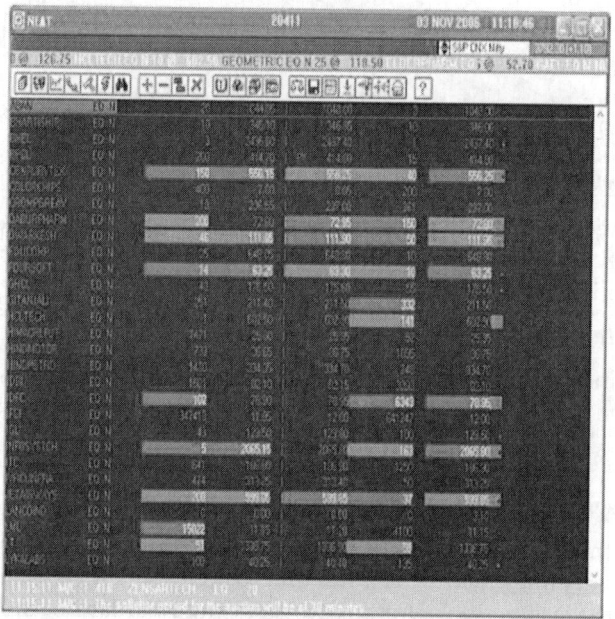

Title Bar:

a) *Logo:* It shows the logo of NEAT system.

b) *Name of the software:* The name of the software i.e. NEAT (National Exchange of Automated Trading) is displayed.

c) *Name of the company:* Name of the Trading Member who has taken membership with exchange, is displayed.

d) *Login ID number:* The login ID of the user is displayed. To get this ID, user has to clear NCFM certification in the desired module.

Current date in format date month year (for example 01.01.2007 should 01 JAN 2007)

f. Current time in format - hours: minutes: seconds

➡️ *Second Sub Title Bar:-*

It shows the current INDEX which is S&P CNX NIFTY with it changes from yesterday's closing in bracket along with +/- sign. For example if the current index is 4000 and the change is 100 points, then it will show like: S&P CNX NIFTY 4000 (100), S&P CNX 500, CNX 100, CNX IT, CNX Nifty Junior, S&P CNX Defty, Bank Nifty and CNX Midcap.

➡️ *Sub Title Bar:*

It shows the ticker window in which last traded trades comes in the sequence of symbol, series, market type, quantity and price in red colour for sell and in white colour for buy.

➡️ *Tool Bar:*

It has 23 icons in total which can be operated by mouse as well as by key-board with shortcut keys.

➡️ *Market Watch:*

This screen is the used to setup and view trading details of the securities that are selected by the user. For each security in the market watch, market information is dynamically updated.

➡️ *System Message Window:*

This window shows the messages regarding order/trade confirmation / modification / cancellation etc.

➡️ *Types of Orders*

Regular Lot (RL) Orders:

The term RL stands for regular lot. An order that has *no special condition associated* with it is a Regular Lot Order. When a dealer places this order, the system looks for a corresponding Regular Lot order existing in that market (Passive orders). If it does not find a match at the time it enters the system, the order *is stacked in the Regular Lot book as a passive order*. By default, the Regular Lot book appears in the order entry screen in the normal market.

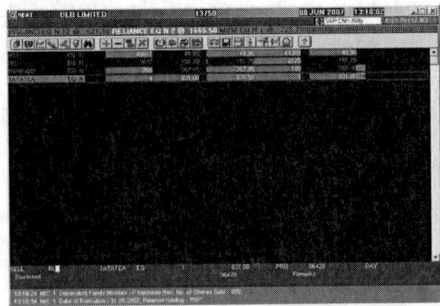

a) *Special Trade (ST) Orders:*

The term ST stands for special terms. All the orders having either AON (all or none) or MF (min fill), come under the category of ST.

Here all or none means that if some one is placing a big quantity order and he doesn't want to get less quantity to be executed, and then he can place an order that either all the quantity should get executed or none.

Same in the case of minimum fill which means that at least this much of minimum quantity should get executed or none. It is also used for buyback of shares.

b) *Stop loss order*

The term SL stands for stop loss order. These orders are placed for minimising/restricting the loss. In the event of a market crash or a rapidly skyrocketing market, it is not possible to place the order immediately and the client might have to suffer huge losses. To avoid such sudden losses and to restrict the loss in case the market moves rapidly in an unfavourable direction, stop loss orders are used. Stop loss orders are stored in this till the trigger price specified in the order is reached or surpassed. When the trigger price is reached or surpassed, the order is released in the regular lot book.

A buy/sell order in the stop loss book gets triggered when the last traded price in the normal market reaches or exceeds the trigger price of the order.

In these types of orders two types of rates are required, one is the trigger price, on which order will be activated in the Normal market and second is, the trade price, which can be market rate also.

For buy stop loss order, the trigger price has to be less than or equal to limit price.

Note:-

(Definition Trigger place

Price at which an order gets triggered from the Stop Loss book is called Trigger price. Limit Price - Price of the orders after triggering from Stop Loss book.)

c) *Negotiated Trade (NT) Orders:*

The term NT stands for Negotiated Trade book, and it contains all negotiated trades captured by the operators before they have been matched against their counter party. These entries are matched with identical counter party.

These orders contain a counter party code in addition to the other orders details.The purpose of Auction Inquiry (AI) is to enable the users to view the auction activities for the current trading day. This window displays information about auctions currently going on and auctions that have been completed.

The detailed line in the auction inquiry screen displays:

No.- Serial Number,

St. - Status of the auction security,

Type - Buy/Sell auction,

Symbol, Series, Best Buy Qty, Best Buy Price, Best Sell Price, Best Sell Qty, Auction Qty, Auction Price and Settlement Period.

The following are the different status displayed for an auction security:

S - Auction is in Solicitor Period

M - System is matching the orders

F - Auction is over

X - Auction is deleted

P - Auction is pending and yet to begin.

d) *Odd Lot (OL) Orders:*

The term OL Stands for Odd Lot book which contains all odd lot orders (orders with quantity less/more than marketable lot).

The operator matches an active odd lot order with a passive odd lot order in the book. Earlier, a market lot used to be of 100 units, so in order to place orders for less/more than 100 units an odd lot market was used. But today, a lot is of 1 unit only, hence the need of odd lot market is not there any more hence, this operation is not working now-a-days.

e) *Retail Debt (RD) Orders:*

The term RD stands for RETDEBT book which contains all RETDEBT orders. The RETDEBT market facility on the NEAT system of capital market segment is used for transactions in Retail Debt Market sessions.

Trading in the Retail Debt Market takes place in the same manner as in the equities (capital market) segment. An operator matches an active order with a passive order.

f) *Auction Market (AU) Orders:*

The term AU stands for Auction in which orders are entered for Auction Market. Auctions are initiated by the Exchange on behalf of trading members for settlement related reasons. The main reasons are Shortages, Bad Deliveries and Objections.

The auction period is initiated at 12:00 P.M to 12:30 P.M.

The matching process for auction orders in this book is initiated only at the end of the auction period. The auction ending period is between 12:30 P.M. and 1:00 P.M.

 ### Key Functions

Outstanding Order (F3): This function is used to enable the User to view the outstanding orders (buy/sell) for a selected security.

An outstanding order is an order that has been entered by the user, but which has not yet been completely traded or cancelled.

The User is permitted to see his own/client's orders and can modify/ cancel the orders till it gets executed. All the figures are till the time of invoking the window.

Invoking Outstanding Orders:

To invoke the Outstanding Order screen, **_press [F3] key._** If a particular security is selected, the details of the selected security defaults in the selection screen or else the current position in Market Watch defaults.

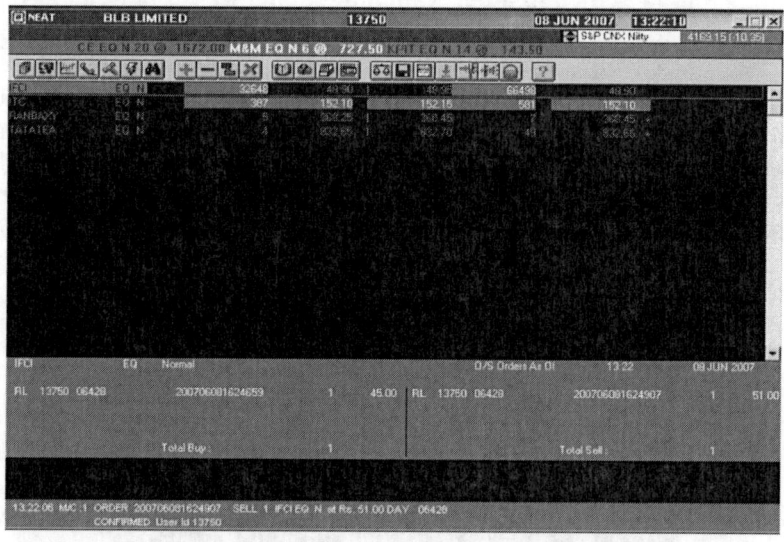

Market Watch screen (F4)

This screen is used to set-up and view trading details of the securities that are selected by the users. For each security in the market watch, market information is dynamically updated. The one line market information displayed is for current best price orders available in the Regular Lot Book.

For each security the following information is displayed:

- Symbol, Series and Market type
- The corporate action indicator "Ex/Cum"
- The total buy order quantity available at best buy price
- Best buy price # Best sell price
- Total sell order quantity available at best sell price
- The last traded price # The last trade price change indicator
- Increase/Decrease indicator
- The no delivery period indicator "ND"

Market By Order (F5):

The purpose of Market by Order (MBO) is to enable the User, to view outstanding orders in the order books, in the order of price/time priority for a selected security. It shows best five orders by price time priority for buyers as well as for sellers for the selected scrip.

This function is not available for Equity market; it only works for Auction markets. This function can be invoked by using F5 key or by clicking on the first icon in the tool bar.

Auction by Order

The Auction No. field is compulsory only to view Auction orders details. Getting Familiar to Neat Screen 19 The User can change any or all information by typing over the appropriate fields. The [Tab] and [Shift Tab] keys can be used to navigate between the fields. After entering the selection details, press [Enter] key. The detailed MBO screen is displayed.

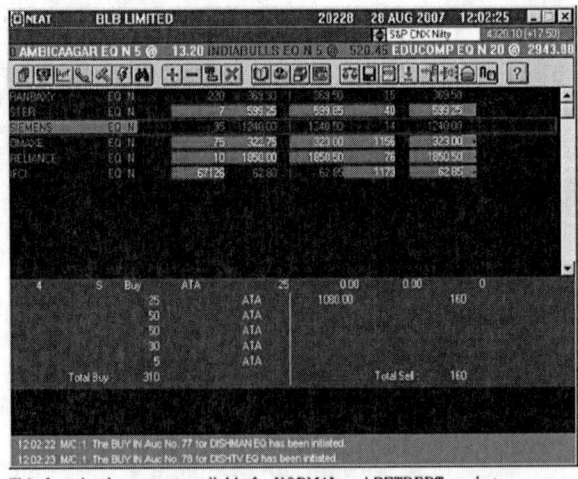

➤ _Market By Price (F6):_

As the name suggests it shows the best five buy/sell rates on the basis of price time priority with quantity available for a specified security. This window is dynamically updated. By pressing F6, the following window displays:

Symbol, Series and Type of the script, is invoked. The output of this function contains the same fields as that of MBO (Market by Order).

Special Features of MBP:

1) Regular lot & special term orders can be viewed in the MBP.

2) The status of a security is indicated in this screen. 'P' indicates that the security is in the pre-open phase and 'S' indicates that the security is suspended.

3) The percentage change for last trade price with respect to previous day's closing price and the average trade price of the security in the given market, are the additional fields in the screens.

4) No un-triggered stop-loss order will be displayed on the MBP screen.

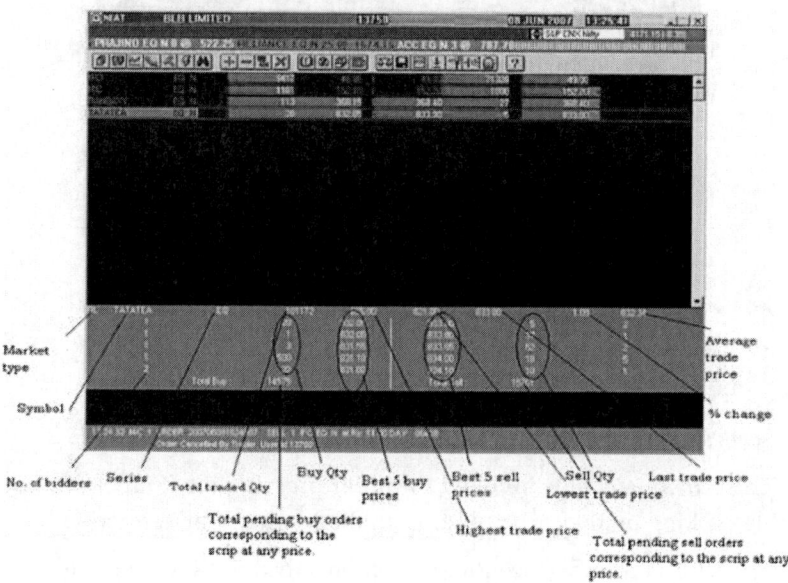

5) Only orders for the best 5 prices information are displayed. Press enter to view the best five buy and sell order

Activity Log (F7):

The Activity Log (AL) shows all the activities which have been **_performed on any order belonging to that User._** These activities include order modification / cancellation, partial / full trade, trade modification / cancellation. It displays information of only those orders in which some activity has taken place. It does not display those orders on which no activity has taken place. All the figures are till the time of invoking the window.

➤ *Invoking AL:*

To invoke Activity Log, press [F7] key. If a particular security is selected, the details of the selected security defaults in the selection screen or else the current position in Market Watch defaults. Details of security in the selection screen can also be defaulted from the last action.

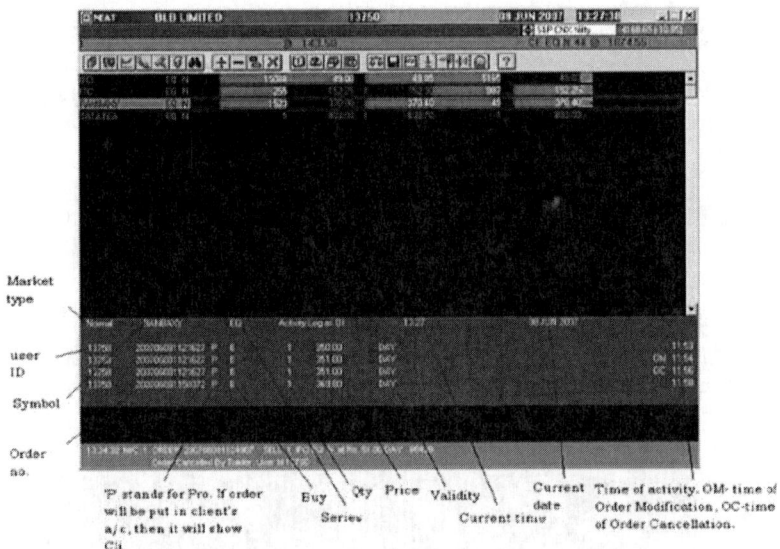

Security Descriptor (Shift + F8):

This function can be invoked by either pressing the [Shift + F8] keys or double clicking on the security setup in the Market Watch screen.

The DPR i.e. Daily Price Range, displays the permissible price band for a security for the current trading day.

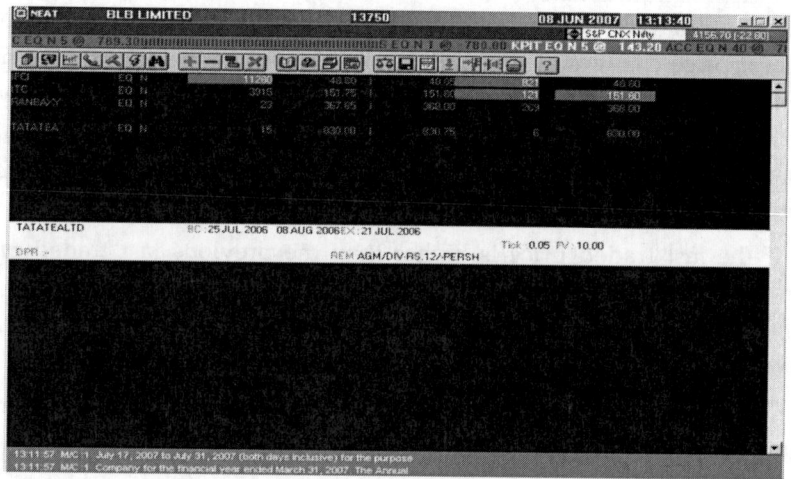

Market Watch (F4):

Getting Familiar to Neat Screen 18 This screen is used to set-up and view trading details of the securities that are selected by the users. For each security in the market watch, market information is dynamically updated. The one line market information displayed is for current best price orders available in the Regular Lot Book. For each security the following information is displayed:

- Symbol, Series and Market type
- The corporate action indicator "Ex/Cum"
- The total buy order quantity available at best buy price
- Best buy price
- Best sell price
- Total sell order quantity available at best sell price
- The last traded price
- The last trade price change indicator
- Increase/Decrease indicator
- The no delivery period indicator "ND"

If the security is suspended, _SUSPENDED' appears in front of the security. *If a question mark (?) appears on the extreme right hand corner for a security,* it indicates that the information being displayed is not the latest and the system will dynamically update it.

Information Update: In the Market Watch screen, changes in the best price and quantities are highlighted on a dynamic basis. For example, if the best price changes as a result of a new order in the market, the new details are immediately displayed. The changed details are highlighted with a change of colour for a few seconds to signify that a change has occurred. *The blue colour indicates that price/quantities have increased, while the red colour indicates that the price/quantities have decreased.*

If the last traded price is higher than the previous last traded price then the indicator= *+ 'appears or if the last traded price is lower than the previous last traded price then the indicator -'appears. If there is no change in the last traded price, no indicator is displayed.*

The list of securities that are available for trading on the Capital Market segment is available in the Security List box.

The user has the option to set up securities directly from the Security List without typing a single character on the market watch screen. This is a quick facility to setup securities. If the user tries to setup a security which is already present in the market watch one gets a message that the security is already setup. The user also has the option to add and delete the security set up in the market watch screen as many times as one desires. The user can print the contents of the Market Watch setup by the user. The user can either print the Market Watch on display or the Full Market Watch.

Market Watch Download: A user has to set up securities after the first download of the software. After setting up the market watch, it is suggested that the user should log out normally. This will help the user to save the freshly set up market watch securities in a file.

If at any given time, when the user has freshly set up a few securities and encounters an abnormal exit, the newly set up securities are not saved and the user may have to repeat the process of setting up securities.

The Market Watch setup is carried over to subsequent days, thus averting the need to set up the Market Watch on daily basis. During the logon stage, the relevant Market Watch details are downloaded from the trading system. The message displayed is _Market Watch download is in progress'. The time taken for the Market Watch download depends on the number of securities set up

Easy Navigation: The details of the current position in the Market Watch defaults in the order entry screen and the inquiry selection screen.

It is therefore possible to do quick order entries and inquiries using this feature. The default details can also be overwritten.

Coporate Actions Indication: An indicator for corporate actions for a security is another feature in market watch. The indicators are as follows:

XD' - ex-dividend (The ex-dividend date for stocks is usually set one business day before the record date. If you purchase a stock on its ex-dividend date or after, you will not receive the next dividend payment. Instead, the seller gets the dividend. If you purchase before the ex-dividend date, you get the dividend.)

_ **XB - ex-bonus** (On and after the ex-date, the shares if bought are no longer eligible to receive the bonus and are called ex-bonus.)

_ **XI' - ex-interest**(n the stock market, "ex-interest" is an adjective that means "not including interest". It's used to describe the price of bonds that doesn't include the right to receive the next interest payment. For example, if someone buys 400 8% Government Securities of Rs 100 each at Rs 102 Ex-Interest Price on September 1, 2016, the price doesn't include the accrued interest for five months from April 1, 2016 to September 1, 2016.)

_ **XR' - ex-rights:**-Ex-rights are stock shares that are trading but without rights attached because they've either expired, been transferred, or been exercised.

CD' - cum-dividend:-Cum dividend" means "with dividend" and refers to a stock whose buyer is eligible to receive a dividend that was declared before the share was purchased. The buyer receives the dividend when it is paid

Similarly :-

CR' - cum-rights

CB' - cum-bonus

CI' - cum-interest

C*' - in case of more than one of CD, CR, CB, CI

X*' - in case of more than one of XD, XR, XB, XI

➡ *Previous trade Window*

The purpose of this window is to provide security wise information to Users for their own trades. The 'Trades' window displays the executed orders. The trade details cannot be modified or cancelled, since the trades reflected in this window are already executed.

The main advantage of this function is that it facilitates viewing the details of each trade separately which cannot be viewed in the Net Integrated Position window, wherein the entire buy/sell quantity is displayed with average price. All the figures are till the time of invoking the window.

Invoking Previous Trades Screen: Getting Familiar to Neat Screen

To invoke Previous Trades screen, press [F8] key. If a particular security is selected, the details of the selected security defaults in the selection screen or else the current position in Market Watch defaults. User is provided with the client account type field. On giving an account type in this field, it is possible to view all previous trades for a particular client. The user can also blank out the Symbol & Series and get all the trades for a particular user id. The page up/page down keys will help the user to move from one security to another. For further details please see the Previous Trades screen.

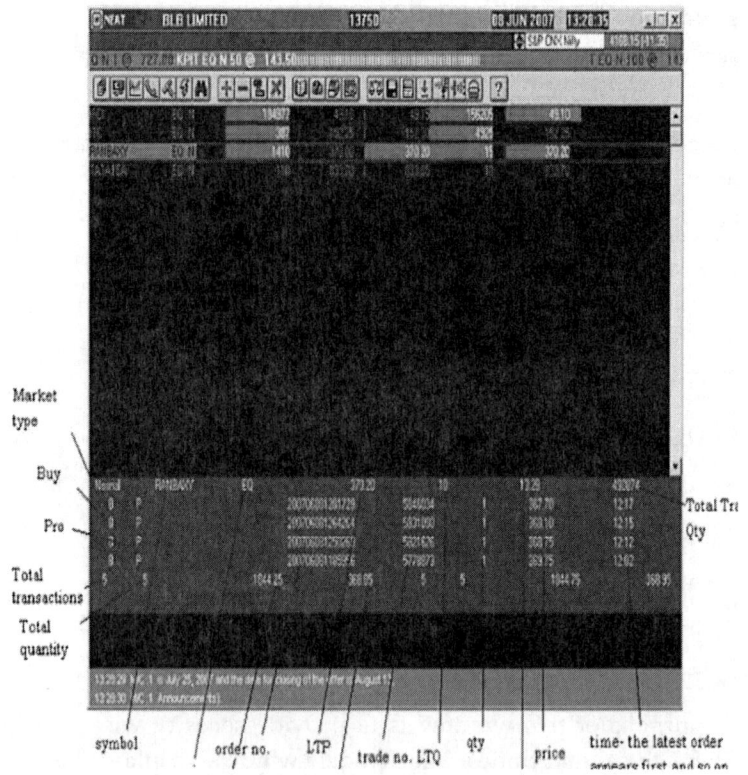

The detailed Previous Trade screen information is split into

1) First Line

2) Detail Line and Summary Line.

a) The first line displays *Market Type, Symbol, Series, Last Trade Price, Last Trade Quantity, Last Trade Time and Total Traded Quantity.*

b) The detail line contains *Buy/Sell Indicator, PRO/CLI indicator (where P – PRO and C - CLI), Order Number, Trade Number, Trade Quantity, Trade Price and Trade Time. The summary line contains Total Number of Buy Trades, Total Buy Quantity Traded, Total Buy Traded Value, Average Buy Traded Price, Total Number of Sell Trades, Total Sell Quantity Traded, Total Sell Traded Value and Average Sell Traded Price.*

Previous Trade Screen displays the client account number also. Pre-open Indicator is displayed as"P‖ for all Pre-open Trades.

Trades are displayed in a reverse chronological order. First all buy trades are displayed and then sell trades are displayed. A facility is provided to users to view their trades for BUY side or SELL side or ALL by selecting the BUY/SELL/ALL filter in primary window.

Special Features of Previous Trades

(a) Trade cancellation can be requested from the Previous Trade screen. This facility is available only for member's own trades. *The Corporate Manager can request for trade cancellation for any branch or any dealer.*

The Branch Manager can request for trade cancellation for any dealer under that branch. The dealer can request for trade cancellation only for trades under that user id.

(b) The user can request the Exchange to modify only the client code field. Currently trade modification facility is not enabled on trading system.

➡ *Snap Quote*

The Snap Quote is a feature available in the system to get instantaneous market information on a desired security. This is normally used for a security that is not setup in the Market Watch window. The information displayed for the set up security is same as that in Market Watch window i

➡ *Order Status*

The purpose of the Order Status is to look into the status of the dealers own specific orders. The screen provides the current status of the orders with the other order details. The order status screen is not dynamically updated. In case the order is being traded, the trade details are displayed.

In case of multiple trades the display of the orders can be seen by scrolling down. It shows the status of orders. To view the status of an order, type the Order Number and press 'Enter'.

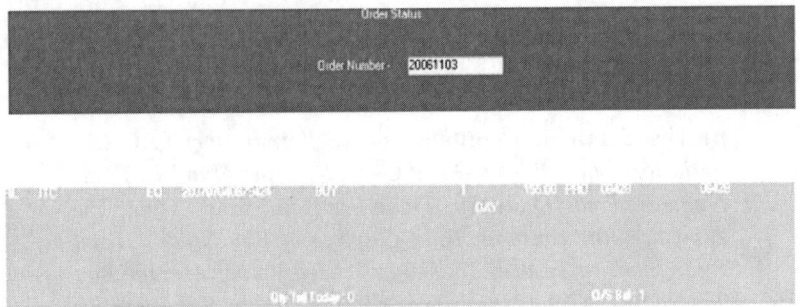

On pressing 'enter', it shows the details of the specified order number. The following example showsa buy order of ITC for 1 share @ Rs. 156.

The detailed OS screen is divided into three parts. The first part covers order related information, the second part covers the trade related information if the order has resulted in a trade and the third part gives summary details.

The first part details are in two lines. The first line gives Book Type, Symbol, Series, Order Number, Type (Buy/Sell), Total Order Quantity, Order Price, PRO/CLI, Client A/C Number and Participant ID.

The second line gives Disclosed Quantity, MF/AON Indicator, MF Quantity, 66 Trigger Price, Day, Indicator 1 (Order Modified - MOD), Indicator 2 (Order Cancelled - CXL) and Indicator 3 (Order Traded - TRD). The second part details are Trade Quantity, Trade Price, Trade Time and Trade Number. The third part details are Quantity Traded Today and Balance Quantity (remaining quantity).

Special Features of Order Status

> a) The OS provides the user the current status of the order i.e. whether order has been modified, order was cancelled, order was traded, or order has been partially traded.

> b) It shows all the order details. It also shows the trade details for each trade done against this order.

> c) The data is presented in chronological order. One line appears for each activity that has taken place today.

d) The dealer can view order status of orders entered under that Dealer ID only.

e) This Inquiry option is not available to Users in Inquiry mode.

➡️ *Market Inquiry*

The purpose of the Market Inquiry is to enable the user to view the market statistics, for a particular market, for security. It also displays the open price andprevious close price for a security.

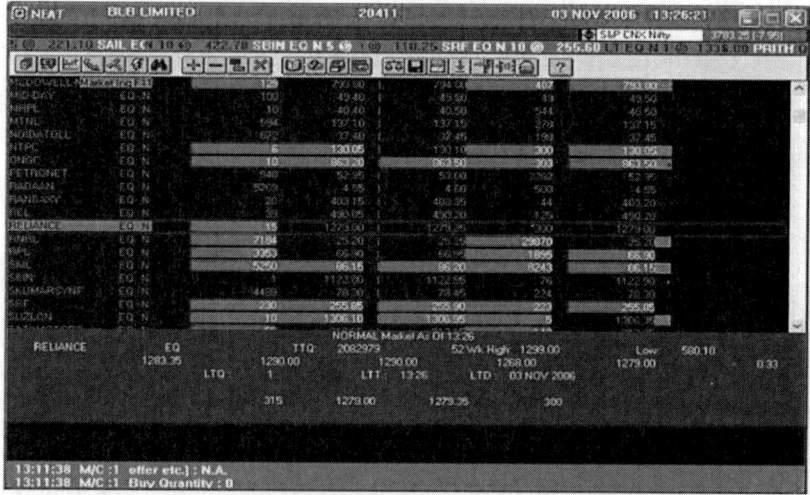

a) This screen is not dynamically updated. It displays the security status of the security selected. _S' indicates that the security is suspended, _P' indicates that the security is in pre open (only for normal market) and in absence of the above indicators the security is open for trading.

b) An indicator for corporate actions for security is displayed on the screen. The indicators are as follows:

1) "CD" = cum-dividend

2) "XD" = ex-dividend

3) "CR" = cum-rights

4) "XR = ex-rights

5) "CB"= cum-bonus

6) "XB" = ex-bonus

7) "CI" = cum-interest

8) "XI" = ex-interest

c) The net change indicator for last trade price with respect to the previous day's closing price and the net change percentage for the last trade price with respect to the previous day's closing price are displayed.

d) The base price of a security for the day is equal to the previous day's closing price of the security in normal circumstances. Thus, in the market inquiry screen the field indicating the closing price also gives the base price for the day.

e) If the base price is manually changed (due to a corporate action) then the market inquiry will not display the new base price in the closing price field.

➤ *Auction inquiry*

Before proceeding with window let us understand what do you mean by auction in Nse

The National Stock Exchange (NSE) conducts auctions for shares every day *between 2–2:45 PM on the T+2 day.*

The purpose of the auction is to invite offers from new sellers for shares that were not delivered to the demat account due to a short delivery. Short delivery happens when a seller fails to deliver shares that were purchased.

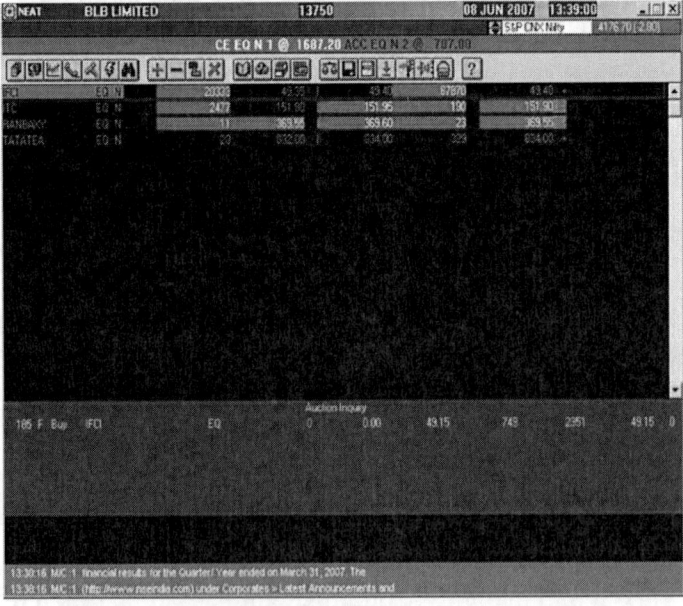

- T day: Shares are only sold for delivery if they are available in the client's demat account.

- T + 2 day (morning): Shares are not delivered.

- T + 2 day (auction session): The exchange invites offers from new sellers for the shares that were not delivered. The exchange sets an upper and lower limit for bids, and the lowest bidder wins the auction. The upper limit is 20% higher than the previous day's closing price. Only shares that are settled in the demat account can be sold during the auction. Members whose clients have defaulted are not allowed to participate in the auction to avoid conflicts of interest

- T + 2 day (post auction): An auction penalty is generated. (The auction penalty in the National Stock Exchange (NSE) is a charge imposed on sellers who fail to transfer shares to the exchange by the designated settlement date. The penalty is intended to: Ensure fair and transparent share transactions, Hold defaulting sellers accountable, and Promote accountability and maintain market integrity). The penalty for a *__periodic call auction in the NSE is 0.50%__* of the trade value for both the sale and the buy, resulting in a 1% penalty for the client on a PAN basis

- T+3 day: The shares are delivered to the buyer.

The purpose of Auction Inquiry (AI) is to enable the users to view the auction activities for the current trading day. This window displays information about auctions currently going on and auctions that have been completed.

The detailed line in the auction inquiry screen displays:

No. - Serial Number,

St. - Status of the auction security,

Type - Buy/Sell auction, Symbol, Series, Best Buy Qty, Best Buy Price, Best Sell Price, Best Sell Qty, Auction Qty, Auction Price and Settlement Period. The following are the different status displayed for an auction security: S - Auction is in Solicitor Period

M - System is matching the orders

F - Auction is over

X - Auction is deleted

P - Auction is pending and yet to begin.

➤ Basket Trading

Basket trading is essential for institutional investors and investment funds that wish to hold a large number of securities in certain proportions.

As cash moves in and out of the fund, large baskets of securities must be bought or sold simultaneously, so that price movements for each security do not alter the portfolio allocation.

A **basket trade** typically involves the sale or purchase of 15 or more securities and is generally used to purchase stocks. Such baskets are typically measured against a **benchmark** or tracked against an entity, such as an index, to measure their returns.

Suppose an investment fund wishes to take advantage of the volatility in an index. The fund manager creates a long/short basket to track the index. The basket does not actually contain securities. Instead, it has a collection of call and put options.

Baskets can also be used to trade currencies and commodities.

For example, an investor may create a basket that includes soft commodities, such as wheat, soybeans, and corn. Most investment or brokerage firms that offer basket trading require a minimum investment amount.

The distribution of dollars between various components of a typical basket can be determined using various types of weightings.

For example, dollar-weighting criteria distribute the overall dollar amount for the basket equally between its components. A basket trading strategy that uses share weighting will divide the overall amount equally between blocks of shares.

Basket trades allow investors to create a trade that is tailored to them, that allows for easy allocation across many securities, and that gives them control over their investments.

➤ Basket Trade Benefits

- ### Personalised Choice:
  Investors can create a basket trade that fits their investment objectives. For example, an investor seeking income may create a basket trade that includes only high-yielding dividend stocks. Baskets might contain stocks from a specific sector, or that have a certain market cap.

- ### Easy Allocation:
  Basket trades make it straightforward for investors to allocate their investments across multiple securities. Investments are typically

distributed using share quantity, dollar amount, or percentage weighting. Share quantity assigns an equal number of shares to each holding in the basket. Dollar and percentage allocations use a dollar amount or a percentage amount to distribute securities. For instance, if an *investor*is using a dollar amount to allocate Rs.50,000 across of basket of 15 securities, Rs.3,333.33 of each security is purchased.

- *Control:*

    A basket trade helps investors control their investment. Decisions can be made to add or remove individual or multiple securities to the basket. Tracking the *performance*of a basket trade as a whole also saves time monitoring individual securities and streamlines the administrative process.

In the basket trading functionality, the user first selects a portfolio from combo box. The portfolio in the combo box is user defined portfolios (which can be created or edited from the Security List screen which is an existing functionality).

All users defined Portfolios are automatically loaded in to the combo box. The User then allocates an amount to the portfolio by mentioning *the amount in the Amount' edit box.*

The amount entered is in lakh and must be less than or equal to Rs. 3000 lakh. If the amount entered is not sufficient to buy/sell a complete basket, a message —Insufficient amount for creating the basketǁ is displayed. Then, the User mentions whether he wants to buy or sell the Portfolio by selecting a choice from BUY/SELL combo box.

The User has to mention the name of offline order file which would be generated. The Output Offline order file is always generated in the Basket directory of the current selected login drive. If a file with the given name already exists then it asks for overwriting the old file.

A Reverse File with *the same name is also generated in R_Basket' directory* of the current login drive. The Reverse File contains reverse order (if user has selected buy then it contains sell orders and vice-versa).

The user can mention order's duration (IOC or day) by selecting from a check box. The User can also specify PRO/CLI orders by selecting from the combo box. In case of CLI orders it is compulsory to mention the account number in the edit box.

The participant name can be mentioned. If mentioned it is verified whether it is a valid participant or not.

The amount mentioned in the _Amount Edit' Box is divided among the securities of the portfolio, depending on their current market capitalisation, and the amount allocated per security is used to calculate the number of shares to be bought / sold for that security which is reflected in the offline order file.

The number of shares is rounded off to the nearest integer. If the basket contains any security whose regular lot is not one, then the file will need to be corrected by the user to accommodate shares in tradable lots. If the portfolio contains a security which is suspended/not eligible in the chosen market then an error message is displayed on the screen.

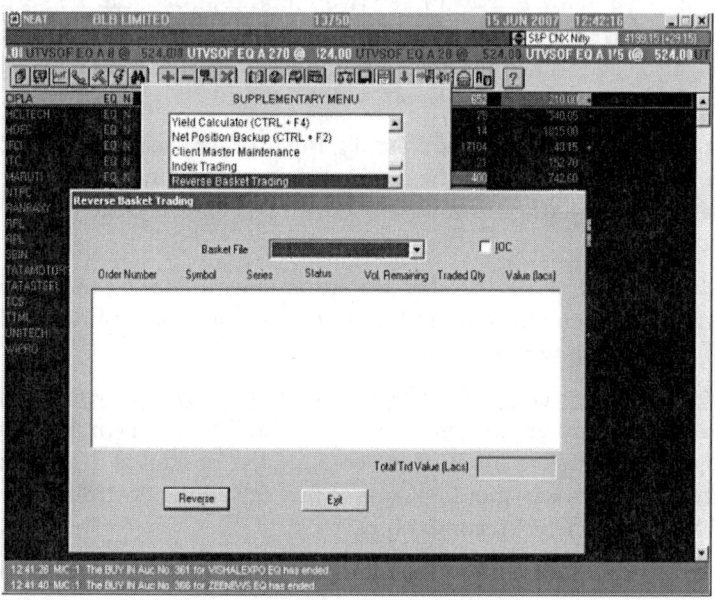

(basket trading screen)

All the orders generated through the offline order file are priced at the available market price. Quantity of shares of a particular security in portfolio is calculated as under

$$\text{Number of Shares of a security in portfolio} = \frac{\text{Amount * Issued Capital for the security}}{\text{Current Portfolio Capitalisation}}$$

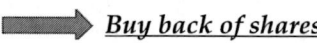 **_Buy back of shares_**

The purpose of Buy Back Trade functionality is to give information to the market about the buy back trades executed from the start of the buy back period till current trading date in the securities whose buyback period is currently on.

The Buyback Trade functionality also provides users with the information about the buyback trades going in various securities.

The front screen shows Symbol, Series, Low price (Today), High price (Today), Weight age.

Average price, Volume (Today), & Previous day Volume.

The user after selecting a particular row from the buyback list box can view further information via Symbol, Series, Start date, End date, Total Traded Qty (Till date), Previous High price, Previous Low price and Wt avg. price till date of buyback scheme.

The Buyback broadcast updates the information.

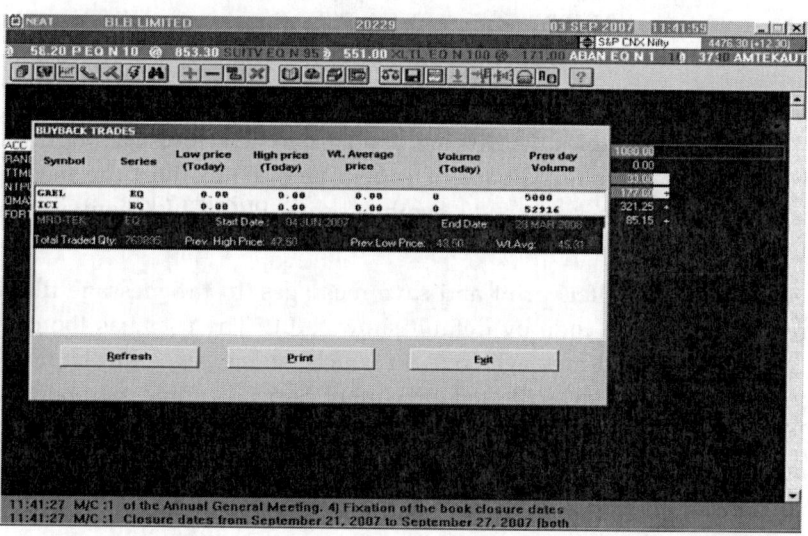

As per **_SEBI Notification, dated November 14, 1998, buyback of securities is permitted in the secondary market_**. This is termed as _Buy-Back from the Open Market'.

➤ **Supplementary Function**

1) _Report selection_

Report selection window allows the user (corporate manager and branch manager) to specify the number of copies to be printed for each report.

All the reports are generated at the end of day. Once the reports are printed, the Report Selection screen shows the date and the time the reports were printed.

The user can request for reprinting of the reports.

The reports that are available to the trading member are Market Statistics and Market Indices

a) Market Statistics: The purpose of this report is to show the market statistics of that trading day.

(*This report gives details related to all the securities traded on that day for all markets.*)

b) Market Indices: This report contains Open, High, Low, Close, Previous Close and % change over the Previous Close of NIFTY 50, NIFTY Defty, NIFTY Junior, NIFTY 500, NIFTY 100, NIFTY Midcap NIFTY IT, Bank Nifty, Nifty Midcap 50, NIFTY FMCG, NIFTY MNC, NIFTY Pharma, NIFTY PSE, NIFTY PSU Bank and NIFTY Service etc.

2) *Full Display message:-*

This option enables the display of all the system messages right from the start of the Opening Phase. It is also possible to filter the messages depending on the message code, symbol, series, PRO/CLI, Client, date and time.

The user can filter, print and save messages. In the message filtering screen the message code by default shows ALL. The user has the option to select the desired message code on which the messages can be filtered. The messages can also be filtered on Symbol, Series, Trading member Code, PRO/CLI/ ALL, Client A/C Number, Date and Time fields

If the user wants to see the messages for trading member account, he need to Specify the messages related to 'PRO', and specify the trading member code.

In case the user desires to see the client message he need to specify the 'CLI' along with the client code.

If the user desire to view all messages 'ALL' has to be specified and Client Account field should be blank

The message filter displays _ALL' by default when the user invokes the full message display screen.

Message Code Description of Messages Selected

ALL- All messages AUC Auction order/trade message

AUI -Auction initiation messages

LIS -All listing related messages

MAR- Margin Violation messages

ORD- Order Related messages

OTH- Miscellaneous

SPD -SecuritySuspension/De-suspension

SYS- System Messages TRD Trades

The user can save messages by invoking the Save option on the Full Message Display screen and by specifying the directory and file name in the pop up box. Here an option is available to the user to both specify the directory and file name to save messages, or to choose the default directory i.e. nsecm\user directory. This file can be viewed in MS-DOS editor.

3) *Colour Selection:*

The user can customise the colours for various inquiry and other trader workstation screens as per choice.

The following is displayed on the colour selection list box:

a) *List of Screens:* Lists all the screens in NEAT system. The user has the option of changing both the foreground and the background colours of any screen.

b) *Display Window:* Displays the screen with the changed colours. To change the colour of a particular screen, the user has to position the highlight bar on the desired screen and select any one of the *sixteen colour buttons.* The user can reset the colour to default setting by selecting the Default option.

(It is to be noted that the user cannot select the same colour for foreground of an inquiry screen)

4) *Print System Messages On/Off:*

The _Print System Messages ON/OFF' enables/ disables printing of the system messages as and when they appear in the messages window. By default the option is set to `OFF'. The user can change the On/Off position by pressing the space bar.

5) *Print Order/Trade Confirmation Slips On/Off:*

The Print Order/Trade Confirmation ON/ OFF' enables/disables printing of the order/trade slips. By default the option is set to `OFF'. The user can change the On/Off position by pressing the space bar. The current mode (On/Off) is displayed for this option on the Supplementary Menu screen itself. Pre open Identifier _P' is displayed for Pre open records.

6) *Ticker Selection:*

The ticker selection screen allows the user to set up the securities that should appear in the user's ticker window. If a security is deleted from the system, it is also removed from the ticker selection display. The selection of securities can be done for each market separately. The user can select one or all security type for display.

7) *Market Movement*:

The purpose of the Market Movement' screen is to provide information to the User regarding the movement of a security for the current day. This inquiry gives the snap shot for a particular security

8) *Most Active Securities:*

This screen displays the details of the most active securities based on the total traded value during the day. The number 'N' is parameterised by the Exchange. The information provided on this screen is not dynamically updated. The user, however, can get the latest information by refreshing the screen.

9) *Reprint Order/Trade Confirmation Slips:*

Although the order and trade slips for **'confirmation', 'modification', 'rejection' and 'cancellation'** slips can be printed as and when a particular operation is performed. The user, however, *can reprint these slips later during the trading day by using this option*. There is facility to select one or more operations for printing the slips.

For example one can select 'confirmation' as well as 'modification' at a time. After the user specifies the type of slip to be printed, the start and end order/trade numbers are automatically filled.(user can customise the range). Initially, the options have such values that all the order related slips can be printed. On selecting Print option all the selected order/trade slips are printed and on selecting the Cancel option, no slips are printed.

10) *Branch Order Value Limit Setup:*

The purpose of this screen is to enable corporate manager to setup a limit on order entry for each branch under the trading member firm. This option *in the supplementary menu is available to the user only if the user is a corporate manager*.

On selection, the Branch Order Value Limit Setup screen appears. To view the limit for a particular branch, *the user has to select the Branch ID and the details for the branch* i.e. branch name, the limit set and the used up value are displayed.

The values for the branch order limit _are displayed in Rs. lakhs._ To change the limit for a branch, the user has to _select the _Limited' option and enter the new limit in the _New Limit Value'_. The new limits are then updated by the system.

The user can also print the details of a branch by selecting the Print option. Viewing and modification is possible during market hours. A corporate manager can set the branch order value limit for any/all branches either before or during trading hours.

Also, the corporate manager can view the set limit and the used limit any time during the trading day. Whenever the corporate manager modifies the branch order limit of any of his branches, the branch manager receives a message to that effect at his trader workstation.

11) _Net Position and Net position Backup:_

The user can interactively view his net position across securities. The Net Position screen displays Symbol, Series, Buy Value (in lacs), Buy Qty, Buy Average Price, Sell Average Price, Sell Qty, Sell Value (in lacs), Net Qty and Net Value (in lacs).

It also displays the Grand Total of Buy Value (in lacs), Buy Qty, Sell Qty, Sell Value (in lacs), Net Value (in lacs) and Net Value Mark to Market (in lacs).

- The user has the option for selecting market type as Normal/Odd Lot/All.
- The user can also select Client Type as CLI/PRO/All.
- The user is provided with an option to select the client code from the drop down menu to view the net position of specific client.
- The user can refresh the screen to update the Net Position and can also print the details of the Net Position screen at any point of time.
- Net position backup is available from the Net position screen. The User can select the fields as Symbol, Series, PRO/CLI and CLI A/c Number on which the output would be filtered. By default the output file is generated and stored as _'Netpos.txt'._
- The user can overwrite and specify any other file name also. The user has the option of generating the output file in any directory he wants to or on a pen drive.

Square off

Squaring off is a trading style that day trade investors use to make profit from the market volatility. The trader buys a number of stocks of one company and sells them off on the same day at a higher price usually, which gives the trader an amount of profit. Or vice versa.

a) *Intraday square off*

Involves buying and selling securities quickly within the same trading day, with a limited holding period. For example, a trader might buy a number of stocks of one company and sell them at a higher price on the same day.

b) *Delivery square off*

Involves closing open positions after holding shares for a longer duration, typically with a long-term investment perspective.

(Square offs usually happen before the stock market closes, which is typically between 3 PM and 3:20 PM in India. They can help traders cut down on losses and make profits on their current position)

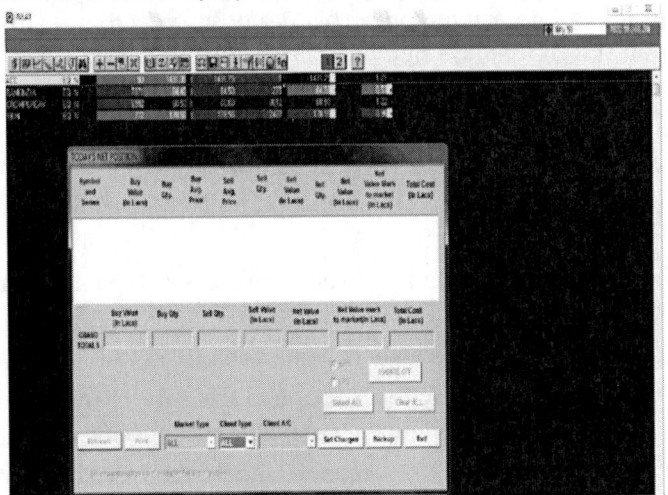

- When user clicks on Square off, an offline file will be generated containing counter orders which will square off the position of that particular user. The offline file generated will be stored in the drive from where the exe is re-inflated.
- The name of the offline file generated will be *"SqrOffPosition.txt"*.
- The position can be squared off *only for Normal Market.*
- If the *ODDLOT market is selected, the Square Off button will get disabled.*
- If ALL is selected from the Market type drop down list, then the positions will be squared off for open position of NORMAL Market only.

- If the user selects PRO or CLI from the Client Type drop down box, then the position would be squared off only for those corresponding Open positions.

- The user is given an option to generate either DAY/IOC (IOC is defaulted) order while generating the offline file.

12) *Online Backup (Alt+F7):*

Online Backup is a facility that the user can invoke to take a backup of all order and trade related information for the user. *The information available is for the current day only.*

Online *backup is in the TXT file* format for the market segments such as Derivatives and

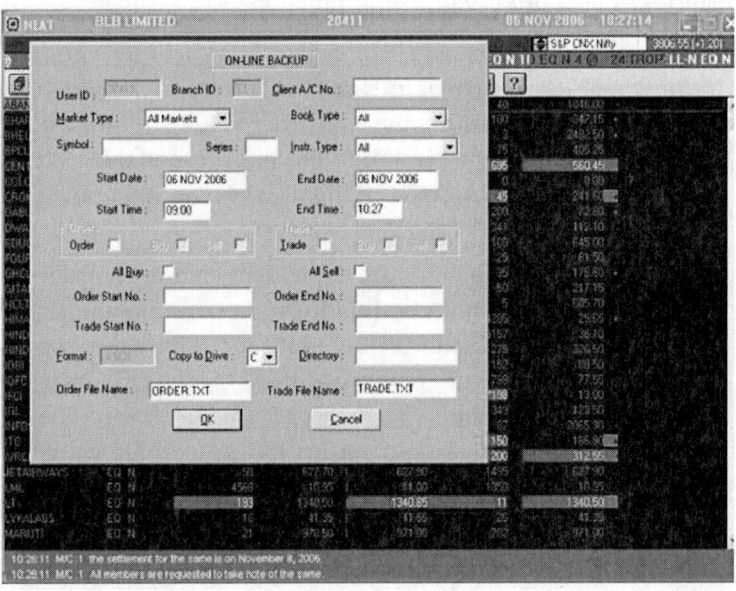

Equities for various functions like Trade, Order, Spread.

The online backup facility involves a *number of filtering options, like the market type, the instrument type and the duration of required report can be specified in terms of date and time.*

13) *One line/Tabular Slips:*

The One Line or Tabular slips' is used to select the format for printing confirmation slips. By default the option is set to _One Line'.

The user can change the format to Tabular slip' by pressing the spacebar. The current mode is displayed on the Supplementary Menu screen.

14) *User Order Value Limit Setup:*

User order value limit is the cumulative value of orders placed by the user during the day across all securities. This enables the corporate manager to set up different limits among the users depending upon the permitted user activity in single/multiple scrips.

For a new user, the user order value limit is set as zero by default. Every order entry will be checked for user order value limit. A user is restricted to enter orders greater than the order value limit specified by his corporate manager. In case the user order value limit is exhausted a message —Order number............request rejected. Used limit cannot exceed the user order value limit.‖ is displayed on the message window screen. Following are the main features of user order value limit functionality:

a) A corporate manager *can set up branch order value limit and user order value* limit for all users. A branch manager can also set up the user order value limit for the users under his branch. While the branch manager can view the user order limits of the users under his branch only.

b) User order value limits are dependent on branch order value limits. It is not possible for a corporate manager to set only branch order value limits and not assign any user order value limit. *It is mandatory for the corporate manager to configure the user order value limit.* The branch manager may also set up the user order value limit for users under his branch.

c) The cumulative value of the user *order value limit should not exceed the corresponding branch order value limit*. Also, the user order value limit cannot be set as unlimited if branch order value limit is set as a specific value. In case the corporate manager tries to revise the branch order value limit to a value less than the user order value limit a message.

d) When the corporate manager sets up the user order value limit as specified, a message —User order value limit for user number ......has been set to Rs. .... "lakh" is displayed on the message window screen of the corporate manager, respective Branch Manager and the concerned user.

e) The user order value limit can be revised during trading hours.

f) The corporate manager/branch manager can also print the user order value limit details.

Example: M/s. Agre Financial Services, a trading member on the NSE, has a branch order value of Rs. 700 lakh for his Chennai branch and Rs. 650 lakh for Kolkata branch. Chennai branch has two users _X' and _Y' with user order value limits of Rs. 250 lakh and Rs. 300 lakh respectively. Kolkata branch has one user _Z' with user order value limit of Rs. 350 lakh. The member applies for a new user at Chennai. What is the maximum user order value that can be set for the new user? The maximum User Order Value limit for Chennai is = Rs. 700 - (Rs. 250 + Rs. 300) = Rs.150 lakh

15) *Offline Order Entry:*

A facility Offline Order Entry' has been incorporated in the tradingsoftware where the user can generate order file in a specific format outside the trading system and upload the file in the system by invoking this facility.

If the system assigns an order number, the same is written against the record. In case of any error(s), the corresponding error code is written against the record. Users can place bulk orders in pre-open with book type as 'PO' The user has to specify the relevant order file name in the Offline Order Entry pop-up box and then initiate the upload process. The user can also interrupt the injection of the orders. It should be noted that the file has to be in the format as specified by the Exchange. The offline order entry facility accepts comma separated file structure (file saved as *.csv where * is the file name).

Advanced Offline Order Entry

A special feature _Advanced Offline Order Entry' has been incorporated in the trader workstation for all types of users (_Corporate Manager ', _Branch Manager' and _Dealer') except _Inquiry users'. The user can create an offline order file using this feature.

16) *Order Limits:*

An Order limit is a facility to enable the user to specify maximum value per order and maximum quantity per order that can be entered from the trader workstation.

At the time of order entry and order modification this limit is checked by the system.

Order limits are set by individual users and are provided as safety measure against any inadvertent error during data entry while entering orders.

In case specific value/quantity is to be specified, data has to be entered in the respective input fields namely Order Value (in lakh)' & 'Order Quantity'. The order limits can be modified during market hours. When the user modifies these limits, a message _Max. Value/Qty for one order has been set to Rs Lakh/ ... ' is displayed on the message window screen. While modifying the values if either of the input fields is left blank, the dealer gets an error message, either Quantity Limit not Entered' or Value Limit not Entered' respectively.

In case the user tries to modify *without entering any new values, a message _Values not changed' is displayed.*

Whenever the user places an order, the order values are validated against these values to confine the checking to the trader workstation. In case the user enters an order that exceeds the specified quantity limit, a message _Order quantity entered exceeds the order limit quantity' is displayed.

In case the user enters an order which exceeds specified order value (order price x order quantity) a message _Order value exceeds order value limit' is displayed.

The quantity check is always done prior to order value check.

- Only if both values are not exceeded, the order is sent to the system for further processing.
- In case of a market order if the order quantity exceeds the order quantity limit, the checking is done at the trader workstation itself as in the case of priced orders.
- For order value check, however, the check is performed by the Host.

17) *Market Price protection functionality:*

This functionality gives an option to a trader to limit the risk of a market order, within a pre-set percentage of the Last Trade Price (LTP). The pre-set Market price protection percentage is by default set to 5% of the LTP. The users can change the pre-set Market price protection percentage from the Order Limit Screen which can be invoked from the Supplementary Menu.

At the time of order entry, the user can check the cursor is in the price field. In case of a buy order, the price value shown is taken as the default price, which is greater than LTP by a pre-set percentage. In case of a sell order, the default value will be lesser than the LTP by a pre set percentage. The time condition in both cases will automatically change to IOC. The user has the option to change any of the fields.

Since the calculations are based on LTP if broadcast for the security is not received, the default value will be =MARKET'.

Order Attribute Selection:

The order attribute selection enables user to set default parameters for two fields – PRO/CLI and Custodial Participant id fields in the order entry screens.

The selection screen provides a facility whereby users can select or deselect required options.

The PRO/CLI and custodial participant ID options as selected by the user is available in the order entry screen. In case the user deselects all options for PRO/CLI the following error message is displayed —Either PRO or CLI must be selected.

If a member sets the default option in the PRO/CLI field as 'PRO', then each time the order entry screen is invoked, PRO' will be displayed and 'CLI'' will not be available to the user for order entry. If a member selects 'PRO' and 'CLI'', then each time the order entry screen is invoked, 'PRO' and 'CLI'' will be available to the user for order entry.

18) Client Master Maintenance:

This facility allows the user to maintain a list of client in trader workstation. The user can add, modify, upload or delete clients.

During order entry when the user selects the cli option and press the down arrow key in the account field, a drop down list of clients will be enabled. The user can select a particular record, by typing the first character of the account number.

On pressing Enter key, the account number of that record will be defaulted in the Account No. field. Also if participant exists for the selected account number, the Participant ID gets populated in the participant field of the order entry screen.

19) Reverse Basket on Traded Quantity:

The purpose of Reverse Basket Trading is to provide the users with an offline file for reversing the trades that have taken place for a basket order. This file will contain orders for different securities of the selected basket file. The Orders will be created according to the volume of trade that has taken place for that basket. This feature can also be used to monitor the current status of the basket file as the latest status of the orders are displayed in the list box. The functionality of creating reverse basket offline order file based on orders at the time of creating the basket will continue to be available.

20) _Display CM Ticker:_

The _Display CM Ticker _ is used to enable or disable CM ticker.

21) _Display FO Ticker:_

The _Display F&O Ticker _ is used to enable or disable F&O ticker.

22) _Trade Confirmation Bell:_

The _Trade confirmation Bell _ is used to enable or disable the bell sound at trade confirmation.

23) _Multiple Trade Cancellation:_

An additional facility _Multiple Trade Cancellation' is provided to the user to cancel all the trades done by him, based on an order number.

24) _Debarred Client Maintenance:_

This facility allows to maintain a list of Debarred Clients. The user is provided option to add, modify, save, upload or delete debarred clients. During order entry, if a user tries to place an order for any debarred client added in the Debarred Client Master, then an error message —The account is debarred from trading will be displayed on the order entry screen.

25) _Reset User ID:_

This will facilitate the members to terminate the active session for users under the trading member. The facility has been provided to all corporate managers and branch managers. A branch manager can terminate the active session for all the users of that branch except for self. Active session of the branch manager can be terminated by the corporate manager. The session of the corporate manager can be terminated only by the Exchange.

26) _Print Bhavcopy On/Off:_

Print Bhavcopy On/Off is used to enable or disable the printing the bhavcopy, interim bhavcopy and index bhavcopy reports. By default,the option will be set to _Enable'. To change the [Enable/Disable] status presses the [Spacebar]. The current status is immediately displayed on the supplementary menu screen.

27) _Reset Password:_

This screen enables Corporate Manager to reset the password and to enable the users of their trading member who got disabled by entering wrong passwords for more than 6 times.

28) _About:_

The _About' window displays the software related version number details and copyright information

The Futures and Options Trading System provides a fully automated trading environment for screen-based, floor-less trading on a nationwide basis and an online monitoring and surveillance mechanism. The system supports an order driven market and provides complete transparency of trading operations.

Orders, as and when they are received, are first time stamped and then immediately processed for potential match. If a match is not found, then the orders are stored in different 'books'. Orders are stored in price-time priority in various books in the following sequence: Best Price

Within Price, by time priority.

➡️ *Order Matching Rules*

The best buy order will match with the best sell order. An order may match partiallywith another order resulting in multiple trades. *__For order matching, the best buy order is theone with highest price and the best sell order is the one with lowest price.__*

(This is because the computer views all buy orders available from the point of view of a seller and all sell orders from the point of view of the buyers in the market.)

Hence, the best buy order is the order with highest price and vice-versa.

Members will enter the orders which will be displayed in the system. Orders which are unmatched will remain as passive order and that come intoMembers can pro actively enter orders in the system which will be displayed in the system till the full quantity is matched by one or more of counter-orders and result into trade(s).

__Orders lying unmatched in the system are 'passive' orders and orders that come in to match the existing orders are called 'active' orders.__ Orders are always matched at the passive order price. This ensures that the earlier orders get priority over the orders that come in later.

➡️ *Order Conditions*

A Trading Member can enter various types of orders depending upon his/her requirements. These conditions are broadly classified into 2 categories: timerelated conditions and price-related conditions.

➡️ *Time Conditions*

DAY - A Day order, as the name suggests, is an order which is valid for the day on which it is entered. If the order is not matched during the day, the order gets cancelled automatically at the end of the trading day.

IOC - An Immediate or Cancel (IOC) order allows a Trading Member to buy or sell a security as soon as the order is released into the market, failing which the order will be removed from the market. Partial match is possible for the order, and the unmatched portion of the order is cancelled immediately.

➡ *Price Conditions*

a) *Limit Price/Order -* An order that allows the price to be specified while entering the order into the system.

b) *Market Price/Order -* An order to buy or sell securities at the best price obtainable at the time of entering the order.

c) *Stop Loss (SL) Price/Order* - The one that allows the Trading Member to place an order which gets activated only when the market price of the relevant security reaches or crosses a threshold price. Until then the order does not enter the market.

A sell order in the Stop Loss book gets triggered when the last traded price in the normal market reaches or falls below the trigger price of the order. A buy order in the Stop Loss book gets triggered when the last traded price in the normal market reaches or exceeds the trigger price of the order.

E.g. If for stop loss buy order, the trigger is 93.00, the limit price is 95.00 and the market (last traded) price is 90.00, then this order is released into the system once the market price reaches or exceeds 93.00. This order is added to the regular lot book with time of triggering as the time stamp, as a limit order of 95.00

The NSE trading system provides complete flexibility to members in the kinds of orders that can be placed by them. Orders are first numbered and time-stamped on receipt and then immediately processed for potential match. Every order has a distinctive order number and a unique time stamp on it. If a match is not found, then the orders are stored in different 'books'. Orders are stored in price-time priority in various books in the following sequence:

- Best Price
- Within Price, by time priority.

Price priority means that if two orders are entered into the system, the order having the best price gets the higher priority. Time priority means if two orders having the same price are entered, the order that is entered first gets the higher priority.

➡ Stop-Loss Book

Stop Loss orders are stored in this book till the trigger price specified in the order is reached or surpassed. When the trigger price is reached or surpassed, the order is released in the Regular lot book.

The stop loss condition is met under the following circumstances:

a) Sell order

A sell order in the Stop Loss book gets triggered when the last traded price in the normal market reaches or falls below the trigger price of the order.

b) Buy order

A buy order in the Stop Loss book gets triggered when the last traded price in the normal market reaches or exceeds the trigger price of the order.

c) Odd Lot Book

The Odd lot book contains all odd lot orders (orders with quantity less than marketable lot) in the system. The system attempts to match an active odd lot order against passive orders in the book. Currently, pursuant to a SEBI directive, the Odd Lot Market is being used for orders that have quantity less than or equal to 500 viz. the Limited Physical Market.

d) Auction Book

This book contains orders that are entered for all auctions. The matching process for auction orders in this book is initiated only at the end of the solicitor period.

➡ Symbol & Series

Securities can be taken as default values from the order entry screen from any of the inquiry screens such as MBP, OO, PT, AL, MI and SQ.

Order entry in a security is not possible if that security is suspended from trading. E.g. If a security is suspended in the normal market a *message —"Security is suspended in the normal market| is displayed on the order entry screen."* The label 'Suspended' is also displayed in the market watch screen for the setup security.

Order entry is also not possible in case the security is not eligible to trade in a particular market. E.g. If a security is not eligible to trade in the normal market a *message —"Security is not allowed to trade in normal market is displayed"* on the order entry screen.

In case the user types the symbol series incorrectly a message —*"Invalid symbol series| is displayed on the screen."*

➤ *Quantity freeze*

All orders with very large quantities will receive a quantity alert at member terminal. Currently, if member enters any order exceeding the lowest of the quantity given below, results in an alert which will read as "Order entered exceeds alert quantity limit. Confirm availability of adequate capital to proceed" and only after the member clicks the button _Yes' the order will be further processed for execution. A global alert quantity limit of more than 25000 irrespective of the issue size of the security, whichever is less.

➤ *Price*

The National Stock Exchange of India (NSE) allows trading members to place different types of orders, including market price orders, limit price orders, and stop loss orders. The price taken for each order depends on the type of order placed:

Market price orders:

Buy or sell securities at the best price available when the order is entered. For example, if the closing price of a stock is Rs. 800 at 3:30 PM, market orders placed between 3:40 PM and 4:00 PM will be executed at Rs. 800.

Limit price orders:

Allow the price to be specified when the order is entered.

Stop loss orders:

Activate when the market price of a security reaches or crosses a specified threshold price

- If a user mentions a price, it should be in multiples of the tick size for that particular security and within the day's minimum/maximum price range, otherwise the order is not accepted by the system and an order rejection message/ confirmation slip is generated.

- Another option provided to Users in the Pre-open phase of the Normal market is "AT"' or the "At Open Price' concept". Market' orders entered in the pre-open are termed as "ATO". Based on the opening algorithm, the system computes a potential opening price. Once the market is open for trading, the ATO orders take these prices.

➤ *Circuit breaker*

Index-based Market-wide Circuit Breakers: The index-based market-wide circuit breaker system applies at 3 stages of the index movement, either way viz. at 10%, 15% and 20%. These circuit breakers when triggered bring about a coordinated trading halt in all equity and equity derivative markets nationwide. The market-wide circuit breakers are triggered by movement of either the BSE Sensex or the Nifty 50, whichever is breached earlier.

TRIGGER LIMIT	TRIGGER TIME	MARKET HALT DURATION	PRE-OPEN CALL AUCTION SESSION POST MARKET HALT
10%	Before 1:00 pm.	45 Minutes	15 Minutes
	At or after 1:00 pm up to 2.30 pm	15 Minutes	15 Minutes
	At or after 2.30 pm	No halt	Not applicable
15%	Before 1 pm	1 hour 45 minutes	15 nMinutes
	At or after 1:00 pm before 2:00 pm	45 Minutes	15 Minutes
	On or after 2:00 pm	Remainder of the day	Not applicable
20%	Any time during market hours	Remainder of the day	Not applicable

 ### *Price band*

A price band is a range of prices within which a stock can move during a trading session on the National Stock Exchange (NSE).

For example, if a stock's price band is 10% and it closed at ₹ 100 in the previous session, it can move between ₹ 90 and ₹ 110 in the current session. Trades outside of this price band are not allowed and are considered invalid

1. Daily price bands of 2% (either way)

2. Daily price bands of 5% (either way)

3. Daily price bands of 10% (either way)

4. No price bands are applicable on scrips on which derivative products are available *

5. Price bands of 20% (either way) on all remaining scrips (including debentures, preference shares etc).

6. Scrips on which no derivatives products are available but which are part of Index Derivatives, are also subjected to price bands.

➤ Quantity Conditions

DQ: An order with a Disclosed Quantity (DQ) allows the user to disclose only aportion of the order quantity to the market.

For example, an order of 1000 with a disclosed quantity condition of 200 will mean that 200 is displayed to the market at a time. After this is traded, another 200 is automatically released and so on till the full order is executed.

Important points:

(For equity and currency trading, the disclosed quantity must be at least 10% of the order. For commodity trading, it must be at least 25% of the order. Disclosed quantity cannot be used for futures and options trading.

Odd lot market

Orders with quantities of 500 or less are placed in the Odd Lot Market. This includes day orders, good till canceled (GTC) orders, good till days/ date (GTD) orders, and immediate or cancel (IOC) *orders.*

Futures and options contracts

The NSE defines the permitted lot size for futures and options contracts based on the underlying. The exchange may also specify a different lot size)

➤ Order modification

All orders can be modified in the system till the time *they do not get fully traded* and only during market hours.

Once an order is modified, the branch order value limit for the branch gets adjusted automatically

 a) A dealer can modify only his own orders.

 b) A branch manager can modify his own orders or orders of any dealer under his branch.

 c) A corporate manager can modify his own orders or orders of all dealers and branch managers

➤ Order Cancellation

Order cancellation functionality can be performed only for orders which have not been fully or partially traded (for the untraded part of partially traded orders only) and only during market hours and in pre-open period.

a) Single Order Cancellation

Single order cancellation can be done during trading hours either by selecting the order from the outstanding order screen or from the function key provided. Order cancellation functionality is available for all book types.

But the user is not allowed to cancel auction initiation and competitor orders in auction market.

b) Quick Order Cancellation

Quick Order Cancellation (Cancel All) is an extension of Single Order Cancellation enabling a user to cancel multiple outstanding orders in various trading books subject to the corporate hierarchy. The different filters available for cancelling orders by using quick order cancellation facility are symbol, series, book type, branch, user, PRO/CLI, client account number and buy/sell.

Quick order cancellation can be performed by invoking the function key provided and cannot be done from the outstanding orders screen.

- If the criterion is not found to be correct by a trading member then an error message is displayed and the focus is set on the incorrect field to enable the user to correct it.

- If the selection criterion is correct then a message appears on the quick order cancellation screen stating the number of buy and sell orders to be cancelled.

Quick order cancellation can be done only during market hours.

c) Order Cancellation for Disabled Member

The Exchange suspends a member from trading due to various reasons. In case a member is suspended from trading by the Exchange, all pending orders in all books of the member are immediately cancelled by the system.

A message: —"**Order Number.......... cancelled due to suspension"** is displayed at the message window screen at the trader workstation.

The National Stock Exchange of India (NSE) uses order matching to pair buy orders with sell orders to execute trades. The process is performed by market specialists and liquidity providers, who use algorithms to match orders.

➡ Order matching rules

The best buy order, which has the highest price, is matched with the best sell order, which has the lowest price. Orders may also match partially, resulting in multiple trades. The system also tries to match active odd lot orders with passive orders in the book. Odd lot orders are orders with a quantity of 500 or less.

Order types

Some types of orders used in NSE include:

Day order: Valid for the day it is entered

Good Till Cancelled (GTC) order: Remains in the system until the trading member cancels it

Orders are stored in price-time priority in different books, with the best price first, and then within price by time priority. Orders that are unmatched in the system are called "passive" orders, while orders that come in to match existing orders are called "active" orders. Matches always happen based on the passive order's price, not the active price at which the match occurs

> a) By Price: A buy order with a higher price gets a higher priority and similarly, a sell order with a lower price gets a higher priority.

E.g. Consider the following buy orders:

* 100 shares @ Rs. 35 at time 9:30 a.m.
* 500 shares @ Rs. 35.05 at time 9:43 a.m.

The second order price is greater than the first order price and therefore is the best buy order.

> b) By Time: If there is more than one order at the same price, the order entered earlier gets a higher priority.

E.g. consider the following sell orders:

* 200 shares @ Rs. 72.75 at time 9:30 a.m.
* 300 shares @ Rs. 72.75 at time 9:35 a.m.

Both orders have the same price but they were entered in the system at different time. The first order was entered before the second order and therefore is the best sell order

Regular Lot Matching

> a) If the combined quantity of one or more matching orders on the opposite side of the regular lot book

* is equal to or more than the quantity of active order, the active order is completely traded.
* is equal to or less than the quantity of active order, the active order is partially traded.

If after trading any quantity is left un-traded, the order is added to the regular lot book.

The orders with the IOC attribute try to match the maximum possible quantity. Any remaining quantity is cancelled.

The orders with DQ attribute disclose only a part of the total order quantity to the market.

⮞ *Co-location*

In January 2010, the NSE began offering a co-location facility to members.

Members could place their servers in the Exchange's premises in return for a fee. This allowed them faster access to the buy and sell orders being disseminated by the exchange's tradingengine.[14] The term 'co-location' means 'a setup wherein the broker's computer is located in the same area as the stock exchange's server.'[15] In addition, High-frequency trading (HFT) or algorithmic trading refers to the use of electronic systems, which can potentially execute thousands of orders on the stock exchange in less than a second.

⮞ *Wireless Application Protocol (WAP)*

SEBI has also approved trading through wireless medium on WAP Platform. NSE-IT launched the Wireless Application Protocol (WAP) in November 2000. This provides access to its order book through the hand held devices, which use WAP technology.

This serves primarily retail investors who are mobile and want to trade from any place when the market prices for stocks at their choice are attractive. Only SEBI registered members who have been granted permission by the Exchange for providing internet based trading services can introduce the service after obtaining permission from the Exchange.

⮞ *Stop loss matching*

Stop Loss Matching All stop loss orders entered into the system are stored in the stop loss book. These orders can contain two prices:

> a) Trigger Price: It is the price at which the order gets triggered from the stop loss book.
>
> b) Limit Price: It is the price for orders after the orders get triggered from the stop loss book. If the limit price is not specified, the trigger price is taken as the limit price for the order. The stop loss orders are prioritised in the stop loss book with the most likely order to trigger first and the least likely to trigger last.
>
> c) The stop loss condition is met under the following circumstances:
>
> • Sell Order: A sell order in the stop loss book gets triggered when the last traded price in the normal market reaches or falls below the trigger price of the order.
>
> • Buy Order: A buy order in the stop loss book gets triggered when the last traded price in the normal market reaches or exceeds the trigger price of the order

Multiple choice questions

1.	Which of the following is not the part of money market a) commercial paper b) derivative c) T-bills **d) None of the above**	1
2.	The first ticker window, by default displays all the _____ _____ traded in the future and option segment a) Derivative b) Nifty securities c) Mid - cap securities d) Nifty junior stocks	1
3.	The ticker selection facility is confined to the securities of ____ _____ segment only. a) Capital market b) Commodity market c) Auction market d) Derivative market	1
4.	The message window enables the user to view messages broadcast by the such as corporate actions any market news etc. **a) Exchange** b) RBI c) Govt d) CRISIL	1
5.	Best sell price for sell is the _____ price and for buy order is ___ price **a) Lowest, highest** b) Highest, lowest c) Minimum bid, highest d) Last, lowest	1

6.	The odd lot book can be selected in order to trade in the odd lot market the book type selected will be a) D **b) OL** c) QP d) EO	1
7.	_____ means that if two orders are entered into the system, theorders having the best price get the highest priority a) Order priority **b) Price priority** c) Time priority d) Participant priority	1
8.	A _____ order as the name suggest is an order that ia valid for the day on which it is entered a) IOC **b) Day** c) MArket order d) Stop loss	1
9.	Order cancellation functionality can be performed only for orders which have not been _____ or a) Traded, Auctioned **b) Fully traded, partially traded** c) Aunctioned, negotiated d) Placed, initiated	1
10.	As per SEBI notification, dated November 14, 1998, buyback of securities is permitted in the market a) Primary market **b) Secondary market** c) Both a and b d) None of the above	1

11.	In case of 20% movement of the indexes, trading shall be halted for the reminder of the a) Week **b) Day** c) Month d) Year	1
12.	In case 10% movement of the index based indices there would be one hour market halt if the movement taken place before _____ **a) 1 PM** b) 2 PM c) 3 PM d) 12 PM	1
13.	Which window/ Trade Screen need to access to put forward the request of trade cancellation a) Market by price b) Activity log c) Previous trade **d) Outstanding order**	1
14.	Find the incorrect information of Auction inquiry window a) S-Auction is in solicitor period **b) F - Auction is over** c) X- Auction is deleted d) P - auction is placed	1
15.	What P indicates in market inquiry a) Pre- orders **b) The security is in pre -open** c) Preliminary orders d) Pending orders	1
16.	How indices do labelled in multiple index broadcast window **a) Vertically** b) Horizontally c) Straight d) Upwards	1

17.	Which of the following is not activity of Normal market open phase a) Order entry b) Order modifications c) Order cancellation **d) Order auction**	1
18.	Which market phase the trading member carry out to set up the market watch **a) Opening** b) Opened c) Normal market phase d) Open	1
19.	What B indicates for Buy order? **a) Match** b) Client c) Quantity d) Security	1
20.	The supplementary menu list box has which of the following options a) Colour selection b) Market movement c) Display FO order **d) All of the above**	1
21.	Name the period after which market close during which you have only inquiry access **a) SURCON** b) Open phase c) Market phase d) None of the above	1
22.	The Neat System provides an order driven market wherein orders match on the basis of a) First comes bases b) Highest price bases **c) Time and price priority** d) None of the above	1

23.	Capital market has many types of markets? a) 5 markets b) 4 markets c) 2 markets **d) 3 markets**	1
24.	Who receive end of the report for all the branches of the Trading member a) Dealer b) Branch manager c) Broker **d) Corporate manager**	1
25.	If the corporate manager forgets his password then he is required to in writing with respect to reset the password a) Inform the client b) Inform the SEBI **c) Inform the Exchange** d) Inform the NSDL	1
26.	Who can view and perform order and trade realted activities only for oneself? a) Broker **b) Dealer** c) Branch manager d) None of above	1
27.	WAP stands for **a) Wireless Application protocol** b) Wireless Application Password c) Wireless Authorised password d) None of the above	1
28.	Which information not displayed on Market Watch Window a) Best buy order b) Best sell order c) Last trade price **d) Auction is over**	1

29.	What information does market movement screen provides to the user? **a) Movement of security on current day** b) Movement of security on P:revious day c) Movement of security on two days later d) Movement of security on three days later	1
30.	Write the name of the market phase session in which the user can set up market watch. a) Current market phase b) pre-Open session c) Closed session d) Market watch session	1
31.	How trading system operates in National Stock Exchange a) Strict time/priority only b) Strict price priority only **c) Strict price/time priority only** d) Strict time/quantity priority only	1
32.	Does Nse allow online trading between two known parties a) Yes it is allowed b) Yes but cashless **c) No** d) Yes buy only in weekend	1
33.	Temporary sign off is useful features that allow the user to disallow the use of the trading software without facility a) Logging in **b) Logging off** c) Typing anything d) Entering order	1
34.	If _____ attempts are made by the user with the incorrect password the user will automatically disabled a) 1 b) 2 c) 3 d) 4	1

35.	The detailed outstanding order screen is splitted into first line and	1
	a) Second line	
	b) Detailed line	
	c) Both 1 and 2	
	d) None of the above	
36.	Broker have terminals installed at the premises are _____ _____	1
	a) VSATs	
	b) Modem	
	c) Leased line	
	d) All of the above	
37.	OECLOB Stands for _____	1
	a) Open Electronic consolidated limit order book	
	b) Open Electronic considered limit order book	
	c) Offer electronic consolidated order limit	
	d) None of the above	
38.	Limit orders are the orders to buy/ sell the securities at_____ _____	1
	a) Stated quantity at specific price	
	b) Active quantity at stated price	
	c) Mutual quantity at mutual price d) None of the above	
39.	The order book visible to all participants is _____	1
	a) Open book	
	b) Limit order book	
	c) Both 1 and 2	
	d) None of the above	
40)	Normal market consist of _____	1
	a) Regular lot order	
	b) Special term order	
	c) Negotiated order and stop loss order	
	d) All of the above	

41)	Odd lot market deals for _____ . a) Auction market **b) Regular lot market** c) Limited physical market d) None of the above	1
42)	On starting the NEAT screen that screen display _____ _____ a) User id b) Trading ID c) Password **d) All of the above**	1
43)	Title bar in Neat screen shows _____ a) Display information of all trades b) Work as a tool bar **c) Display trading system date and time** d) None of the above	1
44)	The difference between the previous trade window and current index system is a) 1 b) 2 c) 3 **d) 0**	1
45)	This screen allows the continuous monitoring of securities which is of specific interest of the user **a) Market inquiry window** b) Inquiry window c) Message window d) All of the above	1
46)	_____ window will allow the user to enter/ modify/ cancel the order and send the request for cancellation and modification a) Market inquiry window b) Inquiry window **c) Order/ trade window** d) All of the above	1

47)	The MBP screen splits into _____ a) First line b) Detailed line c) Summary line **d) All of the above**	1
48)	All buyback of shares are identified by an _____ in the MBP screen before five price **a) *** b) # c) $ d) %	1
49)	In the previous trade window the orders are displayed in _____ chronological order. First all buy trades then all sell trades **a) Reverse** b) Straight c) Horizontally d) Backward	1
50)	The detail AL screen is splitted into _____ **a) First line and detailed line** b) First line and summary line c) First line and second line d) None of the above	1
51)	The user can save the market movement screen by specifying the directory name to save the information. This file can be viewed in directory **a) MS-DOS** b) MS-EXCEL c) MS-EOS d) MS-SOS	1
52)	The indices are labelled vertically and information are displayed **a) Horizontally** b) Vertically c) Elaborately d) Straight	1

Define the following (one mark each)

a) Neat screen

b) Open market phase

c) Snap quote

d) Market inquiry screen

e) SURCON

f) Ex-dividend

g) Ex-bonus

h) Regular lot book

i) Stop-loss book

j) Odd lot book

k) Auction order book

l) Auction Matching

m) Co-location

n) WAP

Answer the following question in 20-30 words (2 marks each)

1) What is the SBTS and Explain its Advantages ?

2) What is the NEAT and Explain its Features ?

3) What are the Types of Markets?

4) What are the Trading system users Hierarchy?

5) Explain the Market Watch Window and Market Inquiry Window under NEAT screen

6) What is MBP? Explain its features?

7) What are the previous trades and explain its features?

8) What are the symbols and series in relation to securities ?

9) What are the circuit breaker ?

10) How to modify the orders ?

11) What is the pre-open matching priority ?

12) What is the internet broking ?

13) What is the stop loss matching ?

14) What are the time /quantity conditions ?

Answer the following questions in 30-50 words (3 mark each)

1) What are the features of User ID and password ?

2) What is the process of logging in and out from the NEAT screen

3) What are the outstanding orders that explain its features ?

4) What is the order status and its features ?

5) What is the index based market - wide circuit breaker ?

6) How to cancel the orders?

7) What is Regular lot Matching ?

8) What are the price conditions while trading ?

Unit 3
Introduction Of Derivatives

Derivative products like futures and options on Indian stock markets have become important instruments of price discovery, portfolio diversification and risk hedging in recent times. The volumes in derivative markets, especially in the case of National Stock Exchange (NSE), have shown a tremendous increase and presently the turnover in derivative markets is much higher than the turnover in spot markets.

At the NSE, the total turnover in the cash segment was Rs.6, 95,049 crore during April-September 2005. The turnover in the NSE's derivative segment continued to be higher than in the cash segment. It increased by 59.2 per cent to Rs.17, 55,790 crore during April-September 2005. Hence, it becomes increasingly important to know its intricacies.

 _DERIVATIVE:_

BASIC CONCEPTS

The term "Derivative" indicates that it has no independent value, i.e., its value is entirely "derived" from the value of the underlying asset. The underlying asset can be securities, commodities, bullion, currency, live stock or anything else. In other words, Derivative means a forward, future, option or any other hybrid contract of predetermined fixed duration, linked for the purpose of contract fulfilment to the value of a specified real or financial asset or to an index of securities.

Derivatives are also known as "deferred delivery of deferred payment instruments". In a sense, they are similar to securitised assets, but unlike the later they are not the obligations, which are backed by the original issuer of the underlying assets or security. With Securities Laws (Second Amendment) Act, 1999, Derivatives has been included in the definition of

Securities. The term Derivative has been defined in Securities Contracts (Regulations) Act, as: A Derivative includes:

> a) a security derived from a debt instrument, share, loan, whether secured or unsecured, risk instrument or contract for differences or any other form of security;
>
> b) a contract which derives its value from the prices, or index of prices, of underlying securities.

The derivative contract also has a fixed expiry period mostly in the range of 3 to 12 months, from the date of commencement of the contract. The value of the contract depends on the expiry period and also on the price of the underlying asset.

For example, a farmer fears that the price of wheat (underlying), when his crop is ready for delivery will be lower than his cost of production. Let's say the cost of production is Rs 8,000 per ton. In order to overcome this uncertainty in the selling price of his crop, he enters into a contract (derivative) with a merchant, who agrees to buy the crop at a certain price (exercise price), when the crop is ready in three months time (expiry period).

In this case, say the merchant agrees to buy the crop at Rs 9,000 per ton. Now, the value of this derivative contract will increase as the price of wheat decreases and vice-a-versa. If the selling price of wheat goes down to Rs 7,000 per ton, the derivative contract will be more valuable for the farmer, and if the price of wheat goes down to Rs 6,000, the contract becomes even more valuable. This is because the farmer can sell the wheat he has produced at Rs .9000 per tonne even though the market price is much less. Thus, the value of the derivative is dependent on the value of the underlying.

If the underlying asset of the derivative contract is coffee, wheat, pepper, cotton, gold, silver, precious stone or for that matter even weather, then the derivative is known as a commodity derivative.

If the underlying is a financial asset like debt instruments, currency, share price index, equity shares, etc, the derivative is known as a financial derivative.

Derivative contracts can be standardisedand traded on the stock exchange. Such derivatives are called exchange-traded derivatives. Or they can be customisedas per the needs of the user by negotiating with the

***other party involved. Such derivatives are called over-the-counter (OTC)
derivatives***

From the example above: If he thinks that the total production from his land will be around 150 quintals, he can either go to a food merchant and enter into a derivatives contract to sell 150 quintals of soybean in three months time at Rs 9,000 per ton. Or the farmer can go to a commodities exchange, like the National Commodity and Derivatives Exchange Limited, and buy a standard contract on wheat. The standard contract on wheat has a size of 100 quintals. So the farmer will be left with 50 quintals of wheat uncovered for price fluctuations. However, exchange traded derivatives have some advantages like low transaction costs and no risk of default by the other party, which may exceed the cost associated with leaving a part of the production uncovered.

 *Classification of derivatives*

Derivatives can be categorised into two primary types:

1) *Exchange-traded derivatives*: These are standardised contracts traded on organised exchanges such as the National Stock Exchange (NSE) or the Bombay Stock Exchange (BSE) Examples include futures and options contracts.

2) *Over-the-counter (OTC) derivatives:* These are customised contracts negotiated between two parties directly, without the involvement of an exchajnge. Common OTC derivatives include forwards and swaps.

In the financial markets, various derivatives are traded. To start with we need to understand the following three:

1) Forward

2) Futures

3) Options

4) Swaps

Types of Derivatives

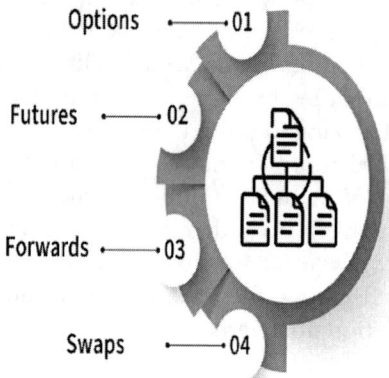

Options •——•01

Futures •——•02

Forwards •——•03

Swaps •——•04

Forward Contract Forward Contracts (forwards) have flourished for many centuries in many countries including India. It is the simplest of all derivatives. A forward contract is a customised contract between two entities, where settlement takes place on a specific date in the future at today's pre-agreed price. It is a one to one bipartite contract, which is to be performed in the future at the terms decided today.

One of the parties in the forward contract assumes a long position and agrees to buy the underlying asset on a certain specified future date for a certain specified period. The other party assumes a short position and agrees to sell the asset on the same date at the same price.

Let us understand the concept with the help of an illustration. Two parties enter into a contract to buy and sell 100 shares of Reliance at Rs 850 per share, two months down the line from the date of the contract. Assume A is the buyer and B is the seller. In the instant case, the product (shares of Reliance), quantity of product (100 shares), product's price (Rs. 850 per share), andtime of delivery (2 months from the date of the contract) have been determined and well understood, in advance by both the parties concerned.

The delivery and payment (settlement of the trade) will take place as per the terms of the contract on the designated date and place.

But there could be risk of default here, suppose Reliance's price two months down the line goes up substantially, seller B would prefer to sell the share the markets rather than selling these shares to A as contracted; because, market would fetch him better price. Therefore he may default. Similarly, in case, price of Reliance goes down, buyer may choose to default because he may find he would find it attractive to buy Reliance share from the market at lower price, instead of honouring the contract. This way, both A and B are exposed to each other's risk of default.

Forwards markets are used in India on a large scale in foreign exchange market to hedge the currency risk. Forward contracts being negotiated by the parties on one to one basis, offer them tremendous flexibility to articulate the contract in terms of price, quantity, quality, delivery time & place. But because they are customised they are plagued with poor liquidity and default risk (credit risk) as explained in the example above.

This example will help us understand it better, two parties might agree today to exchange 500,000 barrels of crude oil for US Rs. 42.08 a barrel three months from today.

A forward contract is specified with four variables:

    1) *The underlier,*

    2) *The notional amount n,*

    3) *The delivery price k, and*

    4) *The settlement date on which the underlier and payment will be exchanged.*

In our example, oil is the underlier. The notional amount is 500,000 barrels. The delivery price is US Rs. 42 per barrel. The settlement date is the actual date three months from now when the oil will be delivered in exchange for a total payment of US Rs. 21.04 MM.

The party who receives the underlier is said to be long the forward. The other party is short. At settlement, the forward has a market value given by $n(s - k)$ [1]

where s is the spot price of the underlier at settlement. This formula derives from the fact that, at settlement, the long party is paying a delivery price k for an underlier then trading at prices.

The difference between those two prices, multiplied by the notional amount, is the market value of the forward. Formula [1] tells us that forwards have linear payoffs.

A forward may be cash settled, in which case the underlier and payment never exchange hands. Instead, the contract settles with a single payment for the market value of the forward at settlement, as given by [1].

If the market value is positive, the short party pays the long party. If it is negative, the long party pays the short party.

Suppose the forward in our oil example were cash-settled. On the settlement date three months from today, no oil would change hands, and there would be no payment of US Rs. 21.04MM. If the spot price at settlement were, say, US Rs. 47.36, then the forward would settle with a single payment of 500,000(47.36 – 42.08) = US Rs. 2.64MM [2] made by the short party to the long party. Forward are generally quoted as delivery prices, which are called forward prices.

Forward prices fluctuate with market conditions. When a forward is entered into, the contract's delivery price is set equal to the quoted forward price. That delivery price then remains fixed until the forward settles.

> *For example, a dealer might quote a three-month oil forward at 41.25/41.29. Those are the bid and offer forward prices. If a counterparty accepts the offer price for 500,000 barrels, then the delivery price on that contract will be USD 41.29. Issues such as the time value of money, short-term supply and demand, market expectations of future spot prices and cash-and-carry arbitrage tend to make forward prices diverge from spot prices, but relevant factors vary from one market to the next. A graph of forward prices for different maturities is called a forward curve.*

➡ Advantages of forward Contract

The following are the advantages of a forward contract –

- Hedging: The preset specifications in the agreement made by the parties allow them to manage risks and protect themselves from market fluctuations that can affect the asset price.

- Customization: The parties involved in the agreement make specific requirements, including expiry date, lot size and pricing.

- Simplicity: These are simpler to understand the price protection and enable proximity among traders with less regulation.

➡ Risks of the forward contract

The following are the risks involved in a forward contract –

- Regulatory Risk: These are executed with the mutual consent of both parties involved. Also, they are not governed by any specific regulatory authority. Because there is no regulatory authority, it increases the risk ability of either of the parties to default.

- Liquidity Risk: The trading decision is impacted in these contracts due to low liquidity. Even though the trader has a strong trading view, they may not be able to execute the strategy because of low liquidity.

- Default Risk: The institution that drafted the agreement is exposed to a high level of risk in the event of default or non-settlement by the client. Thus, these are risky for both parties as it is over the counter investments.

Future contract

Futures Futures contract means a legally binding agreement to buy or sell the underlying security on a future date. Future contracts are the organised/standardised contracts in terms of quantity, quality (in case of commodities), delivery time and place for settlement on any date in future.

The contract expires on a pre-specified date which is called the expiry date of the contract. On expiry, futures can be settled by delivery of the underlying asset or cash. Cash settlement enables the settlement of obligations arising out of the future/option contract in cash.

Unlike forward contracts, futures are normally traded on an exchange. These markets being organised/standardised, are very liquid by their own nature.

Therefore, the liquidity problem, which persists in the forward market, does not exist in the future market. In future markets, clearing corporation /house becomes the counterparty to all the trades or provides the unconditional guarantee for their settlement i.e. assumes the financial integrity of the entire system.

In futures markets, clearing corporations/houses maintains the accounts of all the operations in the market. So it is in a position to tell in the last trading day of the contract, who two are the counterparties to each other and provide the solution to the settlement problem, which is very acute in the forward market.

The following example will help to understand the concept in a better way.

> Referring to the earlier example of A & B entering into a contract to buy and sell Reliance shares. Now, assume that this contract is taking place through the exchange, traded on the exchange and clearing corporation/ house provides the unconditional guarantee for its settlement, it would be called a future contract.

The fundamental difference between futures and forwards is the fact that futures are traded on exchanges. Forwards trade over the counter. This has three practical implications:

*1) Futures are standardised instruments. You can only trade the specific contracts supported by the exchange. **Forwards are entirely flexible. Because they are privately negotiated between parties, they can be for any conceivable underlier and for any settlement date** . Parties to the contract decide on the notional amount and whether physical or cash settlement will be used. If the underlier is for a physically settled commodity or energy, parties agree on issues such as delivery point and quality.*

*2) Forwards entail both market risk and credit risk. **A counterparty may fail to perform on a forward. With futures, there is only market risk. This is because exchanges employ a system whereby counterparties exchange daily payments of profits or losses on the days they occur.** Through these margin payments, a futures contract's market value is effectively reset to zero at the end of each trading day. This all but eliminates credit risk.The daily cash flows associated with margining can skew futures prices, causing them to diverge from corresponding forward prices.*

In view of the above we can say that when standardised and traded on the exchange forward contract becomes futures contract. Therefore all futures contracts are standardised forward contracts.

3) Forward and futures do the same but futures do it better and more efficiently because of transparency and robust risk management in this case. The futures contracts may be settled through physical delivery of asset/ assets or only in cash. Settlement features of futures contracts are well defined in the contract specifications by the exchanges.

A future is transacted through brokerage firms that hold a "seat" on the exchange that trades that particular contract. Working through their respective brokers, two parties will transact a trade. Legally, that trade is structured as two trades both with a clearinghouse owned by or closely affiliated with the exchange.

> *For example, suppose Party A and Party B trades five May natural gas futures at USRs. 3.24. Party A is long and Party B is short. This would be legally structured as Party A being long five May natural gas futures at USRs. 3.24 with the exchange's clearinghouse being the counterparty; and The exchange's clearinghouse being long five May natural gas futures at USRs. 3.24 with Party B being the counterparty. Party A and B then have no legal obligation to each other. Their respective legal obligations are to the exchange's clearinghouse. The clearinghouse never takes market risk because it always has offsetting positions with different counterparties.*

Two parties negotiate (through their respective brokers) a futures transaction. They agree on the price and the number of contracts. *Legally, the transaction is structured as two contracts, each between one of the parties and the exchange's clearinghouse. In this way, the parties are not exposed to each other's credit risk.*

There is credit risk between the respective parties and the clearinghouse, but that is all but eliminated through a margin process. Because the clearinghouse always takes offsetting positions, it never takes market risk.

Before you can trade a futures contract, the broker collects a deposit from you called initial margin. This may be in the form of cash or acceptable securities. broker holds this deposit for you in a margin account and, in the case of a cash deposit, credits interest on the balance. The amount of initial margin is determined according to a formula set by the exchange.

For a single futures contract, it will be a small fraction of the market value of the futures' underlier. For futures spreads, or if you are using futures to hedge a physical position in the underlier, initial margin may be even lower.

Generally, initial margin is intended to represent the maximum one day net loss you could reasonably be expected to incur on a position.

Every day, the profit or loss is calculated on your futures position. If there is a loss, your broker transfers that amount from your margin account to the clearinghouse. If there is a profit, the clearinghouse transfers that amount to your broker who then deposits it into your margin account. This is the daily margining process.

The clearinghouse's margin cash flows net to zero. For every margin payment it receives from one party, it makes an offsetting margin payment to another party. Through the margining process, futures settle every day.

Unlike a forward contract, where all contract obligations are satisfied at maturity, obligations under the futures contract are satisfied every day on an ongoing basis as mark-to-market profits or losses are realised. This essentially eliminates credit risk for futures. Futures can be of many types viz., Index Futures, Stock Futures etc. Futures contracts of this type are based on an index.

Distinguish between Forward and Future Contract

Category	Forward contract	Future contract
Meaning	A forward contract is a private agreement between two parties to buy or sell an underlying asset	A futures contract is a standardised contract to buy and sell an asset on a future date at a fixed price.
Standardisation	Forward contracts are often customised to suit the parties' needs	Futures contracts have standardised terms for consistency and pre-defined lot sizes.
Liquidity and Transparency	Forward contracts lack transparency and liquidity, being private agreements.	Futures contracts are highly liquid and traded on exchanges, providing transparency.
Regulations	Forward contracts are over-the-counter contracts and therefore have minimum to no regulation.	Futures contracts are strictly regulated by exchanges and relevant authorities.
Risk	Forward contracts have higher counterparty risk.	Future contracts have lower counterparty risks
Settlement	Forward contracts are settled at the maturity date and are settled in cash or physical settlement	Future contracts are settled on a daily basis and are settled in cash as the difference between the spot price and the futures price.

Margin	A forward contract has no collateral requirement, as the parties trust each other to honour the contract.	A futures contract has a collateral requirement, as the parties have to deposit an initial margin and maintain a maintenance margin to cover potential losses.
Costs	Forward contracts usually have lower transaction costs.	Futures contracts may involve brokerage, exchange fees, and margin requirements.
Price determination	Forward contract prices are mutually agreed upon between the parties to the contract.	Futures contract prices are determined by open market forces.

➡️ *Advantages of Future*

- *Leverage*:

  Leverage is an investment strategy of using borrowed money— specifically, the use of various financial instruments or borrowed capital —to increase the potential return of an investment. Futures are traded with leverage on margin, allowing investors to control larger positions with a small initial outlay. However, this can be a double-edged sword if the asset's price moves in the unintended direction. Traders should be aware they can lose more than their initial margin when trading futures contracts.

- *Diversification:*

  Investors can trade futures on everything from stock indexes to orange juice, helping to provide a diversified portfolio across multiple asset classes.

- *Hedging:*

  Investors can use futures to protect unrealised profits or minimise potential losses. The wide selection of futures products available allows traders to take a cost-effective hedge against the broader market or specific sectors and individual commodities.

➡️ *Disadvantages of Future*

- *Complex:*

  While anyone can trade futures, there are some complexities involved that can make this a complicated process. You will require a good deal of time and effort if you want this strategy to be successful. This means monitoring the market and keeping on top of current events.

- *Over-Leverage*:

  Leverage is a double-edged sword. On the one hand, it can be advantageous to amplify returns with less of a cash outlay. However, if markets turn against you, you will be responsible for the full amounts of the losses and be subject to margin calls. In other words, leverage will also amplify losses.

- *Managing Expiry Dates*:

  Most futures contracts have an expiry date that traders need to monitor. As the contract approaches its expiry, its price may rapidly lose value or even become worthless. To combatthis, investors frequently roll forward their futures contracts to a longer-dated one as the expiry date approaches.

- *Physical Delivery:*

  If you fail to close your positions or you don't trade them off into offsetting contracts over, you do run the risk of taking physical delivery of the underlying asset. At this time, you'll have to pay the agreed-upon price.

 *Options*

Options Contract is a type of Derivatives Contract which gives the buyer/holder of the contract the right (but not the obligation) to buy/sell the underlying asset at a predetermined price within or at end of a specified period. The buyer/holder of the option purchases the right from the seller/writer for a consideration which is called the premium.

The seller/writer of an option is obligated to settle the option as per the terms of the contract when the buyer/holder exercises his right.

The underlying asset could include securities, an index of prices of securities etc. Under Securities Contracts (Regulations) Act,1956 options on securities has been defined as "option in securities" means a contract for the purchase or sale of a right to buy or sell, or a right to buy and sell, securities in future, and includes a Boom period, a recession,, a put, a call or a put and call in securities.

An Option to buy is called Call option and option to sell is called Put option.

Puts and calls are sometimes called vanilla options to distinguish them from more exotic structures.

Further, if an option that is exercisable on or before the expiry date is called American option and one that is exercisable only on expiry date, is called European option.

The price at which the option is to be exercised is called Strike price or Exercise price. Not that whereas it costs nothing to enter into a forward or futures contract, there is a cost to acquiring an option

As an example, consider a three-month, European exercise, strike US Rs. 45 put option on 100,000 barrels of Brent oil. Such an option might trade OTC. It has: underlier: Brent oil Notional amount: 100,000 barrels Expiration: in three months Strike price: US Rs. 45 It gives the holder the right, but not the obligation, to sell the issuer 100,000 barrels of Brent oil three months from today for a price of US Rs. 45 per barrel.

Another Example is, assume

Mr. A goes to the market and likes the television worth Rs. 12,000. A doesn't have the money to make the full payment at that time and he offers Rs. 2,000 to the shopkeeper with a proposal to take the delivery within two days after paying the balance amount. Further assume that the shopkeeper makes it clear that the television is not brought within two days, contract would expire. This is a typical example of a forward contract wherein a shopkeeper not being confident about the counterparty has taken the advance, which may be treated as margin money in the instant case. It is clear that if Mr A doesn't turn up in 2 days he would be loosing his advance paid. This would be a default situation.

Another way to structure this deal is that Mr A tell the shopkeeper that you pay Rs. 200 – 300 for reserving the television for me. If I want I will come back and pay Rs. 12,000 and buy the television. Otherwise, I will lose the right to buy the same. In the case A is a option buyer and the shopkeeper is the option seller. An option buyer has a right to buy the option but not the obligation. If he comes across another shop selling the same television from the second shop but for a lesser price than he will forget the deal with the first shop and buy the television and buy it from the second shop. In other words A would let his right expire if he finds it unattractive to exercise the option. If A doesn't exercise his right, he is not going to receive back Rs. 200 – 300, paid for reserving the television for 2 days This money may be called the price of the option.

In the case of American options the buyer has the right to exercise the option at anytime on or before the expiry date. This request for exercise is submitted to the Exchange, which randomly assigns the exercise request to the sellers of the options, who are obligated to settle the terms of the contract within a specified time frame.

In the beginning futures and options were permitted only on S&P Nifty and BSE Sensex. Subsequently, sectoral indices were also permitted for derivatives trading subject to fulfilling the eligibility criteria.

Derivative contracts may be permitted on an index if 80% of the index constituents are individually eligible for derivatives trading. However, no single ineligible stock in the index shall have a weightage of more than 5% in the index. The index is required to fulfil the eligibility criteria even after derivatives trading on the index has begun. If the index does not fulfil the criteria for 3 consecutive months, then derivative contracts on such index would be discontinued.

By its very nature, index cannot be delivered on maturity of the Index futures or Index option contracts therefore, these contracts are essentially cash settled on Expiry. In options markets, the exercise (strike or striking) price means the price at which the option holder can buy or sell the underlying asset. If the current price of the underlying asset exceeds the exercise price of a call option, the call is said to be in the money.

Similarly if the current price of the underlying asset is less than the exercise price of a call option, it is said to be out of the money. The near the money call options are those whose exercise price is slightly greater than current market price of the asset. Premium is the price paid by the buyer to the seller of the option, whether put or call. A call option when it is writtenagainst the asset owner by the option writer is called a covered option, and the one written without owing the asset is called naked option.

Options Position There are two sides of every option contract.

On one side there is the investor who has taken long position (i.e., has bought the option).

On the other side is the investor who has taken the short position (i.e., has sold or written the option). The writer of an option receives cash up front, but has the potential liabilities later. The writer's profit or loss is the reverse of that for the purchaser of the option. There are four type of option position:

A long position in a call option

A long position in a put option

A short position in a call option

A short position in a put option

Advantages and Disadvantages of Option Trading

Advantages of options trading

- Excellent hedging tools: Options are good hedging tools, however, one must use them correctly. Traders can reduce their downside risk in equities by using options. For example, if a trader has shares in a company and they have a concern about the price going down, they can buy a put option to limit the downside risk.

- Cost-efficient: Options are cheaper than equities because they are contracts of underlying assets and do not represent ownership. For example, if a trader wants to purchase 100 shares of a company with a share price of Rs 100 each, they will have to spend Rs 10,000. But in the case of options, they can buy one contract of 100 shares at just Rs 500. Traders can use the rest of the money at their discretion, and earn high profits on the bets.

- Potential for higher returns in the short term: Options have a higher potential to give better returns than equities in the short term. However, the trader must use the right strategies. Since traders are spending less money through options and making almost similar profits as equities, the profit percentage is higher in options.

Dis-advantages of options trading

- Complex: Options trading can be very complex as it involves three decisions, direction, time, and price. Traders must consider all three things before implementing an option strategy.

- Additional hurdle: In India, one needs to open a **demat account** and **trading account** to trade shares. Though the same demat account works for options trading, there is an additional hurdle which is a compulsion. *SEBI* mandates all investors to sign the options trading agreement, which lists all risks involved in options trading.

- Uncertainty of gains: Every option strategy works on future expectations and assumptions. The trader earns profits only if the share prices move in a direction as predicted by the trader. Else, the chances of making losses are high.

- Trading fees and commissions: Compared to equities, trading fees and commissions are high in the case of options trading. The more complex the strategy, with more calls and puts, the higher the expenses.

- Tax: All gains in options trading are short-term gains and are taxable as per the **short-term capital gains tax** rate, which is 15%. Hence, the trader loses a part of the gains in the form of taxes.

Things to Remember While Trading in Options

- **_Losses:_** In options trading, the investment is only a small margin amount, lesser than the capital used to buy shares. This can make traders forget the magnitude of losses they will incur if the market doesn't move in their favour.

- **_Liquidity:_** When trading in options, having an exit plan is a must. Trade only in those options with high liquidity. Otherwise, there are chances for funds to block and might also end up making losses. A low-priced option might look attractive, but it is often less liquid than a high-priced one. Hence it is important to balance profitability with affordability and liquidity.

- **_Hedging:_** Option trading can be very confusing at first. Beginners must combine options with a regular trade to minimise risk and better understand how options work. It is better to use options for the purpose of hedging first. Ideally only seasoned trades must use it to speculate and make profits.

- **_Option strategies:_** The option strategies matter the most when traders want to hedge, speculate, or make profits. Using the right strategy is the key to making money and minimising risk.

Swaps

A swap is an agreement between two parties to exchange assets or sets of financial obligations or a series of cash flows for a specified period of time at predetermined intervals. They include both spot and forward transactions in one agreement, and are generally customised transactions. The corporations, banks, individual investors, etc. are now using swaps to arrange complex and innovative financing that reduces borrowing costs, and to increase control over interest rate risk and foreign currency exposure.

While swaps are used for various purposes—from hedging to speculation—their fundamental purpose is to change the character of an asset or liability without liquidating that asset or liability. For example, an investor realising returns from an equity investment cajn swap those returns into less risky fixed income cash flows— without having to liquidate the equities. A corporation with floating rate debt can swap that debt into a fixed rate obligation—without having to retire and reissue debt.

The most common type of swap is a "plain vanilla" interest rate swap. In this, a company agrees to pay cash flows equal to interest at a predetermined fixed rate on a notional principal for a number of years. In return, it receives interest at a floating rate on the same notional principal for the same period of time. The floating rate in many interest rate swap agreements is the London Interbank Offer Rate (LIBOR).

The markets have developed a variety of swaps viz., interest rate swaps, coupon swaps, basis rate swaps, bond swaps, substitution swap, intermarket spread swap, swaps with timing mismatches, swaps with options like payoffs, currency swaps etc. Out of this interest rate swaps & currency swaps are the most commonly used swaps.

An interest rate swap is a transaction between two parties involving an exchange of one steam of interest obligations (payments) for another. It has specific maturity on a notional principal amount, which is simply a reference amount against which the interest is calculated; no principal amount ever really changes hands in such a transaction. Maturities range from under a year to over 15 years, but most transactions fall within a two year to 10-year period.

A currency swap is a contract exchanging foreign currency in the spot market with simultaneous agreement to reserve the transaction in the forward market. Both exchange rate and timing of the forward market transaction are specified at the time of the swap. Put differently, in a currency swap, both the principal and interest in one currency are swapped for principal and interest in another currency. On maturity the principal amount is swapped back.

For Example, a company that has borrowed rupees at a fixed interest rate can swap away the exchange rate risk by setting up a contract whereby it receives rupees at a fixed rate in return for dollars at either a fixed or floating interest rate. Currency swap can help to manage both interest rate and exchange rate risk. By setting up a contract whereby it receives Rs at a fixed rate in return for dollars at either a fixed or floating interest rate.

	Libor + 1.30%	Variable Interest Paid by XYZ to ABC	5% Interest Paid by ABC to XYZ	ABC's Gain	XYZ's Loss
Year 1	3.80%	Rs.38,000	Rs.50,000	-Rs.12,000	Rs.12,000
Year 2	4.55%	Rs.45,500	Rs.50,000	-Rs.4,500	Rs.4,500
Year 3	5.30%	Rs.53,000	Rs.50,000	Rs.3,000	-Rs.3,000
Year 4	6.05%	Rs.60,500	Rs.50,000	Rs.10,500	-Rs.10,500
Year 5	6.80%	Rs.68,000	Rs.50,000	Rs.18,000	-Rs.18,000

Category	Options	Swaps
Liquidity	Generally higher due to standardised contracts and exchange trading.	Varies based on type; liquidity can fluctuate.
Obligations	The seller is obligated to sell the underlying asset if the option is exercised.	Both parties have obligations to exchange cash flows.
Underlying	Involves trading assets based on their true worth.	Involves exchanging cash flows alongside the underlying asset's value.
Trading Method	Can be traded either over-the-counter (OTC) or on exchanges.	Typically over-the-counter (OTC) derivatives are customised and privately traded.
Payment	Requires a premium payment to acquire the option.	Generally does not involve an upfront premium payment.
Exchange Involvement	Tradable on exchanges and privately.	Primarily traded privately and not on exchanges.

History of the financial Derivative Markets

Financial derivatives have emerged as one of the biggest markets of the world during the past two decades. A rapid change in technology has increased the processing power of computers and has made them a key vehicle for information processing in financial markets.

Globalisation of financial markets has forced several countries to change laws and introduce innovative financial contracts which have made it easier for the participants to undertake derivatives transactions.

Early forward contracts in the US addressed merchants' concerns about ensuring that there were buyers and sellers for commodities. *"Credit risk", however, remained a serious problem. To deal with this problem, a group of Chicago businessmen formed the Chicago Board of Trade (CBOT) in 1848.*

The primary intention of the CBOT was to provide a centralised location for buyers and sellers to negotiate forward contracts.

In 1865, the CBOT went one step further and listed the first *"exchange traded" derivatives contract in the US.* These contracts were called "futures contracts". In 1919, Chicago Butter and Egg Board, a spin-off of CBOT, was reorganised to allow futures trading. Its name was changed to Chicago Mercantile Exchange (CME).

The CBOT and the CME remain the two largest organised futures exchanges, indeed the two largest —financiall exchanges of any kind in the world today.

The first exchange-traded financial derivatives emerged in 1970's due to the collapse of fixed exchange rate system and adoption of floating exchange rate systems.

As the system broke down currency volatility became a crucial problem for most countries. To help participants in foreign exchange markets hedge their risks under the new floating exchange rate system, *foreign currency futures were introduced in 1972 at the Chicago Mercantile Exchange.*

During the mid eighties, financial futures became the most active derivative instruments generating volumes many times more than the commodity futures. Index futures, futures on T-bills and EuroDollar futures are the three most popular futures contracts traded today. Other popular international exchanges that trade derivatives are LIFFE in England, DTB in Germany, etc.

Futures contracts on interest-bearing government securities were introduced in mid1970s. The option contracts on equity indices were introduced in the USA in early 1980's to help fund managers to hedge their risks in equity markets. Afterwards a large number of innovative products have been introduced in both exchange traded format and the Over the Counter (OTC) format.

Economic Function of Derivative Market

1) Risk management tool

This is a very important function. Derivative market able to shaft the risk of buyer to seller. Thus the derivatives are very effective risk management tool. Most of the companies use this tool to lower the risk

2) *Price discovery function*

This refers to the ability to achieve and disseminate the price information. Without price information producers, investors, and consumers cannot make informed decisions. Derivatives are exceptionally well suited to provide price information.

They are the tool to assist the price determination value.the wider the use of derivative the wider will be distribution of price information

3) *Liquidity function*

Derivative products provide liquidity to underlying instruments. They provide better avenues for raising money in the market.

Derivative markets often have greater liquidity than the spot markets, this higher liquidity is at lest partly due to the smaller amount of capital required for participation in derivative markets. Since the capital required is less, more participants will operate in the market. This leads to increased volume of trade and liquidity.

4) *Efficiency function*

Derivatives significantly increase market liquidity, as a result, transactional costs are lowered, the efficiency in doing business is increased, the cost of raising capital investment is expanded.

5) *Portfolio management function*

Derivatives help in efficient portfolio management. With a smaller fund disposal,better diversification can be achieved. Derivatives provide much wid menu to portfolio managers who constantly seek better risk return trade off.

6) *Economic development function*

Bright, creative, well educated people with an entrepreneurial attitude wi be attracted towards the derivative markets. Derivative markets energise other create new businesses, new products and new employment opportunity

⇒ *Participants in a Derivative Market*

As with the regular financial markets, derivatives markets have the following participants: Stock Exchange: Where the derivatives are created and traded.

1) *Investors*: Investors in derivatives could be retail investors, institutional investors, banks, corporates. Each investor has different objectives of investing in derivatives. The types of investors are detailed below.

2) **_Regulatory Authorities_**: They ensure smooth functioning of the markets and ensures fair practices are being followed by all participants. SEBI regulates the equity derivative markets, RBI the interest rate and currency derivative markets and FMC (Forward Markets Commission) the commodity markets. FMC is now merged with SEBI, and hence SEBI overlooks both parts of the derivative markets.

3) **_Others:_** Other participants such as Clearing and settlement agencies, credit rating agencies, investor grievances etc are shared between the financial markets and the derivatives markets.

➡ _Types of investors:_

The derivatives market is similar to any other financial market and has following three broad categories of investors:

1) **_Hedgers:_** These are investors with a present or anticipated exposure to the underlying asset which is subject to price risks. Hedgers use the derivatives markets primarily for price risk management of assets and portfolios. Banks, treasury of companies etc fall under this category.

2) **_speculators:_** These are individuals who take a view on the future direction of the markets. They take a view whether prices would rise or fall in future and accordingly buy or sell futures and options to try and make a profit from the future price movements of the underlying asset. Retail investors who invest for the purpose of making profits on gains fall under this category.

3) **_Arbitrageurs:_** They take positions in financial markets to earn riskless profits.

The arbitrageurs take short and long positions in the same or different contracts at the same time to create a position which can generate a riskless profit. Institutional players, proprietary dealers may fall under this category.

Understanding interest rate

What is Continuous Compounding Formula?

Continuous compounding Formula in practical applications is an infinite process of idealisation and serves as a fundamental principle in finance.

Typically, interest is compounded at regular intervals, such as monthly, quarterly, or semiannually, which differs from the theoretical continuous approach.

Continuous compounding formula denotes the *investment* calculation where interest is continuously computed and added to the investment account's balance over the mentioned time interval.

Formula for Continuous Compounding

The formula for continuous compounding is derived from the concept of calculating limit as the number of compounding periods (n) approaches infinity. The Formula for continuous compounding is given as:

$$FV= PVxe(I \times t)$$
e refers to log having value= 2.718

Where,

- PV (Present Value): The initial investment amount.
- i (Interest Rate): The stated annual interest rate.
- t (Time): The duration in years.

Continuous Compounding Definition

Continuous Compounding formula is a method for determining interest, assuming compounding takes place over an unending series of intervals, offering a more accurate assessment of interest accrual.

Continuous Compounding Formula Proof

The formula for continuous compounding is derived from the compound interest formula, and it involves using the mathematical constant 'e.'

- PV (Present Value): The initial investment amount.
- i (Interest Rate): The stated annual interest rate.
- t (Time): The duration in years.

Example 1: Suppose you invest Rs 1,000 at an annual interest rate of 5% compounded continuously. What will be the investment after one year?

Solution:

Given we want to invest Rs 1,000 at an annual interest rate of 5% compounded continuously, the future value (FV) can be calculated as follows:

$FV= PVxe^{(ixt)}$

After one year, the future value (FV) can be calculated as follows:

$FV = Rs\ 1,000 \times e^{(0.05*1)}$

$FV = Rs\ 1000 \times 2.718^{(0.05)}$

FV= Rs 1000 x 1.0512

FV=1051.27

After one year, your investment would be worth approximately Rs 1,051.27.

Example-2

Suppose you deposit Rs. 5,000 into a savings account with a stated annual interest rate of 4.5% that compounds continuously. How much will you have in the account after 3 years?

Solution:

Given we want to invest Rs. 5,000 into a savings account with a stated annual interest rate of 4.5% that compounds continuously, the future value (FV) can be calculated as follows for three years:

$FV=PV \times e^{(i*t)}$

$FV= Rs\ 5,000 \times e^{(0.045*3)}$

$FV= Rs.\ 5000 \times 2.718^{(0.045*3)}$

$FV=Rs\ 5,659.47$

After 3 years, your savings account would hold approximately Rs 5,659.47 .

Example 3: You have Rs. 9,500 to invest in a certificate of deposit (CD) with a stated annual interest rate of 5.5% that compounds continuously. How much will you have in the CD after 4 years?

Solution:

Given we want to invest Rs. 9,500 into a certificate of deposit (CD) with a stated annual interest rate of 5.5% that compounds continuously, the future value (FV) can be calculated as follows for four years:

$FV = PV \times e^{(i*t)}$

$FV = Rs\ 9,500\ xe^{(0.055*4)}$

$FV= Rs\ 11,048.46$

After 4 years, your savings account would hold approximately Rs 11,048.46.

Example 4:-Tina invested Rs. 3000 in a bank that pays an annual interest rate of 7% compounded continuously. What is the amount she can get after 5 years from the bank? Round your answer to the nearest integer.

Solution:

To find: The amount after 5 years.

The initial amount is P = Rs.3000.

The interest rate is r = 7% = 7/100 = 0.07.

Time is, t = 5 years.

Substitute these values in the continuous compounding formula,

A= Pe^{rt}

A= 3000 × e$^{0.07(5)}$ ≈ 4257

The answer is calculated using the calculator and is rounded to the nearest integer. Answer: The amount after 5 years = Rs. 4,257.

Example 5: What should be the rate of interest for the amount of Rs.5,300 to become double in 8 years if the amount is compounding continuously? Round your answer to the nearest tenths.

Solution:

To find: The rate of interest, r.

The initial amount is, P = Rs. 5,300.

The final amount is, A= 2(5300) = Rs. 10,600.

Time is, t = 8 years.

Substitute all these values in the continuous compound interest formula,

A= Pe^{rt}

10600 = 5300 × e$^{r(8)}$

Dividing both sides by 5300,

2= e^{8r}

Taking "ln" on both sides,
ln 2 = 8r

Dividing both sides by 8,
r = (ln 2) / 8 ≈ 0.087 (using calculator)
So the rate of interest = 0.087 × 100 = 8.7

Answer: The rate of interest = 8.7%.

Example 6: Jim invested Rs. 5000 in a bank that pays an annual interest rate of 9% compounded continuously. What is the amount he can get after 15 years from the bank?

Round your answer to the nearest integer.

Solution:

To find: The amount after 15 years.

The initial amount is P = Rs. 5000.

The interest rate is, r = 9% = 9/100 = 0.09.

Time is, t = 15 years.

Substitute these values in the continuous compounding formula,
A= Pe^{rt}

$A = 5000 \times e^{0.09(15)} \approx 19287$

The answer is calculated using the calculator and is rounded to the nearest integer. Answer: The amount after 15 years = Rs. 19,287.

Problem for practice

Q1: Calculate the future value of a Rs 2,500 investment at a continuous annual interest rate of 6% after 4 years?

Q2: If you invest Rs 10,000 at a continuous interest rate of 3.5%, how long will it take for your investment to double in value?

Q3: You open a continuous compounding savings account with an initial deposit of Rs1,200. After 2 years, the account balance is Rs 1,500. What was the annual interest rate?

Q4: Determine the present value (PV) of an investment if you want it to grow to Rs 8,000 after 5 years with continuous compounding at an annual rate of 4.2%.?

Q5: Suppose you invest Rs 18,000 at a continuous interest rate of 5%. How long will it take for your investment to triple in value?

Some examples on compound interest formulas are,

Example 1: Find the Compound Interest when principal = Rs 6000, rate = 10% per annum and time = 2 years.

Solution:

$A = P(1 + R/100)^n$

$A = 6000(1 + 10/100)^2$

$A = 6000(1.1)^2$

$A = 6000 \times 1.21$

$A = 7260$

Compound interest = 7260-6000

Compound interest = 1260

Example 2: What will be the compound interest on Rs 8000 in two years when the rate of interest is 2% per annum?

Solution:

Given,

- Principal P = 8000

- Rate r = 2%
- Time = 2 years

by formula

$A = P (1 + R/100)^n$

$A = 8000 (1 + 2/100)^2$

$A = 8000 (102/100)^2$

$A = 8323$

Compound interest = $A - P$ = 8323 – 8000 = Rs 323

Example 3: Hari deposited Rs. 4000 with a finance company for 2 years at an interest of 5% per annum. What is the compound interest that Rohit gets after 2 years?

Solution:

Given,

- Principal P = 4000
- Rate r = 5%
- Time = 2 years

By formula,

$A = P (1 + R/100)^n$

$A = 4000 (1 + 5/100)^2$

$A = 4000(105/100)^2$

$A = 4410$

Compound Interest = $A - P$ = 4410 – 4000 = 410

Example 4: Find the compound interest on Rs. 2000 at the rate of 4 % per annum for 1.5 years.

When interest is compounded half-yearly?

Solution:

Given,

- Principal p = 2000
- Rate r = 4%
- Time = 1.5 (i.e 3 half years)
  by formula,

$A = P (1 + 4/100 * 6/12)^3$

$A = 2000 (1 + 4/200)$

$A = 2000 \ (204/200)^3$

$A = 2122$

Compound Interest $= A - P = 2122 - 2000 = 122$

Example 5: What is the compound interest on 10000 for one year at the rate of 20% per annum, if the interest is compounded quarterly?

Solution:

Given,

- Principal P = Rs 10000
- Rate R = 12% (12/4 = 3 % per quarter year)
- Time = 1 year (1 × 4 = 4 quarters)

By Formula,

$A = P \ (1 + R/100)^n$

$A = 10000(1 + 3/100)^4$

$A = 10000 \ (103/100)^4$

$A = 11255.0881$

Q1:-Calculate the future value of a Rs 2,500 investment at a continuous annual interest rate of 6% after 4 years?

Q2: If you invest Rs 10,000 at a continuous interest rate of 3.5%, how long will it take for your investment to double in value?

Q3: You open a continuous compounding savings account with an initial deposit of Rs 1,200. After 2 years, the account balance is Rs 1,500. What was the annual interest rate?

Q4: Determine the present value (PV) of an investment if you want it to grow to Rs 8,000 after 5 years with continuous compounding at an annual rate of 4.2%.?

Q5: Suppose you invest Rs 18,000 at a continuous interest rate of 5%. How long will it take for your investment to triple in value?

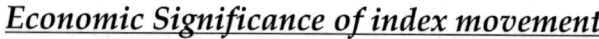

Economic Significance of index movement

They reflect the changing expectations of the stock market about future dividends of the corporate sector. The index goes up if the stock market thinks that the prospective dividends in the future will be better than previously thought. When the prospects of dividends in the future becomes pessimistic, the index drops. The ideal index gives us instant readings about how the stock market perceives the future of corporate sector.

Every Stock price moves for two possible reasons:

    1) News about the company (eg., a product launch, or the closure of a factory).

    2) News about the country (eg. Budget announcements)

The job of an index is to purely capture the second part, the movements of the stock market as a whole (i.e.. news about the country). This is achieved by averaging. Each stock contains a mixture of two elements – stock news and index news. When we take an average of returns on many stocks, the individual stock news tends to cancel out and the only thing left is news that is common to all stocks. The news that is common to all stocks is news about the economy. That is what a good index captures. The correct method of averaging is that of taking a weighted average, giving each stock a weight proportional to its market capitalization.

INDEX CONSTRUCTION ISSUES

A good index is a trade-off between diversification and liquidity. A well diversified index is more representative of the market/economy. However there are diminishing returns to diversification. Going from 10 stocks to 20 stocks gives a sharp reduction in risk. Going from 50 stocks to 100 stocks gives very little reduction in risk. Going beyond 100 stocks gives almost zero reduction in risk. Hence, there is little to gain by diversifying beyond a point. The most serious problem lies in the stocks that we take into an index when it is broadened. If the stock is illiquid, the observed prices yield contaminated information and actually worsen an index.

Example: Suppose an index contains two stocks, A and B. A has a market capitalization of Rs.1000 crore and B has a market capitalization of Rs.3000 crore. Then we attach a weight of 1/4 to movements in A and 3/4 to movements in B.

We will study more on how indices are constructed and the issues therein in the next section.

➤ Index Construction

Index Construction A good index is a trade-off between diversification and liquidity. A well diversified index is more representative of the market/economy. There are however, diminishing returns to diversification.

Going from 10 stocks to 20 stocks gives a sharp reduction in risk. Going from 50 stocks to 100 stocks gives very little reduction in risk. Going beyond 100 stocks gives almost zero reduction in risk. Hence, there is little to gain by diversifying beyond a point. The more serious problem lies in the stocks which are included into an index when it is broadened. If the stock is illiquid, the observed prices yield contaminated information and actually worsen an index.

How is the NIFTY 50 Index Calculated?

The NIFTY 50 index is calculated using a process called the free-float market capitalization-weighted method. It reflects the total market value of all stocks in the index relative to a base period value (November 3, 1995).

Market capitalization, or market cap, is the total value of a company's shares held by all investors, including the organization itself. Free-float market cap captures the total market value of those shares which are available for public trading, that is, that are not held by company owners or the government.

Using the weighted method means that the component of each stock in calculating the index is assigned a weight according to the total value of its outstanding shares.

The total market cap of each stock is computed by multiplying it with a float-factor or Investable Weight Factor (IWF).

It considers only those shares that are available for public trading and exclude the following categories:

- Shares held by company owners and promoters
- Shares held by the government
- Shares held through American/Global Depository Receipts (shares held by foreigners indirectly through foreign financial institutions in India)
- Strategic stakes by corporate bodies
- Investments held under *FDI*
- Shares held by associate companies (cross-holdings)

- **Employee Welfare Trusts** (for example, shares given to employees of the company as some form of security)
- Locked-in shares (shares that cannot be traded, due to some regulation imposed on the company by a regulatory authority)

1. Market capitalization = Shares Outstanding * Current Price

2. Free-float Market Capitalization = Market Cap * IWF

3. Index Value = (Current Market Value/Base Market Capital) * 1000

The current market value is the weighted aggregate market cap of all the 50 companies. The base market capital is the weighted aggregate market cap of all 50 companies as in the base period.

Computing the Index: An Illustration

Let stocks A, B, and C form the NIFTY index. The following information (hypothetical) is given about the stocks (all values in INR).

	Market Cap (Current)	IWF	Free-float Market Cap (Current)	Weight	Weighted Free-float Market Cap
Stock A	1,00,000	0.9	90,000	035	31,500
Stock B	1,50,000	0.8	1,20,000	0.47	56,400
Stock C	50,000	0.9	45,000	0.18	8,100
Current Market Value					96,000

	Market Cap (Base)	IWF	Free-float Market Cap (Base)	Weight	Weighted Free-float Market Cap
Stock A	80,000	0.95	76,000	0.40	30,400
Stock B	1,10,000	0.75	82,500	0.43	35,475
Stock C	40,000	0.8	32,000	0.17	5,440
Base Market Capital					71,315

Free Float Market Capitalisation Weighted index: The free float factor (Investible 164 Weight Factor), for each company in the index is determined based on the public shareholding of the companies as disclosed in the shareholding pattern submitted to the stock exchange by these companies

The Free float market capitalization is calculated in the following manner:

By applying the formula :-

Free float market capitalisation =issue Size*price*Investable weight factor (IWF) (It is calculated on current market price as we calculated above i.e 96000)

Free float base market capitalisation =issue Size*base price* IWF (Calculated as above =71315)

Index = (96000/71315)*1000

Index = 1346

With the capitalization-weighted method, the index components with a higher market cap will have a greater impact on the index. Proportionally, the performance of companies with a small market cap will have less of an influence on the index's performance. Other methods for computing the value of stock market indexes include weighting by price, by fundamentals, and by giving each stock equal importance.

- *Company A: 1 million shares outstanding; the current price per share equals Rs.45*
- *Company B: 300,000 shares outstanding; the current price per share equals Rs.125*
- *Company C: 500,000 shares outstanding; the current price per share equals Rs.60*
- *Company D: 1.5 million shares outstanding; the current price per share equals Rs.75*
- *Company E: 1.5 million shares outstanding; the current price per share equals Rs.5*

Here is the total market cap for each based on the above:

- *Company A market value = (1,000,000 x Rs.45) = Rs.45,000,000*
- *Company B market value = (300,000 x Rs.125) = Rs.37,500,000*
- *Company C market value = (500,000 x Rs.60) = Rs.30,000,000*
- *Company D market value = (1,500,000 x Rs.75) = Rs.112,500,000*
- *Company E market value = (1,500,000 x Rs.5) = Rs.7,500,000*

The entire market value of the index components would equal Rs.232.5 million given the following weights for each company:

- *Company A has a weight of 19.4% (Rs.45,000,000 / Rs.232.5 million)*
- *Company B has a weight of 16.1% (Rs.37,500,000 / Rs.232.5 million)*
- *Company C has a weight of 12.9% (Rs.30,000,000 / Rs.232.5 million)*
- *Company D has a weight of 48.4% (Rs.112,500,000 / Rs.232.5 million)*
- *Company E has a weight of 3.2% (Rs.7,500,000 / Rs.232.5 million)*

Impact cost

Impact cost is the cost that a buyer or seller of stocks incurs while executing a transaction due to the prevailing liquidity condition on the counter.

In other words, it represents the cost of executing a transaction of a given security, with a specific predefined order size, at any given point in time.

In mathematical terms it is the percentage markup observed while buying / selling the desired quantity of a stock with reference to its ideal price (best buy best sell) / 2.

ORDER BOOK			
Buy Quantity	**Buy Price**	**Sell Quantity**	**Sell Price**
1000	237	1500	239
1500	238	1000	240
800	239	1200	241

Suppose a buyer wants to purchase 3,000 shares of, say, ABC. If the best buy order for 1,000 shares is placed at Rs 237 and the best sell order for 1,500 shares is placed at Rs 239, the ideal price for the deal should be:

(Best buy order is always having the highest price and best selling order is always having the lowest price)

Ideal price = (best buy + best sell)/2

Ideal price= (239 + 237)/2

Ideal price = Rs 238

At this price, one can expect the buyer to ideally get the desired quantity of ABC shares.

But suppose that the buyer was able to buy 3,000 ABC shares at an average cost of Rs 239.67 (see the above table)

Average cost (Actual cost)= [(1500x 239) + (1000 x 240) + (500 x 241)]/3000

Or (3,58,500 + 2,40,000 + 1,20,500)/3000

Actual cost = 239.83

The impact cost, therefore, would be 0.70 per cent. To find the impact cost, the formula is: (Actual cost - ideal cost)/ideal cost*100 (#)

In our example, the ideal price is Rs 238, but the average acquisition price for that buyer is Rs 239.67.

By formula, the impact cost should thus be:

Impact cost=(Actual cost-ideal cost)/actual cost

Impact cost=(239.67 - 238)/239.67*100

Impact cost = 0.70

This is a cost that the buyers incur due to lack of market liquidity. The importance of impact cost can be judged from the fact that it is one of the criteria to select a stock for inclusion in the NSE's benchmark index Nifty50.

Consider the second example

	Buyer		Seller	
Sr no	**Quantity**	**Price(Rs)**	**Price (Rs)**	**Quantity**
1.	1000	13.5	14	1000
2.	1000	13.4	14.5	1500
3.	2000	13.1	13.7	500

Impact cost (for a particular quantity) =

(Actual Buy / Sell Price – Ideal Price) ÷ Ideal Price x 100

Ideal Price = (Best Buy Price Best Sell Price) ÷ 2

Actual Buy / Sell Price = Sum of (Quantity x Execution Price) ÷ Total Quantity

Case 1:

If a trader wants to buy 3000 shares of X,

Ideal Price = (Rs 13.5 + Rs 14) ÷ 2 = Rs 13.75

Actual Price = (14 x 1000 + 14.5 x 1500 + 13.7 x 500) ÷ 3000 = Rs 14.2

Impact cost for 3000 shares = (14.2 – 13.75) ÷ 13.75

Impact cost = 0.0327 x 100

Impact cost = 3.27%

Case 2:

Now, if a trader wants to sell 3000 shares of X

Ideal Sell Price = (Rs 14 + Rs 13.5) ÷ 2

Ideal price = Rs 13.75

Actual Sell Price = (13.5 x 1000 + 13.4 x 1000 + 13.1 x 1000) ÷ 3000

Actual sell price= Rs 13.3

Impact Cost = (13.3 – 13.75)÷ 13.75

Impact cost = 0.0303 x 100

Impact cost = 3.03%

Index derivatives

Index derivatives are financial contracts that derive their value from the performance of an underlying index. They allow investors to gain exposure to a group of securities without having to own all the underlying assets.

Index derivatives can include:

1) Index futures

Give investors the right and obligation to buy or sell an index at a predetermined price on a future date. For example, an investor could buy or sell index futures on the S&P 500 to speculate on whether the index will increase or decrease in value.

2) Index options

Another type of index derivative that derives its value from the movements of the underlying index.

Reason why index derivatives are popular

a) Diversification

Index options are less volatile than the individual stocks that make up the index, so they offer more predictability and less wild swings.

b) Hedging

Index options can help hedge against the risk of underlying assets. For example, if you buy positional stocks in cash markets, you can buy a Put option on the derivative market. When the stock falls in the cash market, the value of your Put option will increase.

c) Liquidity

Index options are more liquid than equity-based options, which makes them less exposed to the risk of slippage.

d) Exposure

Index trading allows you to get exposure to an entire economy or sector with one position, instead of opening multiple trades across several companies.

e) Price transparency

Index derivatives offer price transparency and immediate execution and confirmation

Multiple choice questions

1.	The payoffs for financial derivatives are linked to _____ a) securities that will be issued in the future. b) The volatility of interest rates. **c) Previously issued securities.** d) Government regulations specifying allowable rates of return.	1
2.	Financial derivatives include a) Stocks. b) bonds. **c) Futures** d) none of the above.	1
3.	By hedging a portfolio, a bank manager **a) Reduces interest rate risk.** b) Increases reinvestment risk. c) Increases exchange rate risk. d) Increases the probability of gains.	1
4.	Which of the following is not the financial derivative **a) Stock** b) Futures c) Options d) Forward contracts	1
5.	By hedging portfolio, a bank manager **a) Reduce interest rate** b) Increase reinvestment risk c) Increase th exchange rate risk d) Increase the probability of gains	1

6.	Which of the following is the reason to hedge portfolio	1
	a) To increase the probability of gains	
	b) To limit the exposure to risk	
	c) To profit from capital gains when interest rate fall	
	d) All of the above	
7.	Hedging risk for a long position is accomplished by	1
	a) taking another long position.	
	b) Taking a short position.	
	c) Taking additional long and short positions in equal amounts.	
	d) Taking a neutral position.	
8.	Assume you are holding Treasury securities and have sold futures to hedge against interest rate risk. If interest rates fall	1
	a) The increase in the value of the securities equals the decrease in the value of the futures contracts.	
	b) The decrease in the value of the securities equals the increase in the value of the futures contracts.	
	c) The increase in the value of the securities exceeds the decrease in the values of the futures contracts.	
	d) Both the securities and the futures contracts increase in value.	
9.	A contract that requires the investor to buy securities on a future date is called	1
	a) short contract.	
	b) long contract.	
	c) hedge.	
	d) cross.	
10.	A long contract requires that the investor	1
	a) Sell securities in the future.	
	b) Buy securities in the future.	
	c) Hedge in the future.	
	d) Close out his position in the future.	

11.	A person who agrees to buy an asset at a future date has gone	1
	a) long. b) short. c) back. d) ahead	
12.	When in derivative the exchange is fixed at the future time it is called	1
	a) Forward commitment b) Future commitment c) Contingent claim d) Option and swaps	
13.	Swaps and options are comes under _____	1
	a) Future contract b) Forward contract **c) Contingent claim** d) None of the above	
14.	In case of contingent claim if event not happens the contact will be _____	1
	a) Maturured b) Null and void c) Expired **d) Both b and c**	
15.	If derivative contract is based on interest rate the underlying asset will be	1
	a) Fixed asset **b) Debt instrument** c) Any commodity d) All of the above	
16.	Usually forward and some type of options are traded in ____ _____	1
	a) Any exchange **b) OTC market** c) Both a and b d) None of the above	

17.	The management of counterparty is _____ a) Centralised **b) Decentralised** c) Demutualisation d) Any of the above	1
18.	Forward contract are generally popular in _____ a) Debt instrument b) Commodity **c) Interset rate and currency** d) Equity	1
19.	An option can be exercise at expiry of the contract are known as _____ a) American option **b) European option** c) ADR d) GDR	1
20.	In call option buyer is having _____ position **a) Long** b) Short c) Both d) None of th above	1
21.	_____ are the private agreements that between both the patties to exchange the cash flows a) Interest rate option **b) Swaps** c) Future contract d) Forward contract	1
22.	Full form of CBOT a) Central board of trading b) Central business organisation of trading **c) Chicago board of trade** d) Chicago business of trade	1

23.	The first exchange traded derivative is initiated due to _____ _____ a) Introduction of LPG policy b) Collapse of fixed exchange system c) Adoption of floating exchange rate system **d) Both b and d**	1
25.	The first future stock index was traded in _____ a) NSE **b) Kansas city** c) Mumbai city d) New york exchange	1
26.	Currently the most popular stock index is _____ **a) S & p 500 index** b) Nifty index c) Bank nifty d) IT nifty	1
27.	_____ will ensure the smooth functioning of the market and ensure fair practices followed by participants a) SEBI b) NSE **c) Regulatory authority** d) All of the above	1
28.	In derivative market _____ investor will take a view on future direction of market **a) Speculator** b) Hedger c) Arbitrageurs d) Any of the above	1

29.	A good index is trade off between diversification and _____ a) Liquidity b) Market price c) Share price **d) All of the above**	1
30.	A free float market capitalisation refers to _____ **a) Price * issue price * investible weighted factor** b) Price * issue price * investible average factor c) Price * market price * investible weighted factor d) Market price * issue price * investible weighted factor	1
31.	In _____ type of index calculation each stock in index effects the index value in proportion to the market value of all shareholdings a) Free float market capitalisation **b) Market capitalisation weighted index** c) Price weighted index d) Free float average index	1
32.	Index is not vulnerable to _____ a) Price fluctuation b) Risk factor **c) Speculation** d) Safety	1
33.	The securities contract regulation act cames into force in ___ a) 1996 b) 2006 **c) 1956** d) 2002	1

34.	Derivatives can be classified in which of the ways? a) On the basis of nature of underlying asset b) On the bases of nature of derivatives c) On the bases of place of trading **d) All of the above**	1
35.	Interest rate derivative are regulated by _____ a) SEBI **b) RBI** c) Forward market commission d) Ministry of finance	1
36.	Holder of the american option can _____ a) Buy the asset only on expiration b) Sell the asset on or before the expiration **c) Buy the asset on or before expiration** d) Sell the asset only on expiration date	1
37.	Among them which is the computation methodology followed for construction of stock indices a) Market capitalisation weighted index b) Price weighted index c) Free float Market capitalisation index **d) All of the above**	1
38.	Elimination of risk less profit in future market is _____ a) Hedging **b) Arbitrage** c) Speculation d) Underwriting	1
39.	Futures differ from forwards because they are a) Used to hedge portfolios. b) Used to hedge individual securities. c) Used in both financial and foreign exchange markets. **d) A standardised contract.**	1

40.	Options are contracts that give the purchasers the	1
	a) Option to buy or sell an underlying asset.	
	b) The obligation to buy or sell an underlying asset.	
	c) The right to hold an underlying asset.	
	d) The right to switch payment streams	
41.	The price specified on an option that the holder can buy or sell the underlying asset is called the	1
	a) Premium	
	b) Call	
	c) Strike price	
	d) Put	
42.	The seller of an option is to buy or sell the underlying asset while the purchaser of an option has the to buy or sell the asset.	1
	a) Obligated ; right	
	a) Right ; obligation	
	b) Obligated ; obligation	
	c) Right ; right	
43.	A put option gives the owner	1
	a) The right to sell the underlying security.	
	b) The obligation to sell the underlying security.	
	c) The right to buy the underlying security	
	d) The obligation to buy the underlying security.	
44.	A put option gives the seller	1
	a) The right to sell the underlying security.	
	b) The obligation to sell the underlying security.	
	c) The right to buy the underlying security	
	d) The obligation to buy the underlying security.	
45.	The number of futures contracts outstanding is called	1
	a) Liquidity	
	b) Volume	
	c) Float.	
	d) Open interest	

46.	From the following which is not the advantage of option trading	1
	a) Excellent hedging tools:	
	b) Cost-efficient:	
	c) Potential for higher returns in the short term:	
	d) None of the above	

Define the following

a) Derivative

b) Future commitment

c) Contingent claim

d) Index

e) Future contract

f) Option

g) Call option

h) Put option

i) Interest rate swap

j) Swaps

k) Forward contract

l) Hedging

m) Arbitrator

n) Speculator

o) Impact cost

Answer the following question in 20-30 words

a) Classify the derivative on the bases of underlying assets

b) Classify the derivative on the bases of derivative contract

c) Classify the derivative on the bases of place of trading

d) What are the basic derivatives

e) Explain the Free Market Capitalisation Weighted method

f) Explain market capitalization index

g) What are desirable attributes of an index

Answer the following questions in 30-50 words

a) What are the difference between the forward and future contract

b) What are the difference between option and swaps

c) Who are the participants in the derivative market

d) What are the types of investors in derivatives ?

e) What are the economic functions of the derivative market?

f) What is the difference between Free Market Capitalisation Weighted method and Market capitalization index ?

g) What are the reasons for the popularity of index derivatives ?

h) What are the economic significances of index movement ?

Answer the following question in 50-80 words

a) According to you, if you invest in the OTC market of having a future what problems will you face and what advantages will you enjoy?

b) If you want to invest interest rate swaps in which asset you will invest and why?

c) According to you which contract (Forward or Future) is better for the investor and why?

Unit 4
Financial Statement Analysis

Define simple interest

Simple interest is a method of interest that always applies to the original principal amount, with the same rate of interest for every time cycle. When we invest our money in any bank, the bank provides us interest on our amount. The interest applied by the banks is of many types and one of them is simple interest.

Simple interest is calculated with the following formula:

Simple interest = $(P \times R \times T)/100$,

Where

P = Principal,

R = Rate of Interest in % per annum, and

T = Time , usually calculated as the number of years.

<u>*The rate of interest is in percentage*</u> **R% (and is to be written as R/100, thus 100 in the formula).**

To understand more about this formula

- *Principal:* The principal is the amount that was initially borrowed (loan) from the bank or invested. The principal is denoted by P.

- *Rate:* Rate is the rate of interest at which the principal amount is given to someone for a certain time, the rate of interest can be 5%, 10%, or 13%, etc. The rate of interest is denoted by R.

- Time: Time is the duration for which the principal amount is given to someone. Time is denoted by T.

The above formula can be further solved for any variable, P, R, or T. For example, by dividing both sides of the SI formula S.I. = (P × R × T)/100 by R × T, we get P = (100 × S.I.)/(R × T). Similarly, we can solve for either R or T.

$$S.I. = \frac{P \times R \times T}{100}$$

$$P = \frac{100 \times S.I.}{R \times T}$$

Sometimes, the simple interest formula is written as just SI = PRT

$$R = \frac{100 \times S.I.}{P \times T}$$

where R is the rate of interest as a decimal. i.e., if the rate of interest is 5% then R can be written as 5/100 = 0.05.

$$T = \frac{100 \times S.I.}{P \times R}$$

Principal Amount = Rs.1,000, Rate of Interest = 5% = 5/100. (Add a sentence here describing the given information in the question.)

Duration	Simple Interest
1 Year	S.I = (1000 × 5 × 1)/100 = 50
2 Year	S.I = (1000 × 5 × 2)/100 = 100
3 Year	S.I = (1000 × 5 × 3)/100 = 150
10 Year	S.I = (1000 × 5 × 10)/100 = 500

Now, we can also prepare a table for the above question adding the amount to be returned after the given time period.

Duration	Simple Interest	Amount
1 Year	S.I = (1000 × 5 × 1)/100 = 50	A= 1000 + 50 = 1050
2 Year	S.I = (1000 × 5 × 2)/100 = 100	A= 1000 + 100= 1100
3 Year	S.I = (1000 × 5 × 3)/100 = 150	A= 1000 + 150= 1150
10 Year	S.I = (1000 × 5 × 10)/100 = 500	A= 1000 + 500 = 1500

WHAT IS COMPOUND INTEREST?

To quote Albert Einsteein: — *Compound interest is the eighth wonder of the world.*

He who understands it, earns it ... he who doesn't ... pays it

Compound Interest:

Compound interest means that the interest will include interest calculated on interest. The interest accrued on a principal amount is added back to the principal sum, and the whole amount is then treated as new principal, for the calculation of the interest for the next period. Formula for compound interest

$$A = P\left[1 + \frac{R}{100}\right]^n$$

A=amount after compounding

P=Principal amount

R=rate of interest

n=Time period

Important points

- If compound interest need to calculated annually then rate of interest will be calculated for whole year
- If compound interest need to calculated quarterly then rate of interest will be calculated
- =Rate of interest /4
- If compound interest need to calculated semiannually then rate of interest will be calculated =Rate of interest /2
- If compound interest need to calculated monthly then rate of interest will be calculated
- =Rate of interest /12

Time period = n

For example, if an amount of Rs. 5,000 is invested for two years and the interest rate is 10%, compounded yearly:

As we have already discussed, the compound interest is the interest-based on the initial principal amount and the interest collected over the period of time. The compound interest formula is given below:

Compound Interest = Amount – Principal

Example 1:

Jasmine deposits Rs.520 into a savings account that has a 3.5% interest rate compounded monthly. What will be the balance of Jasmine's savings account after two years

Solution:-

To find the balance after two years, A(Amount after two years)

$$A = P \left[1 + \frac{R}{100}\right]^n \quad \text{formula,}$$

The principal, P

P , in this situation is the amount Jasmine used to start her account, Rs.520. The rate,

r

r, as stated in the problem, is 3.5% (or 0.35 as a decimal) and compounded monthly, so

n=12 X 2=24 because time period is 2 years and will be vaulted monthly

r=interest is calculator monthly so 3.5/12=0.29166

$$A = P \left[1 + \frac{R}{100}\right]^n$$

$$A = 520 \left[1 + \frac{0.29166}{100}\right]^{24}$$

A=520[1.07297]

A=557.94

A=557.94 approximately

The balance of Jasmine's account after 2 years is Rs.557.94.

Example 2:

Find the amount if Rs 20000 is invested at 10% p.a. for 3 years.

$$A = P \left[1 + \frac{R}{100}\right]^n$$

$$A = 20000 \left[1 + \frac{10}{100}\right]^3$$

On Solving, we get A = Rs. 26620

Example 3:

Find the C, if Rs 1000 was invested for 1.5 years at 20% p.a. compounded half yearly.

Solution:

As it is said that the interest is compounded half yearly. So, the rate of interest will be halved and time will be doubled.

Rate of interest 20% for whole year but we need compound for semi annual or half yearly so interest will 20/2 =10%

$$C = P\left[1+\frac{R}{100}\right]^n$$

$$C = 1000\left[1+\frac{10}{100}\right]^3$$

A=1000[1 0.10]³

A= 1000 [1.10]³

A=1331

Example 4:

An investment earns 3% each year and is compounded monthly. Calculate the total value after 6 years from an initial investment of Rs. 5,000.

Solution:

Here interest is 3% divided by 12 because interest is calculated monthly

And compounded monthly that means

$\frac{3}{12}=0.25$

n=72 (6 years X12)because interest is compounded monthly

$A= P\left[1+\frac{R}{100}\right]^n$

$C = P\left[1+\frac{0.25}{100}\right]^{72}$

C = 5000 [1.0025]⁷²

C=5000(1.1969)

C=5984

Example 5:

Kristen wants to have Rs. 2,000,000 for retirement in 45 years. She invests in a mutual fund and pays 8.5% each year, compounded quarterly. How much should she deposit into the mutual fund initially?

Solution:

In this problem we want to calculate the present value

Future value is giving i.e 200000

Here interest will be 8.5/4 =2.125 (Because interest is calculated quarterly)

And n=4x45=180

$$A = P\left[1 + \frac{2.125}{100}\right]^{180}$$

2,00,000= P $[1.02125]^{180}$

2,00,000/44.03241620=P

Principal =4542.108

Example 6:

Sean invests Rs.50,000 into an index annuity that averages 6.5% per year, compounded semi-annually. After 9 years how much will be in his account?

Solution:

Rate of interest = 6.5/2=3.25 (because semi-annually we need to compound)

N =9X2=18

$$A = 50{,}000\left[1 + \frac{R}{100}\right]^{n}$$

$$A = 50{,}000\left[1 + \frac{3.25}{100}\right]^{18}$$

A= 50,000 $[1.0325]^{18}$

A=88918

Time value of money

The time value of money is a basic financial concept that holds that money in the present is worth more than the same sum of money to be received in the future. This is true because money that you have right now can be invested and earn a return, thus creating a larger amount of money in the future. (Also, with future money, there is the additional risk that the money may never actually be received, for one reason or another). The time value of money is sometimes referred to as the **net present value** (NPV) of money.

Suppose you are given two options:

a) Receive Rs. 10,000 now

b) Receive Rs. 10,000 after three years.

Which of the options would you choose?

Rationally, you would choose to receive the Rs. 10,000 now instead of waiting for three years to get the same amount.

So, the time value of money demonstrates that, all things being equal, it is better to have money now rather than later. Back to our example: by receiving Rs. 10,000 today, you are poised to increase the future value of your money by investing and gaining interest over a period of time. For option B, you don't have time on your side, and the payment received in three years would be your future value. To illustrate, we have provided a timeline:

$$FV = PV \times [1 + (\tfrac{i}{n})]^{(n*t)}$$

FV = the future value of money

PV = the present value

i = the interest rate or other return that can be earned on the money

t = the number of years to take into consideration

n = the number of compounding periods of interest per year

Using the formula above, let's look at an example where you have Rs.5,000 and can expect to earn 5% interest on that sum each year for the next two years. Assuming the interest is only compounded annually, the future value of your Rs.5,000 today can be calculated as follows:

$$FV = PV \times [1 + (\tfrac{i}{n})]^{(n*t)}$$

$FV = 5000 \times [1 + (5/100)]^{(1*2)}$

$FV = 5000 \times [1 + 0.05)]^{(2)}$

$FV = 5000 \times (1.05)^{(2)}$

$FV = 5000 \times 1.1025$

$FV = 5512.5$

Future value of annuity

The future value of an annuity (FVA) is the total value of a series of payments, or cash flows, at a specific date in the future

$$CF(\frac{(1+r)^{t}-1}{r}$$

Assume, for example, that you're saving £100 per month for ten years into an account which offers an annual interest rate of 6% compounded monthly. Here are the steps to calculate the future value of your annuity:

$$CF(\frac{(1+r)^t-1}{r})$$

$$100(\frac{(1+0.06/12)^{10}-1}{0.06/12})$$

$$100 \times (\frac{(1+0.005)^{10}-1}{0.005})$$

$$100 \times (\frac{1.05114-1}{0.005})$$

100 X 10.22

1022 (approximately)

Example 7:

Suppose you invest Rs.2000 per year in a stock index fund, which earns 9% per year, for the next ten years, what would be the closest value of the accumulated value of the investment upon payment of the last instalment?

Solution:-

From the information given in the question:

A=2000

N=10

r=9%

So that:

$$FV=CF(\frac{(1+r)^t-1}{r})$$

$$FV=2000(\frac{(1+0.09)^{10}-1}{0.09})$$

$$FV=2000(\frac{2.36736-1}{0.09})$$

FV= 2000 x 15.1929

FV= 30385.85 (approximately)

Example 8:

Mr. A decides to deposit a monthly payment of Rs. 2000 for the next four years at the beginning of each month. The ongoing interest rate being charged by the bank is 5%

Solution:-

$$FV=CF(\frac{(1+r)^t-1}{r})$$

$$FV=2000(\frac{(1+0.05/12)^{48}-1}{0.05/12})$$

$$FV=2000(\frac{(1+0.0042)^{24}-1}{0.0042})$$

FV=2000(1.2228-1)/0.0042

FV=2000(53.058)

FV=106116(approximately)

Effective annual return

Effective annual return (EAR), also known as the effective annual interest rate (EAIR), is the actual interest rate that an investor earns on an investment or a borrower pays on a loan.

It takes into account the effects of compounding over time and is usually higher than the nominal rate. EAR is calculated using the nominal rate and the number of compounding periods per year, which can be daily, weekly, monthly, quarterly, or semi-annually.

EAR is a key tool for evaluating investments and loans, and can help people and organisations determine the best financial strategies. It can be used to assess earnings from investments like savings accounts or guaranteed investment certificates (GICs), as well as interest payable on loans or other debts

How to go systematically analysis of the company

Industry analysis

Industry analysis is a marketing process that examines a specific industry, such as manufacturing, service, or trade, to help companies understand their position and develop strategies. It can provide insights into the market potential of a company's products and services, and can help companies identify threats and opportunities, and make the most efficient use of their resources.

For example,National Hydroelectric Power Company (NHPC) Ltd., National Thermal Power Company (NTPC) Ltd., Tata Power Company (TPC) Ltd. etc. belong to the Power Sector/Industry of India.

It is very important to see how the industry to which the company belongs is faring. Specifics like effect of Government policy, future demand of its products etc. need to be checked.

Corporate analysis

Corporate analysis, also known as company analysis or fundamental analysis, is a process that involves studying a company's operations, financials, management, products and services, competitors, market position, and industry trends. The goal of corporate analysis is to gain a comprehensive understanding of the business, and to help investors decide whether to invest in a company's stock. It can also help analysts forecast company performance.

Financial analysis

Financial analysis is the process of evaluating businesses, projects, budgets, and other finance-related transactions to determine their performance and suitability. Typically, financial analysis is used to analyse whether an entity is stable, solvent, liquid, or profitable enough to warrant a monetary investment.

For that you need to understand financial statements of a company i.e. Balance Sheet and Profit and Loss Account contained in the Annual Report of a company

What is the annual report and its features

An annual report is a document that a public corporation must provide to shareholders each year to describe its financial conditions and operations. It can also be used to communicate with other stakeholders, such as investors, employees, and customers.

The report can include the following features:

- *Company profile:* A summary of the business
- *Financial statements:* Detailed information about the company's financial position
- *Operational performance:* An overview of the company's activities over the past year
- *Management discussion and analysis:* A section where management discusses the business and industry, as well as future goals and strategies

- *Letter to shareholders:* Often written by the CEO or Chairman, this letter can summarise the company's performance and highlight key achievements
- Auditors' Report (including Annexure to the Auditors Report)
- Profit and Loss Account.
- Balance Sheet.
- Notes to accounts attached to the Balance Sheet.

Shareholders fund

Shareholder fund is another term for owners' or shareholder's equity. It signifies the funds invested in the company through stock purchases or any other private investments.

The shareholders being the owners, share part of the profit of the company, as dividend. Share capital has been further divided into equity capital and preference capital.

What is the meaning of Equity share capital

Equity Share Capital is the funds generated by a company through issuing Equity shares (also known as ordinary shares). It consists of company shares that the owners decide to sell to individual investors and institutions in the stock market. The Equity Shareholders become stakeholders in the organisation, and these investors are eligible for both ownership and voting rights in the company to select their management.

Some of the features of Equity Shares are as follows:

- Equity Share Capital Remains with the organisation, *and the investors can claim it back only when the company winds up their operations*. It is like a perpetual source of funding for the organisation.
- They *get a percentage of the company's profits, but only after preference shareholders get their dividend.*
- The Equity Shareholders *do not get a fixed rate of dividend. Th*e dividend amount depends on the surfeit capital with the company after paying the preference shareholders.
- Equity shareholders get voting rights in the selection of the company's management.

What is the meaning of Preference Share Capital?

Preference Share Capital is the funds generated by a company through issuing preference shares (also known as **Preference stock**). Preference Shareholders have the first right to receive dividends even before equity shareholders. They are also part owners of the company, but they do not get any voting rights to select its management. They are entitled to a fixed rate of compensation every time the company decides to declare a dividend. They also have the right to claim repayment of capital if the company dissolves.

Some of the features of Preference Shares are as follows:

- Preference Shareholders have the first right to claim the company's assets whenever they decide to wind up their operations.
- Preference Shareholders have the first claim to their dividend.
- The Preference Shareholders get a fixed rate of dividend.
- Preference shareholders do not get voting rights in the selection of the company's management.
- Preference Shares have features of both debt and equity investment. They are also known as a hybrid security option for their investors.

Differences between Equity Share Capital and Preference Share Capital

The main differences between Equity Share Capital and Preference Share Capital are as follows:

Category	Preference Share Capital	Equity Share Capital
Definition	Preference Share Capital is the funds that a company has generated by issuing preference shares.	Equity Share Capital is the funds that a company has generated by issuing Equity shares.
Dividend rate	The Dividend Rate in the case of Preference Share Capital is not changeable.	The Dividend Rate is changeable or fluctuating in the case of Equity Share Capital.
Voting rights	Preference Shareholders do not have any voting rights in the selection of the management.	Equity Shareholders have voting rights in the selection of the management.
Participation in management	Preference Shareholders do not have the right to participate in the management decisions.	Equity Shareholders holders have the right to participate in the management decisions.

Claim to assets of the company	Preference Shareholders have a right to claim over the company's assets whenever they decide to wind up their operations.	Equity Shareholders do not have any right to claim their assets whenever they decide to wind up their operations.
Preference in paying dividend	Preference shareholders get the first preference when the company pays a dividend.	Equity shareholders get second preference when the company pays a dividend.
Types of shares	The different types of Preference Shares are as follows: • Cumulative Preference Shares • Participating Preference Shares • Redeemable Preference • Shares • Convertible Preference Shares • Non-Cumulative Preference Shares • Non-Participating Preference Shares • Non-Redeemable Preference Shares • Non-Convertible Preference Shares	The different types of Equity Shares are as follows: • Authorised Share Capital • Issued Share Capital • Subscribed Share Capital • Paid-up Share Capital • Rights Share • Bonus Share • Sweat Equity Share
Arrears of dividend	Preference Shareholders are eligible to get arrears of unpaid dividends from previous years. They can get it along with the dividend of the current year, except for non-cumulative preference shares.	Equity Shareholders are not eligible to get arrears of unpaid dividends from previous years.

Convertibility	Preference Shares are eligible to get converted into Equity Shares.	Equity Shares can never be eligible to get converted into Preference Shares.
Risk	Preference Shareholders are at a lower risk compared to Equity Shareholders.	Equity Shareholders are at a higher risk compared to Preference Shareholders.

What do terms like authorised, issued, subscribed, called up and paid up capital mean?

a) Authorised share capital

Authorised capital, also called nominal capital, as stated in the **Memorandum of Association (MOA)** is the amount of share capital that a company can raise at any time by issuing new shares. A company cannot issue shares of the value more than the authorised capital. If capital is to be raised beyond the authorised capital, the memorandum has to be amended via a resolution passed at a general meeting of the shareholders. Once this is done and the limit of authorised capital is increased, the company may raise more finance by way of sale of shares.

b) Issued Share Capital

Issued Capital is issued by the company from time to time. The issued capital has to be within the limits of the authorised capital as stated in the memorandum. The issued share capital is either equal to or less than the authorised capital. It can never be more than the authorised capital of the company. It is also called as called-up capital.

c) Subscribed Share Capital

Subscribed capital is increased when members have subscribed to the shares of the company. Subscribed share capital should also be equal to or less than the issued share capital. The oun-allotted capital out of the subscribed share capital is called unsubscribed share capital.

d) Paid-Up Share Capital

Paid-up share capital is the aggregate amount of money received from shareholders for shares issued. Hence, the capital allotted and paid by shareholders is called paid-up capital. This shows the amount received either in cash or in kind by the company from the allottees of sharessubscribed by them. That part of the subscribed capital that remains to be paid is called "Calls in Arrears" or "unpaid share capital". Therefore, paid-up share capital is shown after deducting from the subscribed capital and the unpaid share capital.

Distinguish Between Authorised Capital and Paid-up capital

Aspect	Authorised Capital	Paid-Up Capital
Definition	The maximum share capital a company is legally allowed to issue.	The actual amount of share capital that the company has issued and received payment for.
Legal Documents	Specified in the company's constitutional documents.	Reflected in the company's financial statements.
Purpose	Indicates the potential for raising capital.	Represents the actual capital raised and available for use in business operations.
Changes	Can be altered by amending the company's charter and with shareholder approval.	Changes when new shares are issued and fully paid for by shareholders.
Impact on Business	Represents the growth potential and capacity to raise funds in the future.	Indicates the extent of shareholder investment and capital available for immediate use.
Example	A company with an authorised capital of ₹ 10 crores can issue shares up to that value.	If the company has issued and received payment for shares worth ₹ 5 crores, that is its paid-up capital.

What is the difference between secured and unsecured loans under Loan Funds?

a) Secured loan

A secured loan is a type of loan that requires you to provide Security i.e. tangible security properly charged to the Bank and do not include intangible securities such as guarantees to the lender if you want to borrow money from them. Real estate, vehicles, securities, jewellery, and other such assets of high monetary value are accepted by the banks as collateral.

Secured loans generally help borrowers enjoy a comparatively lower rate of interest and lenient borrowing terms. This is because collateral-backed loans are usually less risky for the lender as they have an assurance of repayment.

b) Unsecured loan

An unsecured type of loan does not require you to provide any Tangible security to the lender when taking a loan from them. These may have comparatively higher interest rates as compared to secured loans due to the absence of security. The creditor grants you the loan mainly by assessing your ability to repay the debt. This is done by analysing your bank account statements and CIBIL score, among other factors. Having a stable source of income can help you procure an unsecured loan with ease. A stable employment history along with references are also considered by banks when reviewing your application for an unsecured loan. Lenders also take into consideration your monthly income in combination with your existing debts. This helps them accurately understand your financial capacity for repaying the loan.

What is meant by application of funds?

The funds collected by a company from the owners and outsiders are employed to create following assets:

a) Fixed Assets: These assets are acquired for long-terms and are used for business operation, but not meant for resale. The land and buildings, plant, machinery, patents, and copyrights are the fixed assets. In case of the XYZ COMPANY LTD., fixed assets are worth Rs. 526.75 crore.

b) Investments: The investments are the financial securities created by investing surplus funds into any non-business related avenues for getting income either for long-term or short-term. Thus incomes and gains from the investments are not from the business operations.

c) Current Assets, Loans, and Advances: This consists of cash and other resources which can be converted into cash during the business operation. Current assets are held for a short-term period for meeting day-to day operational expenditure. The current assets are in the form of raw materials, finished goods, cash, debtors, inventories, loans and advances, and prepaid expenses. For the XYZ COMPANY LTD., current assets are worth Rs. 1165.20 crore.

d) Miscellaneous Expenditures and Losses: The miscellaneous expenditures represent certain outlays such as preliminary expenses and pre-operative expenses not written off. Though loss indicates a decrease in the owners' equity, the share capital can not be reduced with loss. Instead, share capital and losses are shown separately on the liabilities side and assets side of the balance sheet, respectively

Difference between Gross block and Net Block

Gross Block

Gross block is the sum total of all assets of the company valued at their cost of acquisition. This is inclusive of the depreciation that is to be charged on each asset. Net block is the gross block less accumulated depreciation on assets. Net block is actually what the asset are worth to the company.

Simply, Gross Block Means - Total Value of Asset (Its Original Purchase price any capex)

Net Block Means - Original Value Of Asset (As Above) - Till Date Charged Depreciation

Normally an "Accumulated depreciation account " is maintained which is credited by the depreciation charged each year on the asset of the company, Once you debit current period depreciation, such depreciation shall be transferred to Accumulated Depreciation Account .

For Reporting purposes under companies act, it needs to be made like Gross Block -Accumulated Depreciation - Net Block, Pls find example below it shall clear your query more precisely .

Eg. Asset purchased on 1.4.2013, at price of Rs.20,000 Rate of depreciation as per companies act,say 20%, Simply First FY 2013-14 Depreciation shall be of Rs. 4,000 and WDV on 31.3.14 shall be 16,000,For Next FY fy.2014-15, WDV shall be 16,000 depreciation charged shall be Rs. 3,200 .Now How it will be reported in the Block system ?

Ans. - FY 13-14

Net block = Gross Block - depreciation

Net block = Rs.20,000 - 4000(20% of 20000)

Net block =16000(WDV)

Add- For period FY14-15 Rs. 3,200 (Depreciation on 16000 @20%p.a)

Accumulated Depreciation - Rs. 7200 (Total Depreciation 4000 3200)

Net Block (Rs.20,000-7,200)

Net block =Rs.,12800

When it comes to financing, liquidity is a crucial aspect to consider. Liquidity ratio is an essential accounting tool that is used to determine the current debt-repaying ability of a borrower.

What is Liquidity Ratio

Liquidity Ratio is a measure used for determining a company's ability to pay off its short-term liabilities.

This ratio reflects whether an individual or business can pay off short-term dues without any external financial assistance. Considering the liquid assets, present financial obligations are analysed to validate the safety limit of a company.

If the liquidity ratio is higher, it is easier to pay off the debts.

Types of Liquidity Ratios

Possessing a substantial amount of liquid assets provides the ability to pay off short-term financial obligations on time. Here are the liquidity ratio types, along with a detailed liquidity ratio formula–

- **Current Ratio**

The **current ratio** implies the financial capacity of a company to clear off its current obligations by using its current assets.

Formula:

1) $\text{Current Ratio} = \dfrac{Current\ asset}{current\ liabilities} \times 100$

Any current ratio lower than 1 implies a negative financial performance for that business or individual. A current ratio below one is indicative of one's inability to pay off the present-time monetary obligations with their assets.

- **Quick Ratio or Acid Test Ratio**

Quick ratio or acid test ratio is another liquidity ratio that determines a company's current available liquidity.

Easily convertible (in cash) marketable securities and present holding of cash are considered while calculating the quick ratio. Hence, inventories are excluded when the acid test ratio is concerned.

Formula:

2).Quick Ratio = (Marketable Securities Available Cash and/or Equivalent of Cash Accounts Receivable) / Current Liabilities

$$\text{Quick Ratio} = \frac{current\ asset - inventory}{Current\ liabilities} \times 100$$

3) $$\textbf{Proprietary Ratio} = \frac{Proprietors\ Fund}{Total\ Assets} \times 100$$

Proprietor fund = Share capital(Equity & Pref.) + Retained earnings (less loss if any) -Fictitious assets

Total Assets = Fixed Assets + Current Assets-Fictitious assets

4) Problem 1:-

$$\textbf{Debt Equity Ratio} = = \frac{Long\ Term\ Debt}{Proprietors\ Fund}$$

Liabilities	Rs.	Assets	Rs.
Equity Share Capital	5,00,000	Land & Building	1,00,000
Preference share capital	2,00,000	Machinery	4,00,000
General Reserve	1,00,000	Furniture	50,000
Secured Loan	3,00,000	Inventory	3,00,000
Sundry Creditors	1,00,000	Sundry Debtors	3,00,000
		Cash/Bank Balance	50,000
	12,00,000		12,00,000

Calculate Following Ratios from the above balance sheet:

1. Current Ratio

2. Liquid Ratio

3. Proprietary Ratio

4. Stock Working capital Ratio

5. Capital Gearing Ratio

6. Debt Equity Ratio

Solution:

1. Current ratio	= Current assets/current liabilities
	Current assets = inventory (3,00,000)+ s.debtors(3,00,000)+ cash balance(50,000) = 6,50,000
	Current liabilities = S.Creditors = 1,00,000
	= 6,50,000/1,00,000
	= 6.5:1
2. Liquid ratio	= liquid assets/liquid liabilities
	liquid assets = s.debtors(3,00,000)+ cash balance(50,000) = 3,50,000
	liquid liabilities = S.Creditors = 1,00,000
	= 3,50,000/1,00,000
	= 3.5:1
3. Proprietary Ratio	Proprietors fund / total assets
	Proprietor fund = Share capital(Equity & Pref.) + Retained earnings (less loss if any) - Fictitious assets = 5,00,000 + 2,00,000 + 100,000 = 8,00,000
	Total Assets = Fixed Assets + Current Assets-Fictitious assets = 12,00,000
	= 800,000/12,00,000
	= 0.66 : 1
6. Debt Equity Ratio	= <u>Long Term Debt</u>
	Proprietors Fund
	Long term debt = secured loan (300,000)
	= 3,00,000/8,00,000
	= 0.38 : 1

Income statement Ratio

1) **Gross Profit Ratio** = $\frac{Gross\ Profit}{Net\ sales}$ **X100**

Purpose: Indicates the efficiency of production and trading operations .

2) **Operating Ratio** = $\frac{operating\ Profit+cost\ of\ goods\ sold}{Net\ sales}$ **X100**

Purpose: index of managerial ability to control operating expenses.

3) **Expenses Ratio** = $\frac{operating\ Expenses}{Net\ sales}$ **X100**

(Expenditure may be cost of production or Cost of sales, administrative or Selling or distribution expenses or any other Element of Group)

Purpose: Indicates the direction in which economies ought to be effected.

4) **Net Operating Profit Ratio** = $\dfrac{operating\ Profit}{Net\ sales}$X100

5) **Net Profit Ratio** = $\dfrac{Net\ profit\ after\ tax}{Net\ sales}$X100

6) **Inventory turnover ratio** = $\dfrac{cost\ of\ goods\ sold}{Average\ inventory}$

Problem: 1

Following is the Income Statement of Urja Auto. Ltd. For the year ended 31st Dec 2019. You are required to calculate: 1) Gross Profit Ratio; 2) Operating Ratio; 3) Net operating Profit Ratio and 4) Net Profit Ratio.

Particulars	Rs.
Sales	20,00,000
Less: Cost of goods Sold	12,00,000
Gross Profit	8,00,000
Less: Operating Expenses	4,80,000
Operating Profit	3,20,000
Add: Non –operating income	48,000
	3,68,000
Less: Non –operating Expenses	16,000
Profit before Tax	3,52,000
Less: Tax @ 30%	1,05,600
Net Profit After Tax	2,46,400

Solution: (Hint: only needs to replace available figures with respective formula to arrive at answer)

Gross Profit Ratio = $\dfrac{Gross\ Profit}{Net\ sales}$X100

Gross Profit Ratio = $\dfrac{8,00,000}{20,00,0000}$X100=40%

Operating Ratio = $\dfrac{operating\ Profit+cost\ of\ goods\ sold}{Net\ sales}$X100

Operating ratio = $\dfrac{12,00,000 + 4,80,000}{20,00,000}$ X 100 = 84%

Net Operating Profit Ratio = $\dfrac{operating\ Profit}{Net\ sales}$X100

Net Operating Profit Ratio = $\frac{3,20,000}{20,00,000}$ X100=16%

Net Profit Ratio = $\frac{Net\ profit\ after\ tax}{Net\ sales}$ $X100$

Net Profit Ratio = $\frac{2,46,4000}{20,00,000}$ $X100$=12.3%

Multiple choice questions

1.	_____interest is interest paid on the borrowed amount a) Compound interest **b) Simple interest** c) Continuous interest d) Discrete interset	1
2.	_____have quoted that compound interest is eighth wonder of the world a) Alfred marshall b) Robert Solow **c) Albert Einstein** d) Robert reich	1
3.	The relationship between value of rupees today and value of rupee is called _____ a) Effective value of return **b) Time value of money** c) Basis of charge d) None of the above	
4.	In _____ circumstances time value of money is calculated a) Future value of a single cash flow b) Future value of annuity c) Present value of single cash flow **d) All of the above**	1

5.	Present value of single is sum of the _____ of all cash inflows of his annuity **a) Present value** b) Monthly cash flow c) Quarterly cash flow d) Ether a or b	1
6.	Companies producing similar products are subset of _____ _____ **a) Industry analysis** b) Corporate analysis c) Financial analysis d) Any of the above	1
7.	_____ will be coming under corporate analysis a) Earning per share b) P/E ratio **c) Managerial capabilities** d) Either a or b	1
8.	For financial analysis we need to understand _____ a) Balance sheet of the company b) Profit and loss of the company c) Growth plans current operations **d) Both a and b**	1
9.	_____ report is annually issued early by a corporate a) Profit and loss report b) Balance sheet report **c) Annual report** d) Income and expenditure report	1
10.	Shareholders fund is also called as _____ a) Load fund **b) Net worth** c) Investor fund d) Mutual fund	1

11.	The accumulated profit over the years in company is called	1
	a) Reserves and surplus b) General reserve c) Capital reserve d) Security premium reserve	
12.	_____ shareholders are not having voting rights	1
	a) Equity shareholders b) Bonus shareholders **c) Preference shareholders** d) Right shareholders	
13.	_____ is part of the authorised capital which is offered by the company for being subscribed by the member of the public or anybody	1
	a) Authorised capital b) Subscribed capital **c) Issued capital** d) Paid up capital	
14.	Paid up capital refers to part of _____ capital which has been actually paid by the shareholders	1
	a) Authorised capital b) Subscribed capital c) Issued capital **d) Called up capital**	
15.	_____ is known as creation of charge	1
	a) Unsecured loan b) Loans funds **c) Hypothecating asset** d) None of the above	

16.	_____ financial securities are not for the business operations a) Fixed asset **b) Investments** c) Current assets d) Loans and advances	1
17.	The term current asset does not include _____ a) Cash b) Stock in trade **c) Furniture** d) Advance payment	1
20.	The fund used for a new plant under erection, a machine yet to be commissioned are example for __ **a) Capital work in progress** b) Investors fund c) Reserve and surplus fund d) Shareholders fund	1
21.	To extract the information from the financial statement number of tools are used. Most important tool is a) Liquidity ratio b) Leverage ratio **c) Ratio analysis** d) Capital structure ratio	1
22.	_____ ratio will reflects the contribution of debtors and owners to finance the business **a) Debt-Equity ratio** b) Debt- asset ratio c) Debt service coverage ratio d) Debt- income ratio	1

23.	Profit and loss shows _____ of the company	1
	a) Financial position of the company	
	b) Operating efficiency	
	c) Cash flow of the company	
	d) None of the above	
24.	Annual report of the company is issued by company to its _____	1
	a) Shareholders	
	b) Directors	
	c) Auditors	
	d) Management	
25.	Which of the these are not the method of financial statement analysis	1
	a) Ratio analysis	
	b) Comparative analysis	
	c) Trend analysis	
	d) Capitalisation method	
26.	Which among the following is not the solvency ratio	1
	a) Debt equity ratio	
	b) Properterity ratio	
	c) Total asset to debt ratio	
	d) Gross profit ratio	
27.	If Rs. 200 is being lend to at the compound interest of 5% for 2 years.find the rate of amount he will get	1
	a) 2300	
	b) 2315.5	
	c) 2320	
	d) 2310	
28.	Find the compound interest on 1000 @18%p.a for the period of 18 years when interest is compounded half yearly	1
	a) 331	
	b) 1331	
	c) 320	
	d) 325	

29.	What is the present value of 20000 received after 2 years at the discount rate of 10% under continuous discounting a) 16374.615 b) 22000 c) 1637.4615 d) 2200.4615	1
30	Calculate the value of deposit 2000 made it today, 3 years hence if the interest rate is 10%(discrete compounding) a) 2699.72 b) 2099 c) 2090 d) None	1
31.	What is the PV of Rs. 2000 received at the end of each year for 3 continuous years a) 4973.704 b) 4923 c) 4978 d) None of above	1
32.	Inventory turnover ratio is equal to _____ a) Cost of goods sold/closing inventory b) Cost of goods sold/opening inventory c) Average inventory/cost of goods sold d) Cost of goods sold/average inventory	1
33.	The ratio obtained by dividing quick assets by current liabilities is called _____ _____ a) solvency ratio b) Turnover ratio c) Acid test ratio d) None of these	1

34.	interest coverage ratio falls under the group of _____ a) liquidity ratio b) Profitability ratio c) Acidity ratio **d) Solvency ratio**	1
35.	What does a balance sheet indicate out of the following options a) The demographic details of the employees **b) The overall organisation's liabilities, assets as well as stockholders' equity** c) The report regarding the weekly work progress of the organisation d) None of the above	1
36.	In a balance sheet report, the total value of assets should be able to match the worth of the following **a) The total sum of equity and liabilities** b) Total number of employees in the organisation c) The total earnings of the organisation in the past week d) The total number of new employees hires in the organisation during the past year	1

Define the following

a) Simple interest

b) Compound interest

c) Fixed asset

d) Gross block

c) Annual report

f) Shareholders fund

g) Authorised capital

h) Called up capital

i) Secured loan

j) Unsecured loan

k) Current asset

l) Current ratio

m) Acid test ratio

n) Inventory turnover ratio

o) Debtors turnover ratio

p) Leverage

q) Gross profit ratio

r) EPS

Answer the following in 20-30 words

a) Explain the simple interest with formulas?

b) Explain the compound interest with an example ?

c) Explain future value of single cash flow with discrete compounding?

d) Explain the future value of annuity with single cash flow?

e) What is the effective Annual Return?

Answer the following in 30--50 words

a) How to systematically analyse a company ?

b) What is the difference between industry and corporate analysis ?

c) What is the annual report with its features ?

d) What are the types of sources of funds ?

e) What is the difference between shareholders capital and preference capital ?

f) Explain the types of capital?

g) What is the difference between authorised,issued and subscribed capital ?

h) What is the difference between secured and unsecured loans under loan funds ?

Answer the following in 50-80 words

1) What effective annual return is important to calculate and why ? Explain with the help of Example

2) After distributing the profit of the company to shareholders, the retained profit of the company is credited in which account and why?

3) Explain the Time value of money with the suitable example

4) If the performance of an industry as well as of the company seems good, then to check the earring price of the share which analysis will be quite helpful. Justify your answer

5) For the daily operations of the company is it necessary to have current liabilities also? Justify your answer.

Unit 5
Clearing and Settlement process

➤ *Introductions:*

The transactions in the secondary market pass through three distinct phases,viz., trading, clearing and settlement.

While the stock exchanges provide the platform for trading, the clearing corporation determines the funds and securities,obligations of the trading members and ensures that the trade is settled through exchange of obligations.

The clearing banks and the depositories provide the necessary interface between the custodians/clearing members for settlement of funds and securities obligations of trading members .

Several entities, like the clearing corporation, clearing members, custodians, clearing banks, depositories are involved in the process of clearing. The role of each of these entities is explained below:

a) *Clearing Corporation*

The clearing corporation is responsible for post-trade activities such as risk management and clearing and settlement of trades executed on a stock exchange.

The First clearing corporation to be established in the country and also the First clearing corporation in the country to introduce settlement guarantee is the National Securities Clearing Corporation Ltd. (NSCCL), a wholly owned subsidiary of NSE. NSCCL was incorporated in August 1995. It was set up with the objectives of bringing and sustaining confidence in clearing and settlement of securities; promoting and maintaining short and consistent settlement cycles; providing counter-party risk guarantee, and operating a tight risk containment system.

b) *Clearing Members:-*

Clearing Members are responsible for settling their obligations as determined by the clearing corporation. They do so by making available funds and/or securities in the designated accounts with clearing bank/ depositories on the date of settlement.

c) *Custodians:-*

Custodians are clearing members but not trading members. They settle trades on behalf of trading members, when a particular trade is assigned to them for settlement. The custodian is required to con rm whether he is going to settle that trade or not. If he conforms to settle that trade, then the clearing corporation assigns that particular obligation to him. As on date, there are 13 custodians empanelled with NSCCL. They are Deutsche BankA.G., HDFC Bank Ltd., Hongkong Shanghai Banking Corporation Ltd., Infrastructure leasing and Financial Services Ltd., ICICI Bank Ltd., Standard Chartered Bank Ltd., Stock Holding Corporation of India Ltd. etc,

d) *Clearing Banks:-*

Clearing banks are a key link between the clearing members and Clearing Corporation to effect settlement of funds. Every clearing member is required to open a dedicated clearing account with one of the designated clearing banks. Based on the clearing member's obligation as determined through clearing, the clearing member makes funds available in the clearing account for the pay-in and receives funds in case of a pay-out. There are 13 clearing banks of NSE.

 *Settlement Process*

The settlement process begins as soon as a member's obligations are determined through the clearing process. The clearing corporation provides a major link between the clearing banks, clearing members and thedepositories. This link ensures actual movement of funds and securities on the prescribedpay-in and payout day.

The core processes involved in the settlement process are:

a) *Pay-in of Funds and Securities* : The members bring in their funds/securities to the NSCCL. They make available required securities in designated accounts with the depositories by the prescribed pay-in time. The depositories move the securities available in the accounts of members to the account of the NSCCL. Likewise members with funds obligations make available required funds in the designated accounts with clearing banks by the prescribed pay-in time. The NSCCL sends electronic instructions to the clearing banks to debit member's accounts to the extent of payment obligations. The banks process these instructions, debit accounts of members and credit accounts of the NSCCL.

b) ***Pay-out of Funds and Securities:*** After processing for shortages of funds/securities and arranging for movement of funds from surplus banks to deficit banks through RBI clearing, the NSCCL sends electronic instructions to the depositories/clearing banks to release pay-out of securities/funds. The depositories and clearing banks debit accounts of NSCCL and credit settlement accounts of members. Settlement is complete upon release of pay-out of funds and securities to custodians/members.

Settlement is deemed to be complete upon declaration and release of pay-out of funds and securities. Exceptions may arise because of short delivery of securities by CMs, bad deliveries or company objections on the pay-out day. (The detailed explanation of securities and funds settlement follows in the later section).

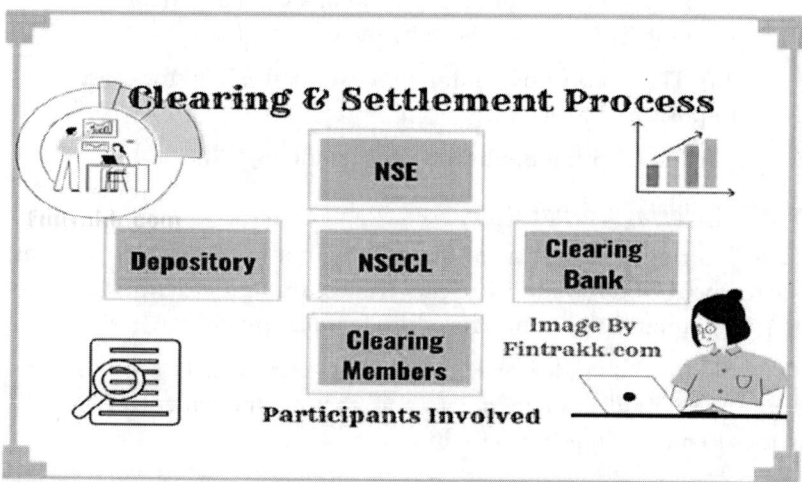

1) The first step involves downloading of the trade information (real time and end of day trade files) from the exchange to the clearing corporation.

2) The clearing house then intimates the clearing member about the trade details who confirm the same. The clearing house performs multi lateral netting Jm to determine the obligations.

3) The clearing members download the trade details and pay-in advice.

4) The clearing member gives instructions to clearing banks to make funds available by pay-in time.

5) They also give instructions to the depositories to make securities available by pay-in time.

6) Pay-in of securities - The clearing house advises depository to debit pool account of custodians/CMs and credit its account. This is carried out by the Depository.

7) Pay-in of funds - The Clearing house advises Clearing Banks to debit account of custodians/CMs and credit its account. This is carried out by the clearing bank.

8) Pay-out of securities - The clearing house advises depository to credit pool account of custodians/CMs and debit its account. This is carried out by the depository.

9) Pay-out of funds - The clearing house advises Clearing Banks to credit account of custodians/CMs and debit its account. This is carried out by the clearing bank.

10) The Depository informs custodians/CMs through depository participants.

11) The Clearing Banks inform custodians/CMs.

▶ *Clearing Corporations*

The Clearing Corporation or the clearing house carries out the clearing and settlement of the trades. It clears trades through a defined settlement cycle and maintains the same procedure for clearing all trades.

It sums up the trades over the trading period, nets the positions to compute the liabilities of members and ensures movement of funds and securities to meet respective liabilities.

Clearing houses conceptualise 'novation' (where the clearing corporation acts as seller to the buyer and buyer to the seller) by eliminating obligations of other counterparties with its own obligation thus minimising counterparty risk ensuring completion of transaction.

Every Stock exchange has a designated clearing house. It empanels clearing banks to provide services to the trading members and with depositories for settlement of trades. Every member is required to maintain a clearing account with the designated clearing bank for clearing operations which includes settlement of funds and other obligations like payment of margin or any other penalties.

- Only clearing members can access their clearing account to make or receive payments as assigned by the clearing house depending on his obligations.

The bank then carries out debit or credit operations with respect to the instructions received from the Clearing Corporation. The Clearing Banks are required to provide the following services as a single window to all Clearing Members of Clearing Corporation and also to the Clearing Corporation:

- Branch network in cities that cover bulk of the trading cum clearing members.
- High level automation including Electronic Funds Transfer (EFT) facilities.

Facilities like,

a) dedicated branch facilities,

b) software to interface with the Clearing Corporation,

c) access to accounts information on a real time basis.

Value-added services to members such as free-of-cost Funds Transfer across centers, etc.

- Trading and Settlement
- Providing working capital funds.
- Stock lending facilities.
- Services as Professional Clearing Members.
- Services as Depository Participants.
- Other Capital Market related facilities.
- All other banking facilities like issuing bank guarantees/ credit facilities etc.

▶ *Normal market segment*

At NSE, trades in rolling settlement are settled on a T+2 basis i.e. on the 2nd working day. Typically trades taking place on Monday are settled on Wednesday, Tuesday's trades settled on Thursday and so on.

	Activity	Day
Trading	Rolling Settlement Trading	T
Clearing	Custodial Confirmation	T+1 working days
	Delivery Generation	T+1 working day

Settlement	Securities and Funds pay-in	T+2 working days
	Securities and Funds pay-out	T+2 working days
	Valuation of shortages based on closing prices (at T+1 closing prices)	T+2 working days
Post Settlement	Auction	T+2 working days
	Auction settlement	T+3 working days
	Bad Delivery Reporting	T+4 working days
	Rectified bad delivery pay-in and pay-out.	T+6 working days
	Re-bad delivery reporting and pickup.	T+8 working days
	Close out of re-bad delivery and funds pay-in & pay-out	T+9 working days

➡️ *Inter institutional deals*

Trading in this market segment is available for _institutional investors' only.

In order to ensure that the overall FII limits are not violated, buying and selling in this segment is restricted to specific clients.

Members are required to enter the custodian participant code at the time of order entry and to ensure that the selling/ buying restrictions are strictly adhered to.

A sell order entered by trading members on behalf of clients should be done only on GDR/ADR/FDI/NRI/PIO/FII or a buy order entered by trading members on behalf of client should be done only on (GDR /ADR/ FDI /NRI/ PIO / FII/FI/Banks/ Mutual Funds/Insurance Companies.

The member entering the invalid order is further liable for disciplinary action, which may include penalties, penal action, withdrawal of trading facilities, suspension etc.

Settlement Cycle For Physical Securities

a) Securities delivery in the name of street or market are considered as a bad delivery.

b) Securities bearing the last transfer date in limited physical market will be considered as bad delivery

c) Any delivery in excess of 500 is marked as short will be completely closed out

d) Shortage if any will be closed out at 20% actual traded price and any unrectified delivery or any bad delivery will be closed out at 20% actual traded price

e) The buyer must compulsorily send the securities for transfer and dematerialisation, latest within 3 months from the date of pay-out.

f) Company objections arising out of such trading and settlement in this market are reported in the same manner as is currently being done for normal market segment.

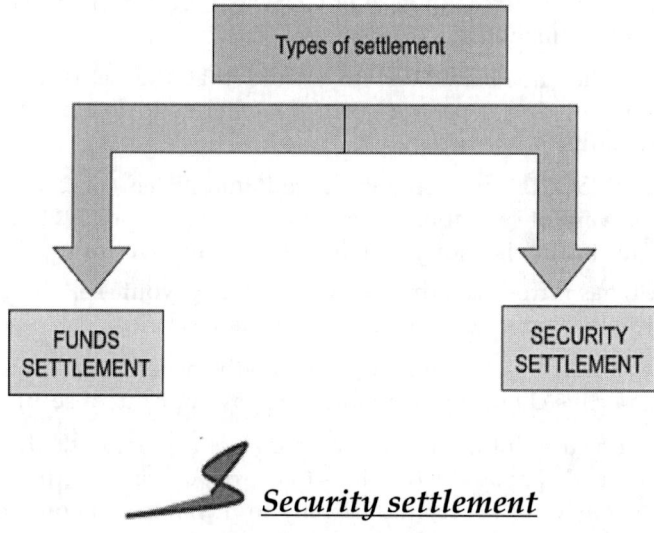

Security settlement

A. The securities obligations of members are downloaded to members/custodians by NSCCL after the end of the trading day.

B. The members / custodians deliver the securities to the clearing corporation on the pay in day in case of physical settlement and in case of dematerialised securities the security are made available with depository participants.

C. Members are required to open accounts with depository participants of both the depositories, NSDL and CDSL.

D. Delivering members are required to deliver all documents to the clearing corporation (in case of physical settlement) between 9:30 a.m. and 10:30 a.m. on the settlement day. Receiving members are allotted specific time slots on settlement day to collect the documents from the clearing corporation at Mumbai.

E. In case of dematerialised settlement, the members receive their obligation by 2.30 pm on T + 1 day. The members need to arrange for the securities as per their obligations and give instructions by 10.30 am on the pay-in day.

F. In case of NSDL, the members need to give instructions to move the securities to the settlement account of NSCCL, whereas in case of CDSL pay-in is done based on settlement ID.

G. The members need to ensure that the settlement number and type are correctly entered to avoid any defaults.

H. NSCCL has also introduced the system of direct delivery of securities to the investors from April 2, 2001. This facility is known as Direct Payout to Investors.

NSCCL has introduced the facility of direct payout (i.e. direct delivery of securities) to clients' account on both the depositories.

It ascertains from each clearing member, the beneficiary account details of their respective clients who are due to receive pay out of securities.

Based on the information received from members, the clearing corporation sends payout instructions to the depositories, so that the client receives the pay out of securities directly to their accounts on the pay-out day.

The client will receive the payout as per instruction received. To the extent of instruction not received, the securities are credited to the CM pool account of the member.

➡️ **Following are the salient features of _Direct Payout' to Investors:**

a) Clearing members are required to provide detail information about payout to clients The file is to be provided as per the structure specified by NSCCL.

b) The time limit for submission of files is up to 9.30.am on the pay out day

c) The files are uploaded by NSCCL and returned with the indication of th success / rejection of the file and the records as per required formats.

d) Clearing members should provide details of beneficiary account of the clients of the trading members.

e) If the quantity requested for direct payout is more than the balance available for payout with clearing members then, the quantity available in that depository is directly credited to members' settlement account in that depository.

In the following situations, the payout is credited to CM Pool / Clearing account of the clearing members :

• Where the clearing members fail to provide details or fails to credit the account of beneficiary

• The remaining quantity received from other depositories as pay out is credited to the CM Pool / Clearing account of the clearing member with the respective depositories.

If the member's client has not cleared the dues and the member has **valid reason** not to release the payout of a client directly, in such a situation the member may not provide the beneficiary details in the file.

But if the investor has cleared the dues and the member is not having a valid reason to release the security, in that case the member needs to provide the details of the beneficiary account.

In case the investor has paid the dues for delivery of securities and there is no valid justification for not releasing pay-out directly to the client, the member has to provide the details of its client's beneficiary account so that direct credit can be given to the client.

➡ *Short Deliveries:*

A short delivery/failed delivery takes place when a broker, a custodian or the clearing corporation delivers fewer securities than what were contracted

On the securities pay-in day, the clearing member informs the clearing corporation about the securities that he will be able to deliver and those securities which he will not be able to deliver. Also informs an amount equivalent to the securities not delivered by him valued at the valuation price. This is called valuation debit.

A valuation debit is also conducted for bad delivery by clearing members.

This problem can arise in case of both physical and dematerialised settlement.

➤ *Bad Deliveries:*

Bad deliveries are required to be reported to the clearing corporation within two days from the receipt of documents.

The delivering member is required to rectify these within two days.

Un-rectified bad deliveries are assigned to auction on the next day. This problem can arise only *in case of physical settlement*

➤ *Company objection*

- Company objections arise when documents for securities transfer are returned due to signature mismatch or for any other reason.

- The original selling CM is normally responsible for rectifying/replacing defective documents to the receiving CM as per pre-notified schedule.

- The CM on whom company objection is lodged has an opportunity to withdraw the objection if the objection is not valid or the documents are incomplete, within 7 days of lodging the complaint against him.

- If the CM is unable to rectify/replace defective documents on or before 21 days, NSCCL conducts a buying-in auction for the non-rectified part of defective document on the next auction day through the trading system of NSE.

- (All objections, which are not bought-in, are deemed closed out on the auction day at the closing price on the auction day plus 20%. This amount is credited to the receiving member's account on the auction pay-out day.)

 **Funds settlement**

Clearing Account:-

Every clearing member is required to maintain and operate a clearing account with any one of the empanelled clearing banks at the designated clearing bank branches.

The clearing account is to be used exclusively for clearing operations.

(i.e., for settling funds and other obligations to the clearing corporation including payments of margins and penal charges.)

Clearing members are required to authorise the clearing bank to access their clearing account for debiting and crediting their accounts, reporting of balances and other information as may be required by NSCCL from time to time as per the specified format.

The clearing bank will debit/ credit the clearing account of clearing members as per instructions received from the clearing corporation. A clearing member can deposit funds into this account in any form, but can withdraw funds from this account only in self-name.

➤ *Change in Clearing Bank*

1) If clearing member need to change the clearing bank then he need to request the clearing corporation either he should

   a) Furnish the NOC by clearing member from the existing bank

   b) If no response will be received after waiting for minimum period the acknowledgement for the above need to be made by clearing member to the existing bank

2) The clearing corporation will receive the letter of introduction for another designated bank

3) On opening of account the clearing member need to furnish the details to clearing corporation along with the account number and also the acknowledged copy issued by clearing member to clearing bank

4) The clearing corporation then will announce the date from which new account will be operational and old bank account will be closed

Settlement of Funds

a) Through the daily data download members came to know about their obligation and debit/ credit transaction date wise. Summary statement provides the detail in summary form

b) The members account debited for a number of obligations and transactions. The member needs to ensure that timely funds need to available in designated clearing bank accounts on a particular date and time.

c) In order to ensure timely fulfilment of obligations the, the member may avail the facility of timely transfer of funds from one bank account to other or temporary overdraft facility. In case a member got that facility he should furnish such details to the bank for timely transfer of funds in order to convenience.

d) The member with funds pay in obligation needs to clear their obligation up-to 11;00 AM on pay in day

e) On pay out day, the clearing member account will be credited on or after 1:30 PM.

➤ Funds shortage

If the funds are in shortage then trading will not be permitted and security payout will be on hold

➤ Shortage handling

On security payout day NSCCL identifies the short delivery and respective clearing member account is debited with an equivalent amount and these securities will be valued at valuation price and it is known as valuation debt. The valuation debt will be conducted for bad delivery also

➤ Valuation price

• The valuation price for Normal and limited physical market for the securities not delivered will be the closing price of the security, immediate trading day preceding the pay in day.

• The valuation price for Normal and limited physical market for the bad delivery securities will be closing price of the security, immediate trading day, preceding the bad day rectification day

➤ *Close out procedure*

All shortages, not brought in are deemed to be closed out at the highest price between first trading day to till the closing date.

➤ For Regular Market:

a) *In the case of failure to give delivery:*

○ At the highest price prevailing in the NSE from the first day of the relevant trading period till the day of closing out

OR

○ 20% above the closing price on the auction day, **whichever is higher.**

In cases of securities having corporate actions all cases of short delivery which cannot be auctioned or where the cum basis auction pay out is after the book closure/record date, would be compulsory closed out.

For compulsory close out, the following formula is applicable:

• Higher of 10% above the closing price of the security in Normal Market on the auction day

• The highest traded price from first trading day of the settlement till the auction day.

a) In the case of non rectification/replacement for bad delivery:

• The highest price prevailing in NSE from the day of trading till the day of closing out

• 20% above the official closing price of auction day (whichever is higher)

b) In the case of non rectification/replacement for objection cases: 20% above price of the auction closing day

▶ *For Limited Physical Market Deals:*

a) In the case of failure to give delivery: At 20% over the actual trade price.

b) In the case of non rectification/replacement for bad delivery: At 10% over the actual trade price.

c) In the case of non rectification/replacement for objection cases: At 20% above the official closing price in the regular market on the auction day.

▶ *Auction Market: (Closing out Procedure)*

In the case of auction non delivery:

When the auction seller fails to deliver in part or full on auction pay-in day, the deal is squared up at

• At the highest price prevailing in the NSE from the first day of the relevant trading period till the day of closing out

- 20% above the closing price on the auction close out day, **whichever is higher.**

and is charged to the auction seller unless otherwise specified.

In the case of an auction bad delivery:

An auction delivery reported as bad delivery is squared up at:

- At the highest price prevailing in the NSE from the first day of the relevant trading period till the day of closing out

OR

- 10% above the closing price on the auction close out day, **whichever is higher.**

and is charged to the auction seller unless otherwise specified.

Rectified/Replaced bad deliveries reported as bad delivery (Re-bad delivery):

For Regular Market Deals:

- At the highest price prevailing in the NSE from the first day of the relevant trading period till the day of closing out

OR

- 10% above the closing price on the auction close out day, **whichever is higher.**

For Limited Physical Deals:

Rectified / replaced shares reported as bad delivery (Re-bad delivery) is squared up at 10% over the actual trade price.

Company objection cases reported as bad delivery:

Rectified /replaced company objection reported as bad delivery is squared up at 10% above the official closing price on the auction day.

Close out price for deleted security :

Security for which trading has been discontinued on the Exchange *close out shall be the last 26 weeks average trade price on the exchange with a close out mark up of 20%.*

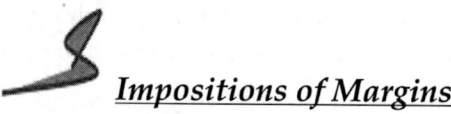

Impositions of Margins

1. Why should there be margin.

Just as we are faced with day to day uncertainties pertaining to weather, health, traffic etc and take steps to minimise the uncertainties, so also in the stock markets, there is uncertainty in the movement of share prices.

This uncertainty leading to risk is sought to be addressed by margining systems of stock markets.

Example:

Suppose an investor purchases 1000 shares of 'xyz' company at Rs.100/- on January 1, 2008. Investor has to give the purchase amount of Rs.1,00,000/- (1000 x 100) to his broker on or before January 2, 2008. Broker, in turn, has to give this money to the stock exchange on January 3, 2008.

There is always a small chance that the investor may not be able to bring the required money by the required date.

As an advance for buying the shares, investors are required to pay a portion of the total amount of Rs.1,00,000/- to the broker at the time of placing the buy order. Stock exchange in turn collects a similar amount from the broker upon execution of the order. This initial token payment is called margin.

Remember, for every buyer there is a seller and if the buyer does not bring the money, seller may not get his / her money and vice versa.

Therefore, margin is levied on the seller also to ensure that he / she gives the 100 shares sold to the broker who in turn gives it to the stock exchange.

Margin payments ensure that each investor is serious about buying or selling shares. In the above example, assume that margin was 15%. That is, the investor has to give Rs.15,000/-(15% of Rs.1,00,000/) to the broker before buying. Now suppose that investor bought the shares at 11 am on January 1, 2008. Assume that by the end of the day price of the share falls by Rs.25/-. That is total value of the shares has come down to Rs.75,000/-. That is buyer has suffered a notional loss of Rs.25,000/-. In our example buyer has paid Rs.15,000/- as margin but the notional loss, because of fall in price, is Rs.25,000/-. That is notional loss is more than the margin given.

In such a situation, the buyer may not want to pay Rs.1,00,000/- for the shares whose value has come down to Rs.75,000/-. Similarly, if the price has gone up by Rs.25/-, the seller may not want to give the shares at Rs.1,00,000/-

. To ensure that both buyers and sellers fulfill their obligations irrespective of price movements, notional losses are also need to be collected.

Prices of shares keep on moving every day. Margins ensure that buyers bring money and sellers bring shares to complete their obligations even though the prices have moved down or up.

2. *What is volatility?*

Different people have different definitions for volatility. For our purpose, we can say that volatility essentially refers to uncertainty arising out of price changes of shares. It is important to understand the meaning of volatility a little more closely because it has a major bearing on how margins are computed.

3. *How is volatility computed? Can you give an example?*

As mentioned earlier, volatility has different definitions and therefore different people compute it differently. For our understanding purpose, let us compute volatility based on close prices of a share over last 6 months.

Since it is based on historical data, let us call it 'historical volatility'.You can easily calculate historical volatility using an excel sheet. All you need to do is to put down close prices of a share for the last six months in a column of the excel sheet. Calculate the daily returns by using 'LN' (natural log) function in excel.

Use the formula LN(today's close price / yesterday's close price) in the next column for calculating daily returns for all the days. Go to the end of the second column (after the last value) and use the excel function 'STDEV' (available under statistical formulas) to calculate the Standard Deviation of returns computed as above. The calculated standard deviation expressed as percentage is the 'historical volatility' of the share for the six months period.

Example: Volatility of Company ABC Ltd. calculated on a spreadsheet

4. *What is the difference between price movements and volatility?*

Prices of shares fluctuate depending on the future prospects of the company. We hear of stock prices going up or down in the markets every day. Popularly, a share is said to be volatile if the prices move by large percentages up and/or down. A stock with very little movement in its price would have lower volatility.

Let us compute volatility of four companies W, X, Y and Z to see how daily price movements of these companies affect the computed historical volatility.

Date	Closing price Of W shares	Daily LN returns	Closing price of X shares	Daily LN returns	Closing priceY of shares	Daily LN returns	Closing price of Z shares	Daily LN returns
1-Jan-08	2800		2420		2825		2510	
2-Jan-08	2850	1.77%	2480	2.45%	2758	-2.40%	2515	0.20%
3-Jan-08	2700	-5.41%	2515	1.40%	2742	-0.58%	2520	0.20%
4-Jan-08	2750	1.83%	2550	1.38%	2725	-0.62%	2512	-0.32%
7-Jan-08	2900	5.31%	2565	0.59%	2708	-0.63%	2508	-0.16%
8-Jan-08	2800	-3.51%	2592	1.05%	2686	-0.82%	2514	0.24%
9-Jan-08	2650	-5.51%	2614	0.85%	2667	-0.71%	2523	0.36%
10-Jan-08	2700	1.87%	2635	0.80%	2635	-1.21%	2510	-0.52%
11-Jan-08	2750	1.83%	2667	1.21%	2614	-0.80%	2505	-0.20%
14-Jan-08	2650	-3.70%	2686	0.71%	2592	-0.85%	2515	0.40%
15-Jan-08	2640	-0.38%	2708	0.82%	2565	-1.05%	2502	-0.52%
16-Jan-08	2520	-4.65%	2725	0.63%	2550	-0.59%	2510	0.32%
17-Jan-08	2670	5.78%	2742	0.62%	2515	-1.38%	2515	0.20%
21-Jan-08	2720	1.86%	2758	0.58%	2480	-1.40%	2511	-0.16%
22-Jan-08	2790	2.54%	2825	2.40%	2420	-2.45%	2514	0.12%
Volatility		3.85%		0.62%		0.62%		0.32%

As you can see from the above, prices of shares of 'W' company moved up and down through out the period and the price changes were ranging from -5.51% to 5.78%. The calculated historical volatility is 3.85% for the period.

Shares of company 'X' moved steadily upwards and the price changes were between 0.58% and 2.45%. Here the historical volatility is 0.62%

Shares of company 'Y' moved steadily downwards and the price changes were between -2.45% and 0.58%. Here the historical volatility is once again 0.62%.

Shares of company 'Z' moved up and down but with smaller percentage variations ranging from -0.52% to 0.40%. Here historical volatility is 0.32% and is the least volatile share of the four under consideration.

Higher volatility means the price of the security may change dramatically over a short time period in either direction. Lower volatility means that a security's value may not change as dramatically.

5. *Is volatility linked to the direction of price movements?*

No. Stock prices may move up or may move down. Volatility will capture the extent of the fluctuations in the stock, irrespective of whether the prices are going up or going down. In the above example shares of 'X' have moved up steadily whereas shares of 'Y' moved down steadily. However, both have same historical volatility.

6. *How does change in volatility affect margins?*

Price movements vary from share to share. Some see larger up or down variations on daily basis and some see lower one way or both way movements.

In our example under question 4, w e considered share price movements of 4 companies W, X, Y and Z during the period January 1, 2008 to January 22, 2008.

On the morning of January 23, 2008, no one knows what would be the closing price of these 4 shares.

However, historical volatility number would tell you that shares of 'W' may move up or down by large percentage whereas shares of 'Z' may see a small percentage variation compared to close price on January 22, 2008. This is only an estimate based on past price movements. Since the uncertainty of price movements is very high for 'W', its shares would attract higher initial margin whereas shares of 'Z' would attract lower initial margin since its volatility is low. Let us deal with this aspect in more detail while exploring different types of margins.

7. *Are margins same across cash and derivatives markets?*

Stock market is a complex place with variety of instruments traded on it. As shown above, one single margin for all shares may not be able to handle price uncertainty /risk.

In our simple example under question 1, even within the cash market, we have seen two types of margins, one at the time of placing the order and another to cover the notional loss. Shares traded on the cash market are settled in two days whereas derivative contracts may have longer time to expiry. That is, derivative market margins have to address the uncertainty over a longer period.

Therefore, SEBI has prescribed different ways to margin cash and derivatives trades taking into consideration unique features of instruments traded on these segments.

8. *What are the types of margins levied in the cash market segment?*

Margins in the cash market segment comprise of the following three types:

1) Value at Risk (VaR) margin

2) Extreme loss margin

3) Mark to market Margin

9. *What is Value at Risk (VaR) margin?*

VaR Margin is at the heart of margining system for the cash market segment. VaR margin is collected on upfront basis. In that respect, it is similar to the margin we have seen in our example under question 1 while placing the order.

Let us try and understand briefly what we mean by 'VaR'. The most popular and traditional measure of uncertainty / risk is Volatility, which we have understood earlier. While historical volatility tells us how the security price moved in the past, VaR answers the question,

"How much is it likely to move over next one day?"

VaR is a technique used to estimate the probability of loss of value of an asset or group of assets (for example a share or a portfolio of a few shares), based on the statistical analysis of historical price trends and volatilities.

A VaR statistic has three components: a time period, a confidence level and a loss amount (or loss percentage).

Keep these three parts in mind and identify them in the following example:

• With 99% confidence, what is the maximum value that an asset or portfolio may loose over the next day?

You can see how the "VaR question" has three elements: a relatively high level of confidence (99%), a time period (a day) and an estimate of loss (expressed either in rupees or percentage terms).

The actual calculation of VaR is beyond the scope of this booklet. However, those who are interested in understanding the calculation methodology may refer any statistical reference material.

Example

Let us assume that an investor bought shares of a company. Its market value today is Rs.50 lakhs. Obviously, we do not know the market value of these shares the next day. An investor holding these shares may, based on VaR methodology, say that 1-day VaR is Rs.4 lakhs at the 99% confidence level. This implies that under normal trading conditions the investor can, with 99% confidence, say that the value of the shares would not go down by more than Rs.4 lakhs within the next 1-day.

In the stock exchange scenario, a VaR Margin is a margin intended to cover the largest loss (in %) that may be faced by an investor for his / her shares (both purchases and sales) on a single day with a 99% confidence level. The VaR margin is collected on an upfront basis (at the time of trade).

10. *How is VaR margin calculated?*

VaR is computed using exponentially weighted moving average (EWMA) methodology. Based on statistical analysis, 94% weight is given to volatility on 'T- 1' day and 6% weight is given to 'T' day returns.

To compute volatility for January 1, 2008, first we need to compute day's return for Jan 1, 2008 by using LN (close price on Jan 1, 2008 / close price on Dec 31, 2007).

Take volatility computed as on December 31, 2007.

Use the following formula to calculate volatility for January 1, 2008:

Square root of [0.94*(Dec 31, 2007 volatility)*(Dec 31, 2007 volatility) + 0.06*(January 1, 2008 LN return)*(January 1, 2008 LN return)]

Example: Share of ABC Ltd.

Volatility on December 31, 2007 = 0.0314

Closing price on December 31, 2007 = Rs. 360

Closing price on January 1, 2008 = Rs. 330

January 1, 2008 volatility = Square root of [(0.94*(0.0314)*(0.0314)+ 0.06 (0.08701)* (0.08701)] = 0.037 or 3.7%

Now, to arrive at VaR margin rate, companies are divided into 3 categories based on how regularly their shares trade and on the basis of liquidity (that is, by how much a large buy or sell order changes the price of the scrip, what is technically called 'impact cost'.

> • Group I consists of shares that are regularly traded (that is, on more than 80% of the trading days in the previous six months) and have high liquidity (that is, impact cost less than 1%).

> • Group II consists of shares that are regularly traded (agai, more than 80% of the trading days in the previous six months) but with

- Group III.

For Group I shares, the VaR margin rate would be higher of

- 3.5 times volatility or
- 7.5%

For Group II shares, computation of VaR margin rate is a little complex. First take higher of

- 3.5 times volatility of the security or
- 3.0 times volatility of index (The volatility of index is taken as the higher of the daily Index volatility based on CNX NIFTY or BSE SENSEX. At any point in time, minimum value of volatility of index is taken as 5%).

The number arrived at as above is then multiplied by 1.732051 (that is, square root of 3). The number so obtained is the VaR margin rate.

For Group III securities VaR margin rate would be 5.0 times volatility of the Index multiplied by 1.732051 (that is, square root of 3).

In the above example, if the shares belong to Group I, then VaR margin rate would be 3.5 * 3.7, which is about 13%.

Actual VaR margin collected at the time of buy or
sell would be 13% of the value of the trade.

For example, if the value of the position (buy or sell) is Rs.10
lakhs, then the VaR margin would be Rs.1,30,000/-

11. *How is the Extreme Loss Margin computed?*

The extreme loss margin aims at covering the losses that could occur outside the coverage of VaR margins.

The Extreme loss margin for any stock is higher of 1.5 times the standard deviation of daily LN returns of the stock price in the last six months or 5% of the value of the position.

This margin rate is fixed at the beginning of every month, by taking the price data on a rolling basis for the past six months.

Example

In the Example given at question 10, the VaR margin rate for shares of ABC Ltd. was 13%. Suppose that standard deviation of daily LN returns of the security is 3.1%. 1.5 times standard deviation would be 1.5 x 3.1 4.65.

Then 5% (which is higher than 4.65%) will be taken as the Extreme Loss margin rate.

Therefore, the total margin on the security would be 18% (13% VaR Margin 5% Extreme Loss Margin). As such, total margin payable (VaR margin extreme loss margin) on a trade of Rs.10 lakhs would be 1,80,000/-

12. *How is Mark-to-Market (MTM) margin computed?*

MTM is calculated at the end of the day on all open positions by comparing transaction price with the closing price of the share for the day.

In our example in question number 1, we have seen that a buyer purchased 1000 shares @ Rs.100/- at 11 am on January 1, 2008. If close price of the shares on that day happens to be Rs.75/-, then the buyer faces a notional loss of Rs.25,000/- on his buy position. In technical terms this loss is called MTM loss and is payable by January 2, 2008 (that is next day of the trade) before the trading begins.

In case the price of the share falls further by the end of January 2, 2008 to Rs. 70/-, then buy position would show a further loss of Rs.5,000/-. This MTM loss is payable by next day.

In case, on a given day, buy and sell quantity in a share are equal, that is net quantity position is zero, but there could still be a notional loss / gain (due to difference between the buy and sell values), such notional loss also is considered for calculating the MTM payable.

MTM Profit/Loss = [(Total Buy Qty X Close price) – Total Buy Value] - [Total Sale Value - (Total Sale Qty X Close price)]

 ## *Cross margining*

An off-setting position for a client in different segments has lower risk as loss on one position is off-set by profit in the other position. An example for an off-setting position can be a buy position of 100 in security —

AI in capital market and short position of 100 in stock futures of security —AI in derivative segment. As the risk of the off-setting positions is lower, the margin requirement for the combined positions has to be lower which is considered as cross margining.

The benefit of cross margining is provided on the following off setting positions:

   a) Index futures and constituent stock futures for same
       expiry in F&O segment

b) Index futures and constituent stock positions in Cash segment.

c) Stock futures in F&O segment and stock positions in Cash segment.

d) The off-seting positions in respect of (a) and (b) above are computed considering the weightage of that security in the index.

13. *What are the types of margins levied in the Futures & Options (F&O) Segment?*

Margins on both Futures and Options contracts comprise of the following:

1) Initial Margin

2) Exposure margin

In addition to these margins, in respect of options contracts the following additional margins are collected

a) Premium Margin

b) Assignment Margin

 ### Risk Settlement

The following two kinds of risks are inherent in a settlement system:

(1) Counterparty Risk: This arises if parties do not discharge their obligations fully when due or at any time thereafter.

This has two components, namely replacement cost risk prior to settlement and principal risk during settlement.

a) *Replacement cost risk*

- The replacement cost risk arises from the failure of one of the parties to transaction. While the non-defaulting party tries to replace the original transaction at current prices, he loses the profit that has accrued on the transaction between the date of original transaction and date of replacement transaction.

- The seller/ buyer of the secur *ity loses this unrealised profit if the current price is below/ above the transaction price.*

- Both parties encounter this risk as prices are uncertain. It has been reduced by reducing time gap between transaction and settlement and by legally binding netting systems.

b) *Principal Risk*

- *The principal risk arises if a party discharges his obligations but the counterparty defaults. The seller/ buyer of the security suffers this risk when he delivers/ makes payment, but does not receive payment/delivery.*

- This risk can be eliminated by delivery vs. payment mechanism which ensures delivery only against payment.

- This has been reduced by having a central counterparty (NSCCL) which becomes the buyer to every seller and the seller to every buyer.

- A variant of counterparty risk is liquidity risk which arises if one of the parties to a transaction does not settle on the settlement date, but later.

- The seller/buyer who does not receive payment/ delivery when due, may have to borrow funds/securities to complete his payment/delivery obligations.

- Another variant is the third party risk which arises if the parties to trade are permitted or required to use the services of a third party which fails to perform.

For example, the failure of a clearing bank which helps in payment can disrupt settlement. This risk is reduced by allowing parties to have accounts with multiple banks.

- Similarly, *the users of custodial services face risk if the concerned custodian becomes insolvent, acts negligently, etc.*

c) *System Risk: This comprises of operational, legal and systemic risks.*

- The operational risk arises from possible operational failures such as errors, fraud, outages etc.

- The legal risk arises if the laws or regulations do not support enforcement of settlement obligations or are uncertain.

- Systemic risk arises when failure of one of the parties to discharge his obligations leads to failure by other parties. The domino effect of successive failures can cause a failure of the settlement system.

 Retail Professional Clearing Member

In case of transactions which are to be settled by Retail Professional Clearing

Members (PCM), all the trades with PCM code are included in the trading member's positions till it is confirmed by the PCM.

Margins are collected from respective trading members until confirmation of trades by PCM. On confirmation of trades by PCM, such trades are reduced from the positions of trading member and included in the positions of PCM. The PCM is then liable to pay margins on the same.

 *Capping of margin*

In Case of buy transaction Var MArgin, Extreme loss margin and MArk to market margin together should not exceed the purchase value of the transaction. In case of sale transaction extreme loss margin and Var margin should not exceed the sale value of transaction and Mark to market should also be levied

 Exemption early in Pay in securities

Early pay in securities is made prior to security pay in date, such position will be exempt from the margin. EPI of securities is allocated only to net obligation securities, on a random basis by member/custodian. They both must ensure that early pay in securities needs to benefit to the relevant client by specifying the client to whom that benefit is allocated.

 Exemption early in Pay in of Funds

Early pay of Funds is made prior to security payout date, such position will be exempt from the margin. EPI of funds allocated only for a specific client and for settlement is allocated against the securities in descending order of net buy value of outstanding position of the client.

 How the online exposure is monitored

NSCCL has an online surveillance system whereby member exposure can be monitored on real time basis. A system will put the alert message both to NSCCL and client at preset levels (Like 70%, 80%, 85%, 90%) when members reach their allowable limits.

The system will allow to check micro details of client also

The online surveillance system generates various alerts, reports on price volume movement not in trend with past trend

Rumours in print media will be taken, where price sensitive information are there, companies will be contacted for verifications. Replies received will be recorded and informed to public.

What is the offline monitoring

It consist of verification and investigation. Trading members are being inspected to see that they are following rules and regulations of the exchange. The inspections will verify that interest of the investors are being protected or not.

What is settlement guarantee mechanism of the exchange

A settlement guarantee fund provides the cushion for my residual risk. In the event of failure to done with settlement the fund is utilised to the extent required for successful completion of the settlement. This has eliminated counter party risk.

This fund will help in settlement process. It is operating like self -insurance mechanism. This fund is funded by NSCCL and NSE from penalties, fines etc recovered by NSCCL.

How the securities are identified as International security identification Number

SEBI being as national numbering agency for India permitted NSDL to allot International security identification number for demat shares.

Numbering system of ISIN:- the numbering structure of security is 12 digit alpha numeric string. The first two character will represents country name i.e IN (refers to india) the third character will represents issuer type

Issuer type	Code Allotted
a) Central government	A
b) State government	B
c) Municipal corporation	C
d) Union territories	D
e) Company, statutory corporation, Banking Company	E
f) Mutual Funds including UTI	F

Maximum issue type can be 35 (A to Z and 0 to 8) the fourth to seventh character represents the company identity of which 3 characters are numeric and 4 will be alpha characters. The numbering begin with 001A to 999A again it will start with 001B. The next two characters are numeric and represent the security type. Both are numeric. The next two characters are serially issued for each security of the issuer entering the system (tenth and eleventh). The last digit is check digit

Security type

Security Type	Code
Equity shares	01
Mutual funds	01
Convertible preference shares	03
Non -convertible shares	04
Secured debentures	07
Unsecured debentures	08
Regular return binds, Promissory notes	09
Floating rate bonds	10
Deep discount bonds	11
Step discount bonds	12
Warrants	13
Commercial papers	14
Pass Through papers	15
Certificate of Deposit	16
Security Receipt	18

What are the SEBI regulations 2008

One of main function of SEBI regulation is to regulate the functioning ofintermediary, so that their will be smooth flow functioning of market and interset of the investors will be protected.

These intermediaries are broker, sub-broker, portfolio manager, mutual fund agencies, creditrating agencies etc.

SEBI has issued guidelines for registration of intermediaries and their regulatory frameworks.

Many of the requirements and regulatory frameworks are common.

SEBI consolidated all and made SEBI regulations act 2008

a) SEBI regulation Act put certain regulations which are common to all intermediaries. The common are that registration certificate, code of conduct, general obligation, taking action in case of default are applicable to all intermediaries.

b) An applicant can file applications in the prescribed form. The existing intermediaries within specified time file the disclosure in the specified format. The disclosure needs to be uploaded in the web side specified by SEBI. if the intermediary wants to operate in a new category, such a person needs to file additional forms disclosing specific requirements of the new category.

c) The registration granted to intermediary is permanent until and unless he is suspended, or registration got cancelled or surrendered by himself as per the regulations

d) The procedure for the action in case of suspension and cancellation is simplified so that short time will be taken without compromising the right of reasonable opportunity to be heard, surrender can be done without following the lengthy procedure.

e) Common requirements need to be followed by all intermediaries. The specific requirements will continue to be followed by individual intermediaries as per their role

What does SEBI Regulations 2015?

That mainly dealt with insider trading .Insider trading means dealing in buying and selling of securities on the bases of price sensitive unpublished information which if published lead to rise or fall in price of securities of that corporate

To deal with this problem SEBI regulation Act 2015 cames into existence

The important definition used in the regulation are:-

a) Dealing in securities means an act of subscribing, buying, selling or agree to buy sell or subscribe by any person either as an principal or an agent

b) Insider means any person connected with the person or deemed to be connected with the person having access of unpublished price sensitive information

c) A connected person include:

- Is a director or deemed to be the director

- Occupies the position as an employee of the company or having business/professional relationship with himself and company either temporary or permanent and having access to price sensitive information

d) A person is deemed to be connected person if

- Such person is working under company having same management, or subsidiary as per the monopolies restrictive act of 1969

- Is an intermediary, investment company AMC or any director or employee of an official stock exchange or of a clearing house or corporation.

- Is a merchant banker, sub-broker, member of board of trustee, member of board of directors of AMC or an employee having fiduciary relationship with the company

e) Is member of the board of director or an employee of an public financial institution

f) Is an official or an employee of a self-regulatory organisation or authorised by board of a regulatory body.

g) Is relative of aforementioned persons

h) Is the banker of the company

i) Relative of the connected person

Price sensitive information means any information which is related directly or indirectly to a company and which if published will material effect the the price of securities of that company.

a) Periodical financial results of the company

b) Intended declaration of dividend

c) Issue of securities or buy-back of securities

d) Any major expansion plans

e) Amalgamation, merger or takeover

f) Disposal of the whole or substantial part of the undertaking

<u>Unpublished information means any information which is not being published by the company or its agents or not specific in natur e</u>

What are the prohibition on communication, dealing, Counselling?

Under this regulation no insider should :

a) Either on himself or on his own behalf on any other person, deal in securities of a company listed on the stock exchange when he is in possession of unpublished sensitive information

b) communicate, counsel or procure,directly or indirectly of such unsensitive information.

c) However this communication does not involve any communication in normal course of business

The regulation require that no company requires to deal with another company, who is in possession of unpublished sensitive information.

What is investigation

If SEBI suspects any person of having violated the provision of insider regulations, it may take inquires with such person or with stock exchange, or mutual fund orother persons associated with securities market.as to form a prima facie evidence that there that any violation of insider trading.

When SEBI form the prima facie opinion that it is required to inspect the books of accounts of stock exchange or mutual fund or other persons associate with the stock exchange or security market, The SEBI may appoint the investigation authority.

The investigation team I requires to submit the report to investigation SEBI after completion of investigation as per rules and regulation

As per the report the SEBI will intimate with the suspect and demand the reply within 21 days. After 21 days getting reply SEBI will take suitable measures to safeguard the interest of investors after due compliances with insider trading regulations.

SEBI also having power to appoint the auditor to audit the books of accounts of stock exchange, mutual funds, other person associated with it

What are the disclosure and internal procedure for prevention of insider trading?

All listed company and organisations associated with securities market need to follow the prescribed format in SEBI regulations without diluting it any manner.

a) Initial disclosure

1) Any person who holds more than 5% of shares and voting rights need to disclose in prescribed format within 2 working days:

- The receipt of intimations of allotment of shares

- The acquisitions of shares or voting rights as the case ma be

2) Any person who is the director or employee of the company must disclose in the prescribed format the number of shares or voting rights held by him within 2 working days of becoming such shareholder

b) Continual disclosure

- Any person who holds more than 5% shares or voting rights in any listed company should mentioned in prescribed format and if any change in voting rights or shareholding even if it results in less than 5% but exceeds 2% of total shareholding or voting rights need to prescribed in proper format

- Any person who is director or employee of the listed company, should disclose in prescribed format the number of shares and voting rights held and if any change is there in such shareholding or voting rights and such change exceeds 5 lakhs in value or 250000 shares or 1% of total shareholding whichever is lower.

The disclosure of the above needs to made within 2 working days

Disclosure by company to stock exchange

Every listed company requires to disclose his continual and initial disclosure to stock exchange within 2 das of receipt of information. The disclosure need to made in electronic mode as per the system devised by the exchange. Further as per insider trading regulation act the SEBI having increased the penalty up to 25 crores or three times the profit he made because of insider trading (whichever is higher)

What does the SEBI regulation 2003 regulates?

The SEBI regulation 2003 regulates enable SEBI to investigate into the cases of market manipulations and fraudulent practices. The regulations specifically prohibit market manipulations, misleading agreement to encourage sale or purchase of

> a) Fraud includes any act expression, omission or concealment whether done in deceitful manner by one person or other or by his aget dealing insecurities.

It includes:

- A knowing misrepresentation of truth

- A promise made without any intention to perform it

- A representation in reckless manner resulting to might be true or false

- Any act or omission which as per law is fraudulent

- A false statement without knowing the reasonable ground that it could be false

- An concealment of the fact by having one knowledge or fact.

Dealing in securities refer to any act of buying and selling or subscribing related to any issue or agreeing to buy or sell or transecting in any way with agent or principal or intermediary under SEBI Act

Prohibition of certain dealing in securities

> a) Buy, sell or otherwise deal in fraudulent manner

> b) Use or employ any manipulative or deceptive device, in connection with issue, purchase or sell of any security

listed or proposed to be listed in a recognised stock exchange.

c) Employ any device or any scheme to defraud in connection with dealing or securities listed or proposed to be listed in any stock exchange

d) Engage in any act, practice, course of business which operates as fraud upon nay person in dealing with issue or nay securities which are listed or proposed to be listed any exchange in contravention of the act

e) Publishing or reporting any information which is not true prior to or in the course of dealing in securities

f) Dealing in any counterfeit or stolen securities whether in physical or dematerialised form

g) An intermediary providing any information to client which is not verified by the client at the time of dealing

h) An misleading advertisement that will influence the decision of investors

i) An intermediary may report the trading transaction in inflated (higher price) manner to increase their commission

j) An intermediary making any fake contract notes

k) Spreading false and misleading news which will lead to effect the market price of the shares

Depositories Act 1996

This Act provides the establishments of the system with the object of ensuring that transfer need to take place with accuracy and with speed also and security by

a) Public limited companies need to freely transferable

b) Dematerialised the securities in the depositories mode

c) Providing the maintenance of book record in book entry form

The terms used in the act are

a) Beneficial owner means whose name are their in depository register

b) Depository means any company, formed and registered under companies act 2013 and got the registration certificate under the SEBI act 1992

c) Issuer means any person who will issue the securities

d) Participant means whose name is registered under the section 12 of SEBI Act 1992 e) Registered owner means whose name in the register of the issuer kept by depository

The Depositories Act, defines the rights and obligations of depositories, participants, issuers and beneficial owners which are mentioned below:

1) *Agreement between Depository and Participant:* A depository is required to enter into an agreement in the specified format with one or more participants as its agent.

2) *Services of Depository:* Any person, through a participant, may enter into an agreement, in such form as may be specified by the bye-laws, with any depository for availing its services.

3) *Surrender of Certificate of Securit* y: Any person who has entered into an agreement with a depository should surrender the certificate of security, for which he seeks to avail the services of a depository, to the issuer in such manner as may be specified by the regulations. The issuer, on receipt of certificate of security, should cancel the certificate of security and substitute in its records the name of the depository as a registered owner in respect of that security and inform the depository accordingly. A depository should, on receipt of information enter the name of the person in its records, as the beneficial owner in respect of that security and inform the depository accordingly.

4) *Registration of Transfer of Securities with Depository:* On receipt of intimation from a participant, the depository

is required to register the transfer of security in the name of the transferee.

5) **_Options to Receive Security Certificate or Hold Securities with Depository:_** Every person subscribing to securities offered by an issuer should have the option either to receive the security certificates or hold securities with a depository. Where a person opts to hold a security with a depository, the issuer should intimate such depository the details of allotment of the security, and on receipt of such information the depository should enter in its records the name of the allottee as the beneficial owner of that security.

6) **_Securities in Depositories to be in Fungible Form_** : All securities held by a depository should be in dematerialised and be in fungible form.

7) **_Rights of Depositories and Beneficial Owner_** : A depository is deemed to be the registered owner for the purpose of effecting transfer of ownership of security on behalf of a beneficial owner. The depository as a registered owner does not have any voting rights or any other rights in respect of securities held by it. The beneficial owner is entitled to all the rights and benefits.

8) **_Pledge or Hypothecation of Securities held in a Depository:_** A beneficial owner may with the previous approval of the depository create a pledge or hypothecation in respect of a security owned by him through a depository for that he needs to give intimation to depository, as it will act as an proof.

9) **_Furnishing of Information and Records by Depository and Issuer_** : Every depository should furnish to the issuer, information about the transfer of securities in the name of beneficial owners at such intervals and in such manner as may be specified by the bye-laws. Every issuer should

make available to the depository copies of the relevant records in respect of securities held by such depository.

10) **_Option to Opt out in Respect of any Security_** : If a beneficial owner seeks to opt out of a depository in respect of any security, he should inform the depository accordingly. After receiving the information, the depository is required to make appropriate entries in its records and inform the issuer. Within thirty days of the receipt of intimation from the depository and on fulfilment of such conditions and payment of such fees as may be specified by the regulations, the issuer is required to issue the certificate of securities to the beneficial owner or the transferee, as the case may be.

11) **_Depository to Indemnify Loss in certain cases:_** In case of any loss caused to the beneficial owner due to the negligence of the depository or the participant, the depository has to indemnify the beneficial owner. Where the loss due to the negligence of the participant is indemnified by the depository, the depository has the right to recover the same from such participant.

Multiple choice questions

1.	The process of delivering securities to the clearing corporation to effect settlement of trade is known as _____ _____ **a) Securities pay in** b) Securities pay out c) Funds pay in d) Funds pay out	1
2.	_____ is responsible for the post trade activity in stock exchange a) Intermediary b) SEBI c) NSE **d) NSCCL**	1

3.	The title of custodian is vested with _____ a) Original holder b) Nominee c) Custodian trustee **d) Any of the above**	1
4.	_____ are the key link between clearing member and NSCCL **a) Cleaning bank** b) NSE c) Broker d) Trading member	1
5	The person who holds the demat account is _____ a) Investor b) Depository **c) Beneficiary owner** d) Custodian	1
6.	_____ procedure adopted by the NSCCL a) Bilateral system **b) Multilateral system** c) Both a and b d) None of the above	1
7.	The settlement process begins as soon as members obligation is decides through/when **a) Clearing process** b) Pay in of securities are done c) Payout of securities are done d) If pay in and pay out both are done	1
8.	Settlement process deemed to be complete if _____ _____ a) **Release of payout of securities** b) Receiving pay in of securities c) Clearing process done d) Al of the above	1

9.	Which of the following statement is false	1
	a) Inter institutional deals re restricted only to specific clients	
	b) Trading in inter institutional deals are available for institutional clients only	
	c) A member are required to enter custodian participant code while entering order	
	d) A sell order or buy order can be neutered for any securities	
10.	In case of NSDL, the member needs to give instructions to move the securities to settlement account of	1
	a) SEBI	
	b) Clearing bank	
	c) Clearing member	
	d) NSCCL	
11.	_____ takes place when a broker a custodian or the clearing corporation delivers fewer securities than what we are contracted for either to another broker	1
	a) Short delivery	
	b) Bad delivery	
	c) Company deliveries	
	d) All of the above	
12.	NSCCL has empanelled _____ clearing banks	1
	a) 12 b) 14 c) 15 **d) 13**	
13.	____ bank comes under NSCCL clearing bank	1
	a) IDBI bank	
	b) Axis bank	
	c) Maharashtra bank	
	d) Punjab national bank	
14.	Clearing account is exclusively used for clearing corporation	1
	a) True	
	b) False	

15.	In case of limited physical limited market failure to get delivery close out the securities at	1
	a) 20% over the actual price	
	b) 10% over of the actual price	
	c) 20% of the official closing price in regular in auction market	
	d) 15 % over of the actual price	
16.	_____ risk arises when one party fails to transect	1
	a) Counterparty risk	
	b) Replacement risk	
	c) System risk	
	d) Any of the above	
17.	The operational risk arises because of _____	1
	a) Failure to fulfil the obligation by one party	
	b) Error, fraud	
	c) Law do not support the enforcement	
	d) None of the above	
18.	Bad deliveries are required to be reported to the clearing corporation within _____ from the receipt of documents.	1
	a) Two days	
	b) 3 days	
	c) 4 days	
	d) 5 days	
19.	On security payout day NSCCL identifies the short delivery and respective clearing member account is debited with an equivalent amount and these securities will be valued at _____ and it is known as_____ _____	1
	a) Valuation price, valuation debt	
	b) Strike price, short handling	
	c) Stock price, short delivery	
	d) None of the above	

20.	The CM on whom company objection is lodged has an opportunity to withdraw the objection with in _____ _____ of lodging the complaint against him. **a) Within 7 days** b) Within 9 days c) Within 10 days d) Within 5 days	1
21.	Any delivery in excess of _____ is marked as short will be completely closed out **a) 500** b) 600 c) 800 d) 1000	1
22.	Unrectified bad delivery and re-bad delivery are compulsorily closed-out at over the actual traded price. a) 10% **b) 20%** c) 30% d) Any of the above	1
23.	The title to the custodian property remains with_____ **a) Original holder** b) Clearing banks c) Depositories d) NSCCL	1
24.	From the following which is the function of clearing banks a) Automation transfer **b)** Providing working capital needs **c)** Services as Depository participants **d) All of the above**	1
25.	Novation refers to _____ a) Determining obligation of the clearing members **b) NSCCL becomes the legal counterparty to the net settlement obligations of every member** c) Providing the major link between clearing member, clearing banks and depositories. d) None of the above	1

26.	In inter institutional deals the buy or sell order entered by the trading member on behalf of client should be 　a) Any securities 　**b) ADR/GDR/FDI/NRI/PIO** 　c) equity/ preference/ debentures 　d) All of the above	1
27.	Which of the following statement is true 　a) In inter institutional deals the order entered should not be other than ADR/GDR/FDI/NRI/PIO 　b) The member entering the invalid order need o be liable for further disciplinary action 　**c) Both a and b** 　d) None of the above	1
28.	_____ are required to be reported to clearing corporation within 2 days 　a) Short delivery 　**b) Bad delivery** 　c) Company objections 　d) All of the above	1
29.	_____ is responsible for rectifying/replacing defective documents to the receiving CM as per notified schedule 　**A) Selling CM** 　B) Purchasing CM 　C) Trading member 　D) Depositories	1
30.	_____ is required to open at least one designated account with clearing bank 　a) Clearing member 　b) Depositories 　c) Trading member 　d) Custodians	1
31.	In _____ market trading member have to do the obligation of clearing member 　a) Whole sale debt market 　b) Capital market 　**c) Retail market** 　d) Regular market	1

32.	_____ risk will arise if parties discharge his obligation but counterparty defaults **a) Counterparty risk** b) System risk c) Replacement risk d) Unsystematic risk	1
33.	In case of deleted security on account of redemption, the security introduced by the exchange will arrive at _____ **a) Closing price** b) Opening price c) Stock price d) Strike price	1
34.	In case where the price of new security is not available for the reason of such security not being traded on the exchange, the closing price of such deleted security will be _____ **a) 20% over the official closing price on the last traded day of deleted security** b) 20% over the official closing price or highest trading price till the auction c) 10% over the official closing price on the last traded day of deleted security d) 10% over the official closing price or highest trading price till the auction	1
35.	_____ means the volatility of the security computed as at the end of the previous trading day **a) Security sigma** b) Security VaR c) Index sigma d) Inx VaR	1
36.	The securities which are traded at least 80% of the days for the previous six months constitute **a) Liquid securities** b) Illiquid securities c) Less liquid securities d) None of the above	1

37.	VaR margin as mentioned above will be charged on _____ _____ for the respective clients a) Closing price **b) Net outstanding position** c) Gross outstanding position d) Opening price	1
38.	In case of _____ the members are not premitted to trade with immediate effect. **a) Margin shortfall** b) Extreme loss margin c) Cross margin d) MTM margin	1
39.	Off-line surveillance activity consists of _____ a) Online exposure monitored b) Offline exposure monitored **c) Inspection and investigation** d) Margin downfall	1
40.	Equity shares are having _____ as a security code **a) A** b) B c) C d) D	1
41	The code 07 allotted to _____ securites a) Equity shares b) Mutual funds **c) Secured debentures** d) Deepdiscount bonds	1
42.	Code F is alloted to _____ issue type a) Central government b) State government c) Municipal corporation **d) Mutual funds including UTI**	1
43.	Which is the function of NSCCL **a) To act as a counterparty to all trades** b) To guarantee settlement c) To provide liquidity d) All of the above	1

44.	What is the purpose of NSCCL	1
	a) To clear and settle trades on NSE	
	b) To regulate the security markets	
	c) To provide depository services	
	d) To facilitate trading	
45.	Which of the following is the benefit of the NSCCL guarantees	1
	a) Reduced risk	
	b) Increased efficiency	
	c) Improved security	
	d) All of the above	
46.	How does NSCCL guarantee settlement	1
	a) By acting as a counterparty to all trades	
	b) By providing liquidity	
	c) By regulating market	
	d) By setting trades on a net basis	
47.	What is the process of mark to market process in the clearing and settlement cycles	1
	a) To adjust the values of securities based on market prices	
	b) To settle trades on net basis	
	c) To provide liquidity	
	d) To regulate markets	
48.	How often does NSCCL settle trades	1
	a) Daily	
	b) Weekly	
	c) Monthly	
	d) Yearly	
49.	How does the NSCCL novate the trades	1
	a) By replacing the original trades with two new trades	
	b) By guaranteeing the settlement	
	c) By providing liquidity	
	d) By regulating the market	

50.	What is the purpose of settlement guarantee fund	1
	a) To cover losses due to default	
	b) To provide liquidity	
	c) To regulate the market	
	d) To facilitate trading	

Define the following

a) NSCCL

b) Bad delivery

c) Short delivery

d) Company objection

e) Clearing bank

f) Custodian

g) Depository

h) Margin

i) Deleted securities

j) Offline monitoring

k) Online monitoring

l) Margin

Answer the following in 20-30 words

a) What is the clearing and settlement of trades ?

b) Key terminologies used in the clearing and settlement process ?

c) Functions of the clearing banks ?

d) What is the settlement process ?

e) What is the settlement cycle for Dematerialised securities ?

f) What is the securities settlement ?

g) What are the problems pertaining to securities settlement ?

h) Explain the process of funds statement ?

i) What are the valuation price?

Answer the following in 30-50 words

a) What are the close out procedure for the regular market in case of shortages?

b) What should be the valuation price of the deleted security in case of regular market

c) What should the closing price of the securities in case of merger, amalgamation scheme?

d) What are the types of counterparty risk?

e) What is the process of categorisation of newly listed securities

f) Explain the numbering system of ISIN.

g) How are the margins imposed?

Answer the following in 50-80 words

1) In case of funds settlement, if the clearing member bank account got changed, What process needs to be followed by the clearing member to inform Nse?

2) The counterparty risk comprises Legal and operational risk and System risk comprises Replacement and Principal risk. Do you agree with the statement ? Justify your answer.

3) In which SEBI regulation the main role is to register and regulate the functioning of intermediaries and persons associated with the securities market? Explain the functions of that regulation?

4) What is the difference between initial and continual disclosure for prevention of insider trading?

5) What are the rights and duties of depositories as per the depositories Act 1996.

6) If an intermediary is promising a certain price in respect of buying and selling of a security to a client and waiting till discrepancy will arrive and retaining the difference in prices as profit. According to you, can an intermediary be allowed to do such practice? Justify your answer.

Unit 6
Future Contracts, Mechanism and Pricing

A forward contract is a customised agreement between two parties to buy or sell an asset at a predetermined price on a specified future date. Here are some features of forward contracts: Two parties are involved

1) Long position :- want to buy the underlying asset on agreed price at the specified future date

2) Short position :- a party want to sell the underlying asset at the specified future date Other contract details like delivery date, price, negotiated as per the customised terms and conditions. Forward contract are generally traded at OTC market

The silent features of forward contract

a) A forward contract is a bilateral contract, which means it's an agreement between two parties that requires both parties to fulfil their obligations:Though the standard contract laws apply to these contract these contracts are not overseen by the exchange or regulatory bodies. These contract are generally between two parties so it may be possible that one party will not honour their part of agreement

b) Each contact is unique in respect of terms and conditions as it is customised as per the terms and conditions of both the parties. So it is highly flexible, which is not true in case of future contact

c) The co tact price is not available in public domain

d) The forward can be cash settled on the expiry date. In cash settlement one party receive/ give the gain/loss arising from the contract tp other party

e) Forward contact can be reversed but it will easy to reverse the contract with same counter party which results high price to be charged because other party with same terms and conditions will be quite difficult to find out

f) Forward contract is having lower cost transaction as compare to future contarct

Limitation of forward contract

a) Counterparty risk

If one party defaults on the contract, the other party may suffer a significant financial loss. Since forward contracts are private agreements, there's no guarantee that the other party will fulfill their obligations.

b) Price risk

Both parties are exposed to price risk. If the asset price moves against the contracted price, one party can face a significant financial loss.

c) Liquidity risk

Forward contracts are not traded on an exchange and are often illiquid. This can make it difficult for parties to exit their position or find a counterparty to take the other side of the trade

d) Non-standard nature

Forward contracts are only settled on the settlement date and are not marked-to-market like futures.

e) Complexity

Forward contracts are more complicated than a standard contract.

f) Non-public details

Forward contracts are negotiated privately between the two parties involved and because they trade over the counter, their details are not made public.

What is the future contact and its limitation

A futures contract is an agreement to buy or sell a commodity or asset at a specific price on a future date. Here are some features of futures contracts: the future contract are created by the stock exchange and made available in open market for trade

Features of future contract

- *Underlying assets* : Futures contracts can be based on a variety of assets. Like commodity asset, financial asset.

• *Contract size:* Each contract has a standardised quantity of the underlying asset.

• *Contract price:* The price at which the asset will be bought or sold is specified in the contract.

• *Contract expiry date* : Futures contracts have a predetermined expiration date.

• *Margin requirements:* Futures trading involves margin requirements.

• *Mark-to-market:* This is a major feature of futures contracts, where money is collected from the buyer or seller depending on whether the price of the underlying asset goes up or down.

• *Hedging:* Futures contracts can be used to hedge against unfavourable market shifts.

• *Regulation and oversight:* Futures contracts are traded on organised exchanges, which provide a transparent and regulated platform

Limitation of future contract

• **Leverage:** Futures contracts can amplify both gains and losses, and investors can lose money quickly if the price moves against them.

• **Limited flexibility:** Futures contracts are standardised agreements with predetermined terms, which can be a disadvantage for investors with specific needs.

• **Counterparty risk:** Although exchanges act as intermediaries, there is still a risk that one party may not fulfil their obligations.

• **Expiration dates**: Futures contracts have expiration dates, after which they must be settled. As the expiration date approaches, the asset value may look less attractive.

• **Price swings**: Investors have no influence over future events and price swings.

• **Over-trading:** Low commission charges can lead to over-trading by traders

Dintigusih between Forward contract and Future contract

Category	Forward Contract	Futures Contract
Meaning	A forward contract is a private agreement between two parties to buy or sell an underlying **asset**	A futures contract is a standardised contract to buy and sell an asset on a future date at a fixed price.
Standardisation	Forward contracts are often customised to suit the parties' needs	Futures contracts have standardised terms for consistency and pre-defined lot sizes.
Liquidity and Transparency	Forward contracts lack transparency and liquidity, being private agreements.	Futures contracts are highly liquid and traded on exchanges, providing transparency.
Regulations	Forward contracts are over-the-counter contracts and therefore have minimum to no regulation.	Futures contracts are strictly regulated by exchanges and relevant authorities.
Risk	Forward contracts have higher counterparty risk.	Future contracts have lower counterparty risks
Settlement	Forward contracts are settled at the maturity date and are settled in cash or physical **settlement**	Future contracts are settled on a daily basis and _are settled in cash as the difference between the spot price and the futures price._
Margin	A forward contract has no collateral requirement, as the parties trust each other to honour the contract.	A futures contract has a collateral requirement, as the parties have to deposit an initial margin and maintain a maintenance margin to cover potential losses.

Costs	Forward contracts usually have lower transaction costs.	Futures contracts may involve brokerage, exchange fees, and **margin** requirements.
Price determination	Forward contract prices are mutually agreed upon between the parties to the contract.	Futures contract prices are determined by open market forces.

List the various Futures Terminologies

Long Position: The investor who buys the contract, and therefore the underlying asset, is said to assume a long position in the transaction

Short Position: The investor, who sells the contract, and therefore the underlying asset, is said to assume a short position in the transaction. These are terms also used in case of other derivative contracts.

Spot Price: The price at which an underlying asset trades in the spot market.

Futures Price: The price that is agreed upon at the time of the contract for the delivery of an asset at a specific future date.

Contract Cycle: It is the period over which a contract trades. The index Futures contracts on the NSE have one-month, two-month and three-month expiry cycles which expire on the last Thursday of the month. Thus, a January expiration contract expires on the last Thursday of January and a February expiration contract ceases trading on the last Thursday of February. On the Friday following the last Thursday, a new contract having a three-month expiry is introduced for trading.

Expiry Date: Is the date on which the final settlement of the contract takes place.

Contract Size: The amount of asset that has to be delivered under one contract. This is also called as the lot size.

Basis: Basis is defined as the Futures price minus the spot price. There will be a different basis for each delivery month for each contract. In a normal market, basis will be positive. This reflects that Futures prices normally exceed spot prices.

Cost of Carry: Measures the storage cost plus the interest that is paid to finance the Asset less the income earned on the asset.

Initial Margin: The amount that must be deposited in the margin account at the time a Futures contract is first entered into is known as initial margin.

- Marking-to-Market: In the Futures market, at the end of each trading day, the margin account is adjusted to reflect the investor's gain or loss depending upon the Futures closing price. This is calledmarking-to-market.

Maintenance Margin: Investors are required to place margins with their trading members before they are allowed to trade. If the balance in the margin account falls below the maintenance margin, the investor receives a margin call and is expected to top up the margin account to *the initial margin level before trading commences on the next day.*

Key terminologies in option contract

a) Call Option: It gives the holder the right but not the obligation to buy an asset by a certain date for a certain price.

b) Put Option: A It gives the holder the right but not the obligation to sell an asset by a certain date for a certain price.

c) Holder of an Option: The buyer of an option is the one who by paying the option premium buys the right but not the obligation to exercise his option on the seller/writer.

d) Writer of an Option: The writer of a call/put option is the one who receives the option premium and is thereby obliged to sell/buy the asset if the buyer exercises on him.

e) Option Price/Premium: It is the price which the option buyer pays to the option seller. It is also referred to as the option premium.

f) Expiration Date: The date specified in the options contract is known as the expiration date, the exercise date, the Strike date or the maturity.

g) Strike Price: The price specified in the options contract is known as the strike price or the exercise price.

h) American Options: These can be exercised at any time up to the expiration date.

i) European Options: These can be exercised only on the expiration date itself. European Options are easier to analyse than American Options and properties of an American Option are frequently deduced from those of its European counterpart.

j) Index Options: Have the index as the underlying. They can be European or American. They are also cash settled. All Indian Index Options are European options

k) Stock Options: They are options on individual stocks and give the holder the right to buy or sell shares at the specified price. They can be European or American. All stock options on NSE are European options since 1st January 2012.

l) In-the-money Option: An in-the-money (ITM) option would lead to a positive cash flow to the holder if it were exercised immediately. A call option on the index is said to be in- the-money when the current index stands at a level higher than the strike price (i.e., spot price > Strike price). If the index is much higher than the strike price, the call is said to be deep ITM. In the case of a put, the Put is ITM if the index is below the strike price.

m) At-the-money Option: An at-the-money (ATM) option would lead to zero cash flow if it were exercised immediately. An option on the index is at-the-money when the current index equals the strike price (i.e., spot price = strike price).

n) Out-of-the-money Option: An out-of-the-money (OTM) option would lead to a negative cash flow if it were exercised immediately. A call option on the index is out-of-the-money when the current index stands at a level which is less than the strike price (i.e., spot price < strike price). If the index is much lower than the strike price, the call is said to be deep OTM. In the case of a put, the put is OTM if the index is above the strike price.

o) Intrinsic Value of an Option: The option premium has two components - Intrinsic Value and Time Value. Intrinsic value of an option at a given time is the amount the holder of the option will get if he exercises the option at that time. The intrinsic value of a Call is Max [0, (S-,K)] which means that the intrinsic value of a call is the greater of 0 or (S-K). Similarly, the intrinsic value of a Put is Max [0, K-S.], i.e., the greater of O or (K-S.). K is the strike price and S, is the spot price.

p) Time Value of an Option: The time value of an option is the difference between its premium and its intrinsic value. Both calls and puts have time value. The longer the time to expiration, the greater is an option's time value, all else equal. At expiration, an option should have no time value

What is the future pay off?

The payoff of a futures contract is the likely profit or loss that a market participant will receive when the contract expires.pay off is positive if it brings profit to the holder and payoff is negative if it brings loss to holder of the position

In finance, the payoff of a position is the estimated profit or loss that a market participant could make if the price of the underlying asset changes.

Pay off for the buyer (long position)

Pay off for the buyer means similar to profit or loss for the holder of the asset. He can earn unlimited profit or unlimited loss.

Take the case if an investor invest in future contract of Nifty for two months future contract

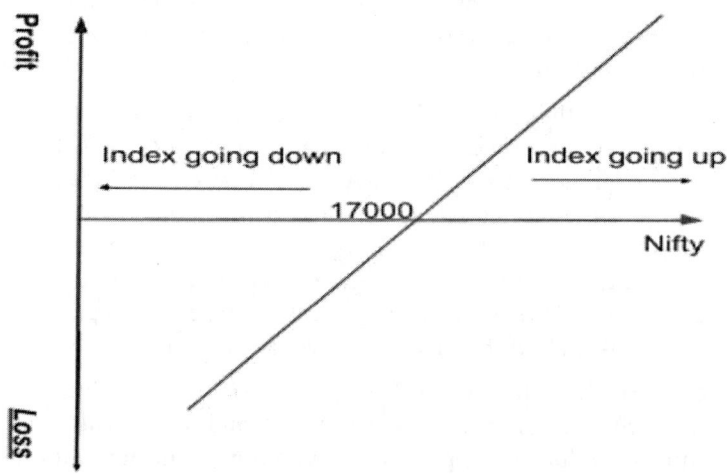

If you see the following diagram the investor have make the future contract when the underlying asset was 17000 after two months the contract got expired now if in the market,the underlying asset got increase the buyer of the contract will earn profit because even if the asset got increase the buyer need to pay only the amount mentioned in the contract In short we can say if underlying asset goes up the future position starts making profit and vice-versa

Pay off for the seller of future contract

Pay off for the seller of the future is the same as a person shorts the assets. He can earn unlimited profit or losses depending upon the market volatility. Take the case of an investor selling the future contract of Nifty at rupees 17000. When the index moves down the seller will earn profit and if the index moves up the seller will incur the loss.

In short position seller will earn profit or loss depends upon the Nifty ups and down

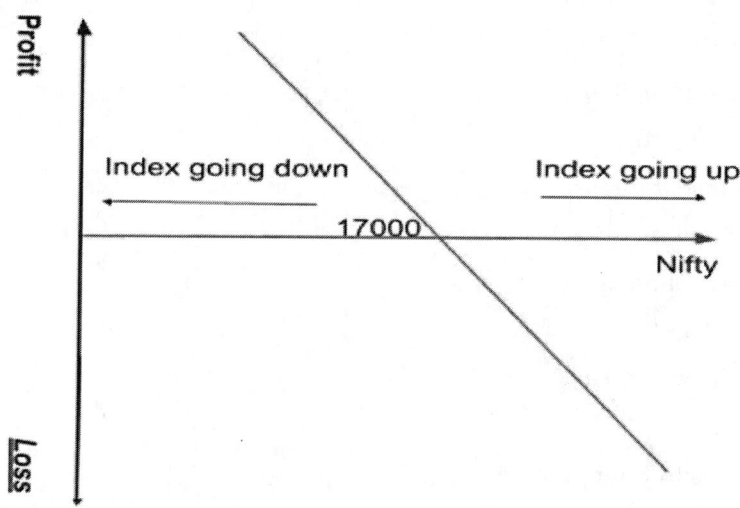

How to price future contract

Pricing of the future contract is very simple. Cost of carry includes financing cot brokerage, interest cost, margin expenses. Using cost of carry we can calculate the fair value of the future contract.

Every time the observed price is deviate from the fair value and that why the arbitrage position arises and helps them to earn riskless profit.

Arbitrage is a condition where you can simultaneously buy and sell the same or similar product or asset at different prices, resulting in a risk-free profit.

In short we can say that if we are holding asset for the period of two months the interest of 2 months will be forgone that we need to add to arrive at fair value of future contract

S=Price in the spot market

r=Cost of financing

T=Time till expiration in years e=2.71828

Example

XYZ had made a contract for the period of month at 1150. Money can be invested at interest rate of 11%p.a. Calculate the fair value of contract

$F = Se^{rT}$

$F = 1150 \times 2.71828^{0.11 \times (1/12)}$

$F = 1150 \times 2.71828^{0.0091666666...}$

F=1160.

Second method

F=S(1 + rt)

r=rate of interest

t=time

S= spot price

F=1150(1 + (0.11x1/12)

F=1150(1.0091667)

F=1160

Questions for practice

1) ABC ltd made a contract for the period of 3 months at 3000. Money can be invested at an interest rate of 12% p.a. Calculate the fair value of contract.

2) Alpha ltd made a contract for the period of 15 days at 5000. Money can be invested at the interest rate 10%p.a. Calculate the fair value of the contract

How to price equity index future

A future contract gives the owner the right and obligation to buy and sell th portfolio of index characterised by the stock index. Index will reflect the performance of the worlds securities market.

Equity index is not having holding cost like other commodities are having like insurance, storage etc. but rather it is having dividend stream

So while calculating the equity index we need to consider the dividend which is negative if we are having long position and positive if we are having short position

**The more accurate you forecast the dividend, the better contract price will be estimated**

Let's assume that the spot price of scrip X is Rs 1,500 and that the current dividend rate is 8 per cent.what should be the cost of carry and price of the future contract

Solution:-

$F = Se^{rT}$

$F = 1500 \times 2.71828^{0.8 \times 30/365}$

$F = 1,509.86$

Cost of carry = future price-spot price

Cost of carry = 1509.86-1500

The cost of carry here is Rs 9.86.

**How to price index future with expected dividend yield**

If the dividend flow is uniform then we need to apply the following formula. In that formula the cost of interest will be reduced by the dividend earned

**For example if by having the future contract for the sake of two months you are forgoing the interest rate that you might earn if you invest it that interest rate will be cost need to reduced by the expected dividend dividend you will earn**

**Example:-**

If two month future contract. The cost of financing is 10% and dividend yield is 2% for the contract value 17000 then reaming 8% will be considered

Solution:-

Future value = $Se^{(r-q)t}$

Future price = $17000 \; 2.71828^{(0.1-0.02) \times 60/365}$

Future price = 17225.04

Practice questions

> 1) A one-year long forward contract on a non-dividend-paying stock is entered into when the stock price is $40 and the risk-free rate of interest is 10% per annum with continuous compounding. What should be the price of the future contract
>
> 2) The risk-free rate of interest is 7% per annum with continuous compounding, and the dividend yield on a

stock index is 3.2% per annum. The current value of the
index is 150. What is the six-month futures price

*At the expiration of the contract the basis is reduced and at the
expiration date the basis will become zero. It it is not then an arbitration
opportunity arises. Arbitrage opportunities will arise when their is
difference between spot price and future price or when there is price between
two future contracts.*

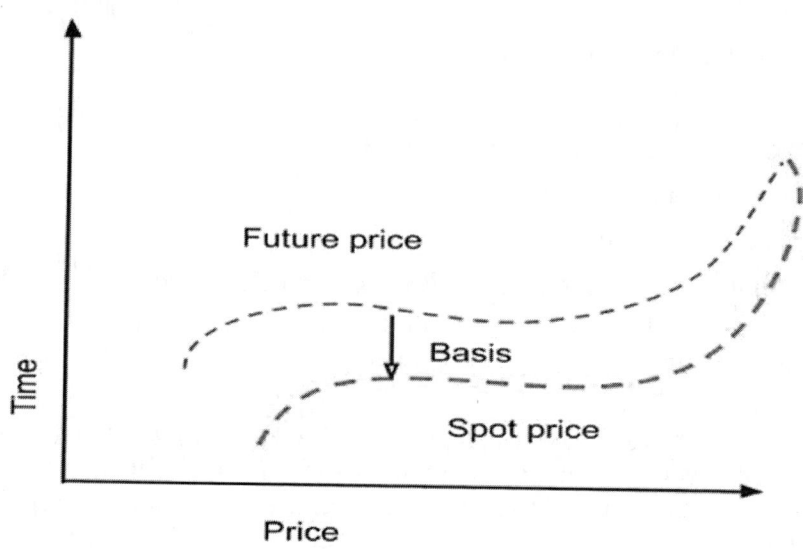

As you see in the above diagram as and when expiration date is coming
near the basis is reduced and finally becomes zero, because, as the contract
nears its expiration date, the futures price naturally moves to align with
the spot price of the underlying asset, meaning there is no price difference
between the two, resulting in a zero basis.

How to price stock futures when no dividend is expected

The pricing of the stock ia also based on the cot of carry model, when
no dividend is expected then pricing of the future stock will be spot price
multiple by the cost of carry

Cost of carry refers to financing cost like brokerage, margin etc.

For example,

**Assume a security is currently trading at $100 per unit. An investor
wants to enter into a forward contract that expires in one year. The current
annual risk-free interest rate is 6%. Using the above formula, the forward
price is calculated as:**

Solution:-

$F = Se^{rt}$

$F = 100 \times e^{0.06 \times 1}$ **(for whole year if is in the form of days then we need to divide the days by 365)**

$F = 106.18$

Practice questions:-

    a) X represents the number of days to expiry. The spot price of XYZ Corp. = Rs 2,380.5 Risk-free rate = 8.3528 percent. Days to expiry = 7 days.

What is beta

Beta measures the sensitivity of the stocks responsiveness to market factors. generally It is seen that when market Rises most stock prices rise and vice versa.

Beta is a measurement of how a stock's price moves in relation to the market's overall movement. It's a key concept in finance that helps investors assess the risk and performance of an investment relative to the market.

Here's what beta means:

- Beta of 1: The stock's price tends to move in line with the market.

- Beta greater than 1: The stock is more volatile than the market.

- Beta less than 1: The stock is less volatile than the market

Examples of Beta

High β – A company with a β that's greater than 1 is more volatile than the market. For example, a high-risk technology company with a β of 1.75 would have returned 175% of what the market returned in a given period (typically measured weekly).

Low β – A company with a β that's lower than 1 is less volatile than the whole market. As an example, consider an electric utility company with a β of 0.45, which would have returned only 45% of what the market returned in a given period.

Negative β – A company with a negative β is negatively correlated to the returns of the market. For example, a gold company with a β of -0.2, which would have returned -2% when the market was up 10%.

What is the hedging: Long security, sell Futures?

Future can be a risk management tool. Investor can hedge the risk in the market by taking the opposite position in the spot and future market

For Example if an investor holds the shares, and the price of these shares are falling, he will suffer the loss in the absence of a future market. He need to tolerate the upheaval in the market

Assume that the investor holding the asset has spot price 390 (market is expected to fall) and simultaneously he purchased two months future contract worth Rs. 402 to sell th security. And at the time of expiration, the market falls to 340. He can set off the losses of Rs. 40 which he might incur in case of absence of future contract. That means because of short position he started making a profit.

What is speculation:Bullish security, Buy Futures?

Investors can speculate on the underlying asset. A bullish speculator buys undervalued stocks and waits for their value to rise, so they can be resold for a profit. Bullish speculations are typical of buy and hold investments that's why bullish positions are also known as long positions.

For example, the stock is Rs.10,000 in value, a bullish speculator would buy it when its value has fallen down to Rs.8000 and would hold it until the stock reaches Rs.11000 thus earning him a profit of Rs.3000.

Today the speculator can take exactly the opposite position on the security by using future contract.

Let us take the example (for purchasing the securities)

A security traded at Rs.1000 with a two month future contract at Rs.1006 per security(total securities 100).Just for the sake of how its works. Minimum contract value is Rs.100000 and for two month contract he paid the margin of Rs.20000. Two months later the security closes at Rs.1010.

Now we had paid margin of Rs. 20000 (as an investment)

Future contract price is 1006

Spot price is 1010

That means being as an buyer speculator earned a profit of Rs.400 (1010-1006)x100

Therefore we earned 12% return on investment of 20000(margin money)

$$400 \times \frac{100}{20000} = 12\%$$

What is the speculation bearish security, sell futures?

A bearish speculator is one who expects the prices of securities to fall in the future. A bearish speculator sells short securities, aiming to profit from being able to repurchase them at a lower price at some point in the future.

Consider the opposite scenario of bullish security. If an investor expects that particular security is overvalued and in future his market price is about to fall. In the absence of derivative market he will suffer the loss.

Simple arbitrage ensures the future contract moves correspondingly with market price. If the security price rises, future contract price will also rise and vice-versa

Assume, he will enter the two month future contract at Rs.240 for 100 securities with small amount of margin

At the expiration date future price and market price converge and market close at Rs.220. That means he clearly eared a profit of Rs. 2000(20x100)

What is an arbitrage: overpriced futures: Buy spot, Sell future

Now in the future market if an arbitrage holding the security and expecting the value of this underlying asset is overpriced and expected that price of this underlying asset will fall in future. In that case the arbitrage will borrow the money to purchase the underlying asset in spot market

Take a example:-

a) Borrow funds, and buy the security in spot market at Rs.1000

b) At the same time sell the future contract worth Rs. 1025

c) Hold the security for one month which you had purchase in spot market

d) At the expiration day of contract say security closes at 1015, sell the security

e) Now if you see future contract will give you profit of Rs.10 (1025-1015)

f) Spot market gives you the riskless profit of Rs.15

g) Return the borrowed funds

h) Total profit you earned is Rs.25 (Rs.10 from future contract and 15 from spot market) Note:-arbitrage will gives you profit if cost of borrowing is less than the arbitrage profit, then only it will make sense to go for arbitrage position

What is an arbitrage: underpriced future: buy future, sell spot

When the future price deviates from the spot price the arbitrage opportunities arise. It could be the case that the future you hold is underpriced and expecting that the underlying asset of these future contracts will rise. Assume that XYZ ltd trades at Rs.1000. One month future contract nd expected to rise in future.

Take a example

a) Sell the security in open market worth Rs.20000

b) At the same time buy the future contract worth Rs.19800

c) On the expiration day the future price and spo price will converge security closes at Rs.19900

d) Your future position expires on profit of Rs.100

e) The result is riskless profit of Rs.100 on spot market and Rs. 100 from future position

If the return you get by investing in riskless instrument is more than the return from the arbitrage trades, it makes sense for you to arbitrage this concept is known as reverse-cash-and -carry arbitrage.

Types of risks

a) Systematic risk

Also known as market risk, this type of risk affects all investments and assets across an entire market. It's caused by macroeconomic factors like inflation, exchange rates, political instability, and natural disasters. Systematic risk is unavoidable and can't be diversified away. This risk cannot be controlled by diversification of your portfolio

b) Unsystematic risk

It is also known as company specific and diversified Risk This type of risk affects specific investments or industries. It can be caused by company-specific events like poor management, regulatory changes, litigation, asset mispricing, legal issues, and technological disruptions. Unsystematic risk can be managed through diversification and asset allocation. This risk can be reduced by diversification

Systematic Risk	Unsystematic Risk

Affects the entire market or economy	Specific to a particular industry, sector, or company
Cannot be eliminated through diversification	Can be reduced or eliminated through diversification
Arises from external factors beyond an investor's control	Arises from internal factors specific to a company or sector
Examples include inflation, recession, or interest rate risk	Examples include management issues or product recalls
Cannot be eliminated through prudent investment decisions	Can be mitigated through careful analysis and research
Often referred to as market risk	Also known as company specific or diversified risk
Diversification does not lower its impact	Diversification helps reduce its impact
Measured by beta coefficient	Measured by alpha coefficient
Impacts the entire portfolio	Impacts only specific investments within a portfolio
Can lead to losses in both bull and bear markets	Mostly affects investments during unfavourable conditions

Hedging is the one way to reduce the unsystematic risk. Hedging can be done into ways by an investor who has an exposure to the underlying stock. By selling index futures or by selling stock features and buying the stock in the spot market. let us now look at how this work agent

By selling index futures

For Example

If an investor buys 125 shares of infosys @ Rs. 3000 per share(approximate portfolio value of Rs. 375000). However the investor fears that the market will fall and thus needs to hedge. He uses NIFTY December future to hedge

- Infosys trades Rs.3000
- Nifty index 5950
- Nifty future is trading Rs.6000
- The beta of infosys is 1.2

- To hedge investor needs to sell (375000 x 1.2=450000) worth of NIFTY futures (450000/6000)75 nifty
- On December market falls
- Infosys trades at 2750
- December NIFTY future trading at Rs.5600

We need to calculate net profit and loss earned by the Hedger

The investors loss in Infosys is Rs.(3000-2750)x125=31250.

The infosys stock value now drop to 343750 from Rs. 375000(because of decreasing stock price from 3000 to 2750..

However December NIFTY future position gains by RS. 30,000(400x75). (Earlier Nifty was 6000-5600=400 profit)

Thus the final portfolio value is 375000 30000-31250

What is the difference between Options and Future.

An options contract gives the buyer the right to buy or sell an asset at a specific price within a certain time frame, but it's not an obligation. There are two types of options: calls and puts. Call options allow the buyer to purchase an asset, while put options allow the buyer to sell an asset. Option prices are made up of the intrinsic value and the time value. The intrinsic value is the difference between the current stock price and the strike price.

The main difference between options and futures is that futures are a contract that obligates the buyer to purchase an asset, while options give the buyer the right to buy or sell an asset

Particulars	Futures	Options
Meaning	Futures contracts are contracts to trade an underlying asset at a predetermined price at a future date. The buyer and seller are both bound to complete the transaction on that date. Futures are standardised contracts that can be bought and sold on an exchange by investors.	Options contracts are standardised contracts that allow investors to trade an underlying asset at a predetermined price before a specific date (the expiry date for the options). Call and put options are the two types of options available. The buyer of a call option has the right (but not the responsibility) to purchase the underlying asset at a predetermined price before the expiration date, whereas the buyer of a put option has the right to sell the security.

Particulars	Futures	Options
Risk	They are subject to higher risks.	They are subject to limited risk.
Profit or Loss	It could reap unlimited profit and loss.	It could again bring you unlimited profit and loss, although it reduces the chances of incurring a potential loss.
Obligation	The buyer is obliged to buy the asset on the certain stated future date.	In this, the buyer will have no obligation to buy or execute the contract.
Contract Execution	A futures contract is executed on the date agreed upon. On this certain date, the buyer buys the underlying asset.	Options contracts can be executed by the buyer anytime before the expiry date. Hence, an individual is open to buying the asset whenever the conditions seem correct.
Advance Payment	In a futures contract, there is no upfront cost when entering. Although, the buyer is supposed to pay the agreed price for the asset ultimately.	The buyer in an options contract is supposed to pay a premium. The premium payment allows the options buyer the chance to not purchase the asset on a future date if it tends to become unattractive. Note that if the options contract holder opts not to buy the asset, the premium paid is the amount he is supposed to lose.

Example of option and future contract

Future contract

The terms of the contract are as follows

    a) Quantity -100KG

    b) Future price - Rs. 20/kg

    c) Period - 3 months

At the end of 3 months the spot price of wheat is Rs, 25/kg. However, since the farmer has entered into the future contract at Rs. 20/kg and because the future contract is binding, he has to sell at 20/kg/ if he did not enter into the contract he could have sold in the spot market and earn the profit of Rs. 500/-. But this is not possible. Hence he makes the loss of 500 over the contract.

Let us see what happens if he had purchased an option contract

Quantity =100 kg

Strike price= Rs. 20/kg

Period - 3 months

Option premium - Rs. 100

At the end of the month, the spot price for wheat is Rs. 25kg

Now since the farmer is getting a better price in spot market, and because it is a put option of which he is the holder, he has no obligation to sell the distributor at the strike price. He was interested in selling on the spot market, thus entering into the market,. Thus his profit will be Rs.400. However he has paid an option premium Rs. 100 while entering into the contract. Thus his profit will be Rs.400.

Options payoff

In option market the losses for the buyer of the option is limited, however the profits are unlimited. For the writer of the option exactly opposite. It is called non-linear payoff for options. There are total six non-linear payoff generate various payoff by using the combinations of options and the underlying

Pay off profile for the buyer of Asset: long Asset (

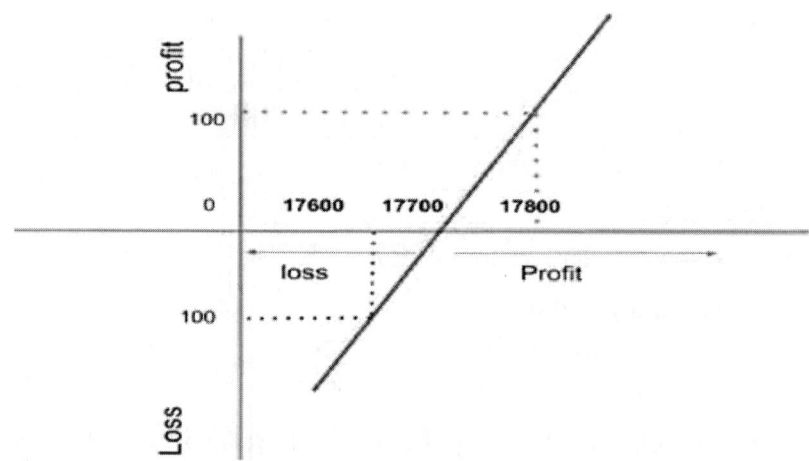

Pay off for the investor who went long NIFTY at 17700

From the above diagram X axis represents Nifty as an underlying asset and Y axis represents the profit and loss earned by buyer purchasing the asset as per future contract

If the buyer as per future contract want to purchase the asset, we can say the buyer is having long position.

Assume that buyer agree to purchase the underlying asset at Rs. 17700 as per the future contract and at the time of expiration if the asset goes up like 17800 then in that case buyer will earn the profit of Rs. 100 because buyer will pay only 17700 as per the future contract agreement.

Similarly if the price of the underlying asset goes down like 17600 then the buyer will incur loss of Rs. 100 because as per future contract buyer have to pay Rs.17700.

Above diagram shows the profit or loss from the long position on the index (Nifty)

Pay off profile for the seller of Asset: Short Asset

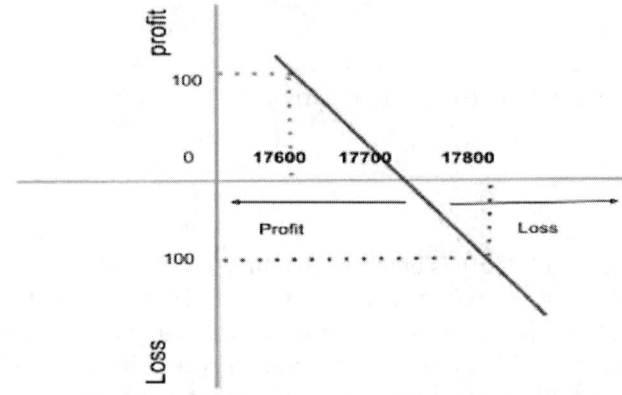

Pay off for seller who need short NIFTY at Rs.17700

In the above diagram the seller of the underlying asset (index) makes the future contract to sell it on 17700 if at the expiration date, asset value increase to 17800 it will lead to loss for him Rs. 100, because even though it is increased to 17800 in market but he will sell it to buyer at Rs. 17700. Similarly if the underlying asset fall to 17600 in the market that seller will earn the profit Rs.100 because he will receive the 17700 as per the future contract.

Payoff profile for Buyer of call option:long option

In call option the buyer is having right to purchase the underlying asset but not obligation for that he needs to pay premium to writer of the contract

The profit or loss of that buyer will depend upon the spot price of the underlying asset. If at the expiration the post price is more than strike price (contract price) then buyer will exercise the option and earn the profit. But if at the expiration date the spot price is less than the contract price then the buyer will un -exercise the option, the only loss he can make is the premium he paid

Following figure will depicts the details

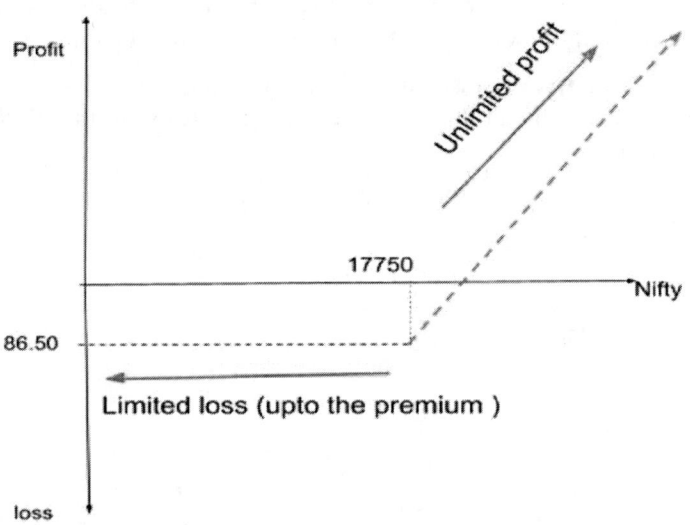

In the above diagram Nifty is being shown in X-axis and Profit and loss is shown in Y-axis. Now consider that the value of Nifty increased in the market above to 17750. In that case the investor will purchase the asset as per future contract (he will execute the contract) because he will earn the profit. (in the market that asset is proven to be costly for the investor). If in the market the security value will fall, in that case the buyer will not exercise the option because he can purchase the same asset in the market at a cheaper rate. The only, loss he will bear is the option Premium

So it is being said that payoff option the buyer is having limited loss but unlimited profit

For Example:-

Strike price =17750

Spot price = 17100

If is 17100 the buyer will purchase the asset from the market and let the contract expired That means the net profit of the buyer will be

17750(Strike price) -17100(market price) - 86.50 (premium paid) =563.50

Pay off profile for the writer of the option

A call option will become a short option for the buyer when buyer sell the option to seller. For selling the option,the writer of the option will charge premium. If the buyer of the option sell the option he is having the right to purchase the asset. Now if in case at the maturity period the spot price exceeds the strike price seller or writer of the option will starts making lossesbecause seller have to sell the asset to buyer only as per term and condition. He is having right as well as obligation to sell the asset to buyer only until and unless buyer will let the contract expired.

Now if in any case if spot price is less than the strike price then buyer will have an unexercised the option and purchasing it from the market at spot price because that will be more profitable. So he will earn unlimited profit and seller profit will limited to the premium paid by the buyer of the option.

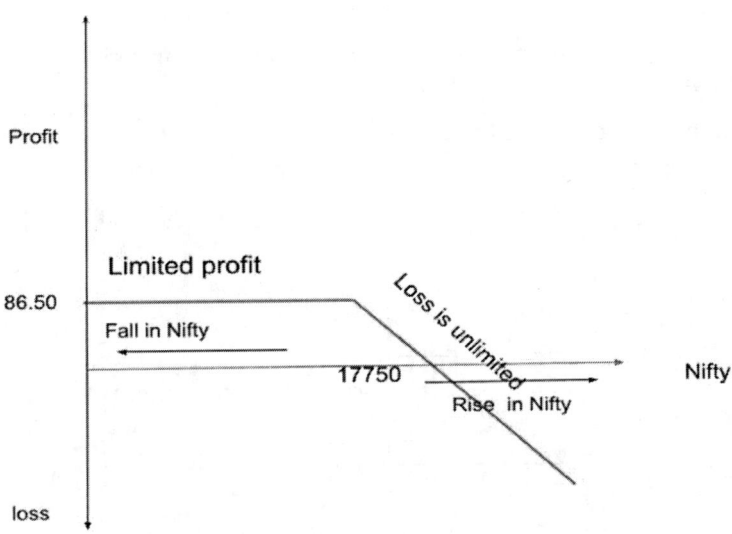

Pay off for the Buyer of call option

From the above diagram if you see that option contract was made with Rs.17750. If spot price rises then the seller will suffer from the loss (because he have to sell to the buyer only at 17750 only) and that will be unlimited as how much market price will rise that will be unpredictable.

If the market proves that spot price is less than the strike price (contract price) then the buyer will an-exercise the option (he will purchase that asset from the market where he can get it at lower price) and the loss suffered by him will be only the premium paid by him to the seller.

For Example

Contract price 17750 (strike price)

Now if spot price is 17800 (seller will suffer the loss)

loss= 17800 - 17750 = 50

Because he sold the option to the buyer, he has the right and obligation to sell the asset to the buyer only, until and unless the buyer will let the contract expire.

Pay off option for the buyer of the put option

A put option gives the buyer (who buys the put option) the right to sell the underlying asset at the specified price. If the market price of the underlying asset goes up the buyer of this put option will suffer loss and if the spot price in the market goes down the buyer of the put option will make profit.

(buyer of put option means seller of the asset having right to sell the asset to buyer but not the obligation)

Note:- put option refers to seller of asset

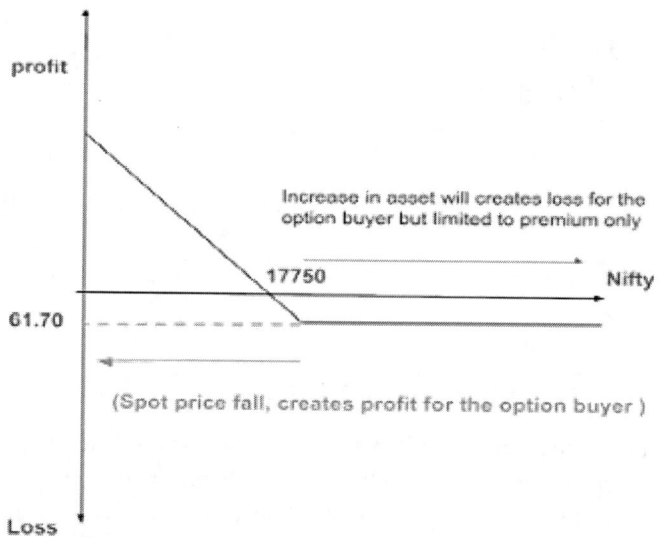

In the above diagram if you see that option buyer (who sells the asset) will earn the profit if the spot price will fall because he needs to sell the asset as per the specified price (strike price) which is more than the spot price.

For example:-

If spot price is 17000 then the option buyer will earn the profit 17750 - 17000 = 750 Net profit will be 750 less premium paid.

Speculation Bullish Security:Buy call or sell put option

There are the points where investor think that security price will increase in future.

The question is that which policy need to implemented by the investor to fetch higher profit.

There are the ways to do

Buy call option

Or

Sell put option

The downside of the buyer of the option is limited upto the premium paid but upside will be unlimited. (that means buyer profit is unlimited if price will rise in the market and loss will limited up-to the premium, he paid)

Let's consider the following illustration which strike price the buyer should choose while investing in options. Consider that current price of security in the market 2000 and rate of risk 12% and volatility 30%

A one month call with strike price of 1900

A one month call with strike price of 1950

A one month call with strike price of 2000

A one month call with strike price of 2025

A one month call with strike price of 2050

A call is said to be deep in the money when there is _**significant higher difference between strike price and spot price that means strike price < spot price (Difference should be** more)_

A call is said to be deep in the money when there is a slight difference between strike price and spot price. (Difference should be less)

A call is said to at the money when strike price and spot price are equal

A call is said to out of the money when there is slighter difference between strike and spot price (strike price> spot price)

A call is said to deep out of the money when there is significant difference between strike and spot price (strike price> spot price) ——--> Difference should be more

Spot price	Strike price	Call premium	Put premium
2000	1950	108.95 (deep in the money)	39.20 (Deep out of money)
2000	1975	93.7 (in the money)	48.76 (out of money)
2000	2000	79.99 (At the money)	59.71 (At the money)
2000	2025	67.60 (out of money)	72.70 (in the money)
2000	2050	56.60 (Deep out of money)	85.82 (Deep in the money)

Similarly we can say from the above table:-

• *A put can be said in the money when spot price is less than strike price (Difference should be less)*

• *A put can be said Deep in the money when spot price is less than strike price (Difference should be More)*

• *A put can be said out of the money when spot price is more than strike price (Difference should be less)*

• *A put can be said deep out of the money when spot price is more than strike price*

(Difference should be more)

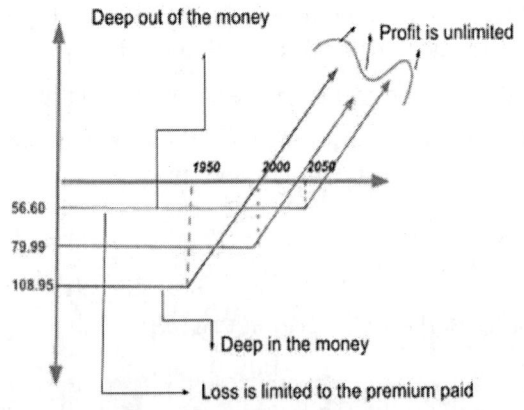

From the above figure it is shown that one month call option deep in the money(1950) are traded at higher premium 108.95 rate and whereas deep out of the money(2050) are traded at lowest premium 56.60.

If buyer of the call option, at the expiration found that spot price falls in the market then he will purchase that asset from the market only and

The loss incurred by him will be limited to the premium paid by him.

In case of deep in the money 56.50

In case of deep out of the money 108.95

Similarly on the expiration date if he found that spot price is higher than the strike price then he will execute the contract and profit will be unlimited. (depends upon the spot price).

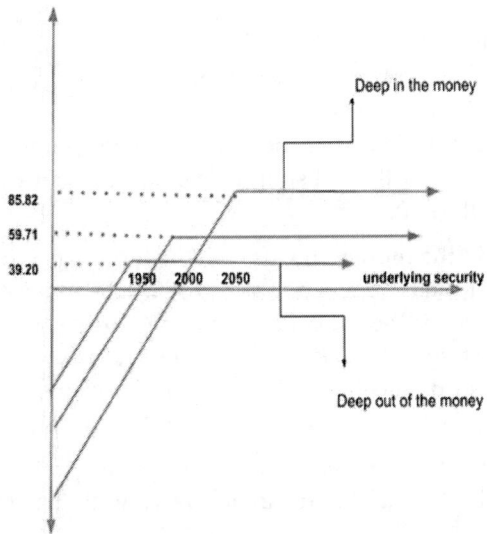

Figure :-Writer of the call option

In the above diagram the option deep in the money are traded at highest premium and deep out of money are traded at lowest premium.

Similarly if the writer of the one month call option faces that spot price at the expiration date is more than the strike price then he will incur the unlimited loss.(because buyer of the option will exercise the contract because he will get the asset as per contract at cheaper rate as compare to market price)

But if the spot price is more than the strike price the writer of the option will earn the profit limited to the premium he received at the time expiration of the contract.(Because the buyer of theoption will let the contract expired and purchase the asset from the market itself at the cheaper sell rate)

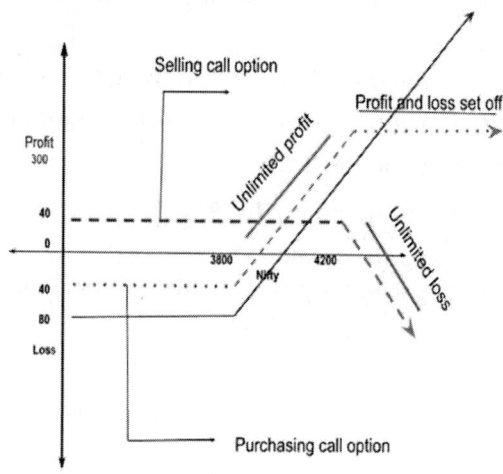

In the above diagram if we see the investor have purchased the call option at the premium of Rs. 80 and sold the call option at rupees 40 so net off of the premium will be 40.

Now if the call is in the money the loss will be limited up-to 80 only but when call comes out of the money(spot price >3800) the investor will starts earn the profit and loss will be set off Similarly the investor have sold the call option in the hope that the market will fall. So when the call option is in the money the investor profit is limited up-to 40 only when market price of the underlying asset go up the investor will incur the unlimited loss

So unlimited profit in purchasing call option and unlimited loss in selling call option will set off and that can be shown with the straight line.

	A	B	C	D
	Buy call option at 3800 Max (0, Market price -strike price)	Sold call option 4200 Min (strike price- market price)	Cash flow (A-B)	(C-premium) (-80+40)-C (-40-C)
3700	0	0	0	-40
3750	0	0	0	-40

3800	0	0	0	-40
3850	+50	0	+50	10
3900	+100	0	+100	+60
3950	+150	0	150	+110
4000	+200	0	200	+160
4050	+250	0	250	+210
4100	+300	0	300	+250
4150	+350	0	350	+310
4200	+400	0	400	+360
4250	+450	-50	400	+360
4300	+500	-100	400	+360

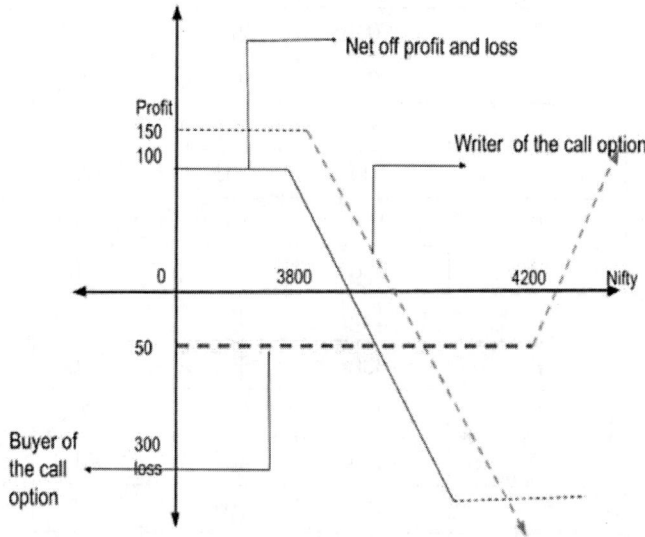

Payoff for a bear spread created using call option

In the above diagram investor will face the bearish market that means market is expected to fall. But it can happens that market will rise that spot price of the securities will rise. In that case investor will purchase one call option and sell one call option (opposite position). Net premium paid by the investor will be 100. So if you see that in the market if the market will fall, the buyer of the call option will have the profit limited to premium paid i.e up-to 150, but in case when the market will rise the seller of the call option will have the unlimited profit but loss will be limited up-to the premium only

So whatever loss investor make on one call option can be set off with profit he made in another call option.

	A	B	C=(A-B)	D= (Premium-C) i.e(100-C)
Nifty (market price)	Buy call option 4200 Max (0, Market price -strike price)	Sell call option at 3800 Minimum of (0,Strike price–market price)	Cash Flow	profit/Loss
3700	0	0	0	+100
3750	0	0	0	+100
3800	0	0	0	+100
3850	0	-50	-50	+50
3900	0	-100	-100	0
3950	0	-150	-150	-50
4000	0	-200	-200	-100
4050	0	-250	-250	-150
4100	0	-300	-300	-200
4150	0	-350	-350	-250
4200	0	-400	-400	-300
4250	+50	-450	-400	-300
4300	+100	-500	-400	-300

Multiple choice questions

1.	A forward contract is _____ contract that will leads to counterparty risk **a) Bilateral contract** b) Unilateral contract c) Quasi contract d) None of the above	1

2.	A forward contract is highly _____ a) Flexible b) Unique c) Customised **d) All of the above**	1
3.	The forward contract are like _____ market a) Capital market b) Equity market **c) Real estate market** d) Derivative market	1
4.	The forward contact are created by _____ a) SEBI b) Exchange **c) Parties** d) Any of the above	1
5.	The initial margin requirement is in _____ - contract a) Forward contract **b) Future contract** c) Interest rate swaps d) Options	1
6.	The buyer is obligated to purchase the specified asset in _____ _____ contract **a) Future contract** b) Forward contract c) Options d) Swaps	1
7.	Because of customised nature of forward contract it will difficult to trade _____in market **a) Open market** b) Capital market c) Stock exchange d) Derivative market b	1

8.	The difference between spot price and future price is called __	1
	a) Cost of carry b) Opening cost **c) Basis** d) Financing cost	
9.	One-year forward contract is an agreement where	1
	a) One side has the right to buy an asset for a certain price in one year's time. **b) One side has the obligation to buy an asset for a certain price in one year's time.** c) One side has the obligation to buy an asset for a certain price at some time during the next year. d) One side has the obligation to buy an asset for the market price in one year's time	
10.	Which of the following term is best described as spot price	1
	a) The price of immediate delivery b) The price for delivery at future date c) The price of an asset has been damaged d) The pricing of renting of an asset	
11.	An investor sells a futures contract as an asset when the futures price is Rs.1,500. Each contract is on 100 units of the asset. The contract is closed out when the futures price is Rs.1,540. Which of the following is true:	1
	a) The investor has made a gain of Rs. 4000 **b) The investor made a loss of Rs.4000** c) The investor has made a gain of Rs. 2000 d) The investor made a loss of Rs.2000	
12.	Which of the following describes European options?	1
	a) Sold in Europe b) Priced in Euros **c) Exercisable only at maturity** d) Calls (there are no puts)	

13.	Which of the following is NOT true about call and put options:	1
	a) An American option can be exercised at any time during its life	
	b) A European option can only be exercised only on the maturity date	
	c) Investors must pay an upfront price (the option premium) for an option contract	
	d) The price of a call option increases as the strike price increases	
14.	The price of a stock on February 1 is $48. A trader sells 200 put options on the stock with a strike price of $40 when the option price is $2. The options are exercised when the stock price is $39.The trader's net profit or loss is	1
	a) Loss of $800	
	b) Loss of $200	
	c) Gain of $200	
	d) Loss of $900	
15.	If the return you get by investing in riskless instrument is more than the return from the arbitrage trades, it makes sense for you to arbitrage this concept is known as	1
	a) reverse-cash-and -carry arbitrage	
	b) Cash-and-carry arbitrage	
	c) Cost of carry concept	
	d) Cost of carry model	
16.	arbitrage will gives you profit if _____ is less than the arbitrage profit, then only it will make sense to go for arbitrage position	1
	a) cost of borrowing	
	b) Cost of carry	
	c) Both and b	
	d) None of the above	
17.	Hedging is _____ mechanisim	1
	a) Risk mitigation	
	b) Risk aggravation	
	c) Risk avoidance	
	d) Risk management tool	

18.	_____ is being used to reduce the unsystematic risk by dealing in stock index and future index a) Arbitrage **b) Hedging** c) Cost of carry model d) None of the above	1
19.	_____ type of risk is also called company specific risk **a) Unsystematic risk** b) Systematic risk c) Operational risk d) Liquidity risk	1
20.	If an investor deals in TATA steel company and because of government policy, the share price of TATASTEEL gets affected. This will comes under risk **a) Unsystematic** b) Systematic c) Undiversified d) Market	1
21.	_____ options are on individual stock and gives the holder the right to buy or sell shares at the specified price a) Index option **b) Stock options** c) American options d) European options	1
22.	When spot price is less than strike price that is called _____ **a) In the money** b) At the money c) Out of the money d) Deep out of the money	1
23.	In case of linear payoff the profit option payer is _____ and loss is_____ a) Limited, limited b) Limited, unlimited **c) Unlimited, limited** d) Unlimited, unlimited	1

24.	A long call is used when one expects that market will	1
	a) Rise	
	b) Fall	
	c) Does not change	
	d) None of the above	
25.	What is in the money (ITM) call option contract?	1
	a) Spot price is greater than strike price	
	b) Spot price is Lower than strike price	
	c) Spot price is equal to strike price	
	d) None of these	
26.	What is out of the money (OTM) put option contract?	1
	a) Spot price is lower than strike price	
	b) Spot price is greater than strike price	
	c) Spot price is equal to strike price	
	d) None of these	
27.	Option has an advantage over futures because _____ _____	1
	a) Option provides hedge without removing opportunity to make profit	
	b) Option provides more certain hedge than futures	
	c) Option is likely to be cheaper	
	d) In option, it is less likely to require delivery of underlying asset	
28.	If the value of underlying asset rises, then the call premium	1
	a) Falls	
	b) No change	
	c) Fall in strike price	
	d) Rises	
29.	What is the maximum potential gain for seller of an option contract till the expiry of the contract?	1
	a) Unlimited	
	b) Limited to the spot price of the underlying	
	c) Limited to the premium received upfront	
	d) Limited to the futures price of the same expiry	

30	If a commodity call option has a strike price of Rs 1800/- and the current market price of the underlying asset is Rs.1950/-, what will be its intrinsic value a) Rs.50 b) Rs.100 **c) Rs.150** d) Rs.200	1
31.	If call option has a strike price of Rs 1210/- and the current market price of the underlying asset is Rs.1320/- and option premium is Rs.200, then what will be the time value a) Rs. 70 **b) Rs. 90** c) Rs. 100 d) Rs. 140	1
32.	A put option gives the owner right _____ **a) But not the obligation to sell the assets** b) And the obligations to sell the assets c) Bit not the obligation to buy the assets d) And the obligations to buy the assets	1
33.	The higher the exercise price:_____ **a) The higher the call price** b) The lower the call price c) Has no effect on call price d) The higher the stock price	1
34.	Suppose an investor buys a call option with an exercise price of $25. If the stock is trading at $30, the option is_____ _____ **a) In the money** b) Out of the money c) At the money d) Deep out of the money	1

35.	Suppose an investor sells a put option. What will happen if the stock price on the exercise date exceeds the exercise price? a) The seller will need to deliver the stock to the owner of the option b) The seller will be obligated to buy the stock from the owner of the option **c) The owner will not exercise the option** d) None of the above	1
36.	Which of the following investor will be happy to see the stock rise sharply **a) An investor who owns call option** b) An investor who owns put option c) a n investor who owns the stock but has sold call option d) An owner who sold an call option	1
37.	Suppose the price of a share of IBM stock is $200. An April call option on IBM stock has a premium of $5 and an exercise price of $200. Ignoring commissions, the holder of the call option will earn a profit if the price of the share a) Increases to $204. b) Decreases to $190. **c) Increases to $206.** d) Decreases to $196.	1
38.	What is the advantage of American Options over European options? **a) American Options can be exercised anytime.** b) American Options can only be exercised at the expiration date. c) American Options available in the US. d) American Options available outside of US as well.	1
39.	Co. B is trading for $179, which option is ITM (In the Money)? **a) Call 171** b) Call 186 c) Put 171. d) None of the above	1

40.	What is the expiration date of an option?	1
	a) The last day on which the option can be exercised	
	b) The first day on which the option can be exercised	
	c) The day on which the option was bought	
	d) The day on which the option was sold	
41.	What is the buyer of a call option hoping to achieve?	1
	a) To buy the asset at a lower price	
	b) To sell the asset at a higher price	
	c) To profit from a price increase	
	d) To hedge against a price decrease	
42.	What is the seller of a put option hoping to achieve?	1
	a) To buy the asset at a higher price	
	b) To sell the asset at a lower price	
	c) To profit from a price decrease	
	d) To hedge against a price increase	
43.	What is the effect of a increase in volatility on the premium of a call option?	1
	a) Decrease	
	b) Increase	
	c) No change	
	d) Depends on the strike price	
44.	What is the effect of a decrease in the underlying asset price on the value of a put option?	1
	a) Decrease	
	b) Increase	
	c) No change	
	d) Depends on the strike price	
45.	Which of the following is a benefit of buying a call option?	1
	a) Limited upside potential	
	b) Unlimited downside risk	
	c) Flexibility to buy the asset at a lower price	
	d) Ability to profit from a price decrease	

Answer the following in 20-30 words

1) What are the forward contracts and explain its silent features?

2) What are the limitations of the forward contract?

3) What are the future contract and explain its standard items

4) List out the key future terminologies?

5) What is the difference between trading underlying and Trading Single Stock Futures?

6) What are the future payoff? Explain payoff for the buyer of the futures?

7) How to price future Future contract?

8) How to price Equity Index Futures?

9) How to price index future given expected Dividend amount?

10) How to price stock futures when no dividend when no Dividend Expected?

11) How to price stock futures when dividend are expected?

12) Which types of risk will be minimised by using hedging?

13) What are the differant option terminologies?

14) What is the difference between future and option?

Answer the following in 50-80 words

1) Explain the payoff for buyer of the call option having long call

2) If being as an investor you are thinking that market is going to drop. How you will make profit by adopting the position in the market.? How does one implement a trading strategy to benefit from the downward movement in the market?

3) There are the times when you think that market is going to rise, however in the event that the market does not rise, which kind of spread strategy you will use to

Solved papers

General Instructions:

1) Please read the instruction carefully

2) This question paper consist of 24 question in two section – Section A and Section B

3) Section A has objective type question whereas Section B contains

Subjective type question

4) **Out of given (6 + 18=) 24 question, a student has to answer (6 + 11=)17 question in the allotted time of 3 hours**

5) All questions of a particular section must be attempted in the correct order

6) **SECTION A – OBJECTIVE TYPE QUESTION (30 MARKS)**

I. This section has 06 question

II. There is no negative marking

III. Do as per instruction given

IV. Marks allotted are mentioned against each question/ part

7) **SECTION B - SUBJECTIVE TYPE QUESTION (30 MARKS)**

1) This section contain 18 question

2) A student has to do 11 question

3) Do as per instruction given

4) Marks allotted are mentioned against each question/ part

	SECTION A –OBJECTIVE TYPE QUESTION	
Q1.	**Answer any 4 out of the given 6 questions on Employability Skills (1 x 4 = 4 marks)**	
I.	—------------------- sentences ask a question. It always ends with question mark a) Declarative b) Exclamatory c) Imperative d) Interrogative	1
II.	What are the smart methods to set goals in self-management skills? a) Specific & Measurable b) Achievable & realistic c) Time bound d) All of the above	1
III.	Self-management is also known as —----,is the ability to effectively control ones emotions, behavior and thoughts a) Self-control b) self- motivation c) Self-design d) None of the above	1
IV.	Mr. Gupta has the spreadsheet with a list of 500 items in his shop. A customer comes and asks for a particular item. How should he arrange the data so that he can find that item fast? He will: a) Apply filters b) Sort of data c) Use a password d) Format data	1

V.	Mohan knows what business he wants to do but does not know what steps to be taken to get it running. The barrier stopping him is _____ a) Building the light team b) Lack of plan c) Self-doubt d) Risk taking	1
VI.	_____ are free from chemical fertilizers residues of synthetic fertilizers and hence, are good for our health a) Organic fruits b) Organic vegetables c) Both a and b d) None of the above	1
Q2.	**Answer any 5 out of the given 7 questions (1 x 5 = 5 marks)**	
I.	Which one of the following is not the key indicator of securities market a) Secondary market b) Index c) Market capitalizations d) Turnover	1
II.	Commercial paper has the maturity period of_____ a) 15 days to 1 year b) 1 day to 1 year c) 10 days to 1 year d) More than one year	1
III.	Which of the following stock exchange has its named Sensex a) India commodity market b) Bombay stock exchange c) Calcutta stock exchange d) National stock exchange	1
IV.	In_____ membership, member is entitled to future and option segment, currency derivative and Debt segment a) Trading cum self-clearing member b) Trading cum clearing member c) Professional clearing member d) Both b and c	1

V.	_____ measure the market volatility over the near term	1
	a) Nifty index	
	b) Volatility index	
	c) Both and b	
	d) None of the above	
VI.	Who is defined as a person whose name is recorded with the depositary	1
	a) Participant	
	b) Issuer	
	c) Beneficial owner	
	d) Depositary	
VII.	Define the investor service cell	1
Q3.	**Answer any 6 out of the given 7 questions (1 x 6 = 6 marks)**	
I.	All the orders can be modified in the system till the time they do not get fully — & only during market hours	1
	a) Auctioned	
	b) Traded	
	c) Partially traded	
	d) Partially auctioned	
II.	In case of 20% movement of the index trading will be halted for the reminder of the	1
	a) Week	
	b) Day	
	c) Month	
	d) Year	
III.	_____ cancellation can be done during trading hours either by selecting the order from the outstanding order screen or from the function key provided	1
	a) Single order cancellation	
	b) Quick order cancellation	
	c) Order cancellation	
	d) Order cancellation for the disabled member	

IV.	The ticker selection facility is confined to the securities of____ _____ segment only a) Derivative market b) Capital market c) Commodity market d) Auction market	1
V.	How does the user select the portfolio for the basket trading a) Open Amount Edit box b) Open combo box c) Open portfolio box d) Open market watch window	1
VI.	While matching order, the system perform _____ a) Auction matching b) Regular lot matching c) Stop loss matching d) Validation check	1
VII.	Define Snap quote	1
Q4.	**Answer any 5 out of the given 6 questions (1 x 5 = 5 marks)**	
I.	_____ is responsible for the post trade activities of a stock exchange a) NSE b) NSCCL c) CRISIL d) RBI	1
II.	NSCCL determines the cumulative obligation of each member on___ a) Every month b) Every week c) End of trading day d) Each day	1
III.	Define clearing account	1
IV.	_____ problem can arise only in case of physical settlement and dematerialized settlement a) Bad delivery b) Short delivery c) Unrectified delivery d) Delivery	1

V.	Which account is used by the clearing member to interface with his client	1
	a) Pool account	
	b) Delivery account	
	c) Receipt account	
	d) All of the above	
VI.	In ISIN what does the code 08 signifies	1
	a) Non-voting rights	
	b) Unsecured debentures	
	c) Warrants	
	d) Step discount bonds	
Q5.	**Answer any 5 out of the given 6 questions (1 x 5 = 5 marks)**	
I.	_____ means the daily volatility of market index computed as at the end of the previous trading day	1
	a) Security sigma	
	b) Security VaR	
	c) Index sigma	
	d) Index VaR	
II.	----------- measures the profit available to the equity shareholder that is the amount they can get on every shareholder	1
	a) Price earnings ratio	
	b) Dividend of the share	
	c) Earnings per share	
	d) Return	
III.	At 6% annual inflation rate an item costing Rs. 100 today would cost Rs. after two years	1
	a) 124.30	
	b) 122.46	
	c) 224	
	d) 112.36	
IV.	An annuity refers to series of	1
	a) One time lump sum payment	
	b) Irregular cash flows	
	c) Unequal cash flows	
	d) Equal periodic cash flows	

V.	The concept of time value of money is based on the principle that: a) Money grows at a constant rate over a time b) Money is affected by inflation rate c) Money has the same purchasing power over the time d) Money can be invested to earn return over time	1
VI.	The frequency with which interest is paid (compounded) will have an effect on a) Effective rate of return b) Reflective rate of return c) Rate of return d) Rate of simple interest	1
Q6.	**Answer any 5 out of the given 6 questions (1 x 5 = 5 marks)**	
I.	A good market index should have which of the following attributes a) It should be professionally maintained b) The stocks included in the index should be highly liquid c) Both a and b d) None of the above	1
II.	_____ must be deposited in the margin account at the time a future contract is first entered into a) Initial margin b) Initial deposit c) Maintenance margin d) Either a or c	1
III.	As the date of expiration comes neat of the contract the basis_____ a) Reduces b) Increases c) Remains constant d) Either a or b	1

IV.	The primary purpose of using future contract is to _____	1
	a) Look in a future price for an underlying asset	
	b) Speculate on the price movement of an underlying asset	
	c) Obtain physical delivery of the underlying asset	
	d) Avoid the counterparty risk associated with forward contract	
V.	Which of the following are the features of future contract?	1
	a) Trading on the stock exchange	
	b) Illiquidity	
	c) Counterparty Risk	
	d) All of the above	
VI.	Options are the derivative that give the holder the right to:	1
	a) Buy or sell an asset at a predetermined price within a specified period	
	b) Borrow money from a bank	
	c) Issue new shares of a company	
	d) Trade currencies in the foreign exchange market	
	SECTION B: SUBJECTIVE TYPE QUESTIONS	
	Answer any 3 out of the given 5 questions on Employability Skills (2 x 3 = 6 marks) Answer each question in 20 – 30 words.	
Q7.	What is the importance of effective communication?	2
Q8.	What are the five parameters that will describe individual personality?	2
Q9.	Why have the spreadsheet program so popular? write any two features	2
Q10.	Explain any two qualities of an Entrepreneur?	2
Q11.	Explain the role of green jobs in eco-tourism?	2
	Answer any 3 out of the given 5 questions in 20 – 30 words each (2 x 3 = 6 marks)	
Q12.	What are the various order types and conditions?	2

Q13.	What are the types of settlement?	2
Q14.	Which feature of an annual Report should one read carefully?	2
Q15.	What are the participants in the derivative market?	2
Q16.	Distinguish between underlying assets and derivatives?	2
	Answer any 2 out of the given 3 questions in 30– 50 words each (3 x 2 = 6 marks)	
Q17.	What is the process of cancellation of registration?	3
Q18.	What are the different order books?	3
Q19.	Explain the process of transaction cycle	3
	Answer any 3 out of the given 5 questions in 50– 80 words each (4 x 3 = 12 marks)	
Q20.	What are the reform in Indian security market	4
Q21.	"Numbering system of ISIN is quite simple. The Numbering system is in compliance with the structure of ISIN adopted by SEBI. ISIN is allotted when security is admitted to NSDL" Justify the above statement	4
Q22.	"A spread trading strategy involves taking position in two or more option of the same type that is, two or more calls or two more puts" Explain the above statement with the help of diagram.	4
Q23.	How the trading System developed over the years?	4
Q24.	Explain the difference between free float market capitalization and weighted capitalization index with formula	4

Answer key

	SECTION A –OBJECTIVE TYPE QUESTION		
Q1.	**Answer any 4 out of the given 6 questions on Employability Skills (1 x 4 = 4 marks)**	**Marks Allocation**	**Marks**
I.	d) Interrogative		1
II.	d) All of the above		1
III.	a) Self-control		1
IV.	b) Sort of data		1
V.	c) Lack of plan		1
VI.	c) Both a and b		1
Q2.	**Answer any 5 out of the given 7 questions (1 x 5 = 5 marks)**		
I.	a) Secondary market		1
II.	a) 15 days to 1 year		1
III.	c) Bombay stock exchange		1
IV.	d) Both b and c		1
V.	b) Volatility index		1
VI.	c) Beneficial owner		1
VII.	Investor Services Cell of the Exchange deals with the complaints of investors against the Trading Members of the Exchange, or against the listed companies.		1
Q3.	**Answer any 6 out of the given 7 questions (1 x 6 = 6 marks)**		
I.	a) Traded		1
II.	b) Day		1
III.	a) Single order cancellation		1
IV.	b) Capital market		1

V.	b) open combo box		1
VI	a) Regular lot matching		1
VII.	The snap quote feature allows a trading member to get instantaneous market information on any desired security.		1
Q4.	**Answer any 5 out of the given 6 questions (1 x 5 = 5 marks)**		
I.	a) NSCCL		1
II.	c) End of trading day		1
III.	NSE Clearing carries out the clearing and settlement of the trades executed in the equities and derivatives segments of the NSE.		1
IV.	b) Short delivery		1
V.	a) Pool account		1
VI.	b) Unsecured debentures		1
Q5.	**Answer any 5 out of the given 6 questions (1 x 5 = 5 marks)**		
I.	c) Index sigma		1
II	c) earning per share		1
III.	d) 112.36		1
IV.	a) Equal periodic cash flows		1
V.	a) Money is affected by inflation rate		1
VI.	a) Effective rate of return		1
Q6.	**Answer any 5 out of the given 6 questions (1 x 5 = 5 marks)**		
I.	a) Both a and b		1
II.	a) Initial margin		1
III.	a) Reduces		1
IV.	a) Avoid the counterparty risk associated with forward contract		1
V.	d) all of the above		1

VI.	a) Buy or sell an asset at a predetermined price within a specified period		1
	SECTION B: SUBJECTIVE TYPE QUESTIONS		
	Answer any 3 out of the given 5 questions on Employability Skills (2 x 3 = 6 marks) Answer each question in 20 – 30 words.		
Q7.	**What is the importance of effective communication?**		2
Ans	1) Needed to communicate effectively with people and customers	1 1	
	2) It equip the person with knowledge and skills, which are necessary to take the advantages of the opportunities the 21st century of first		
	3) Person knowing many languages will be able to convert with people and read sign by travelling to different places		
Q8.	**What are the three parameters that will describe individual personality?**	1	2
Ans	**1) Openness:-** Generally, creative, curious, active, flexible, adventurous. if a person is interested in learning new things meeting new people and making friends and likes visiting new places the person can be called open minded	1	
	2) Consciousness:- individual who listen to other conscience our self-discipline, do their work on time take care of other before themselves and care about others feeling		
	3) Extraversion:- Who love interacting with people around and are generally talkative. A person who can easily make friends and make any gathering lively is confident and extrovert		

Q9.	Why the spreadsheet program have is popular? write any two features	1 1	2
Ans	**Spreadsheet:** - electronic document, which has rows and columns. it is used to store data in a systematic way and do calculations		
	Features:-		
	1) **Sorting**		
	Spreadsheets can sort data in ascending or descending order based on different fields.		
	2) **Formulas and cell addresses**		
	Spreadsheets use formulas and cell addresses for mathematical calculations, including statistical and trigonometric calculations.		
Q10.	Explain any two qualities of an entrepreneur?	1	2
Ans	1) **Initiative**:- an entrepreneur must be able to initiate action and take advantage of an opportunity. once a person misses out and opportunity, it may not come again	1	
	2) **Willingness to take risk**:- in any business, there is a element of risk involved. It implants that it is not necessary that every business shall on Profit. However and entrepreneur always volunteers to take rest to run a business and be successful.		
Q11.	Explain the role of green jobs in eco-tourism?	1 1	2
Ans	1) Eco tourism is intended to provide an experience to the visitors to understand the importance of conserving resources, reducing where enhancing the natural environment and reducing pollution		
	2) This helps improve public image as the visitors feel good about being in an environment friendly place		
	3) Green jobs in ecotourism include Eco tour guide Eco tourism operators		

	Answer any 3 out of the given 5 questions in 20 – 30 words each (2 x 3 = 6 marks)		
Q12.	What are the various order types and conditions?	1	2
Ans	Several combinations of the above are allowed thereby providing enormous flexibility to the users. The order types and conditions are summarized below: **1) Time Conditions (a) DAY:** All orders entered into the system are currently considered as Day orders only. (b) IOC: An Immediate or Cancel (IOC) order allows the user to buy or sell a security as soon as the order is released into the system, failing which the order is cancelled from the system. Partial match is possible for the order, and the unmatched portion of the order is cancelled immediately.		
	2) Quantity Conditions DQ: An order with a Disclosed Quantity (DQ) allows the user to disclose only a portion of the order quantity to the market. For e.g. if the order quantity is 10,000 and the disclosed quantity is 2,000, then only 2,000 is released to the market. After this quantity is fully matched, a subsequent quantity of 2,000 is disclosed. Thus, totally five disclosures with the same order number are shown one after the other in the market.	1	
Q13.	What are the types of settlement?		2
Ans:	1) In case of NSDL, the members need to give instructions to move the securities to the settlement account of NSCCL, whereas in case of CDSL pay-in is done based on settlement ID through which members are required to provide separate balances for each settlement.	1	

	2) The securities obligations of members are downloaded to members/custodians by NSCCL after the end of the trading day. (b) The members / custodians deliver the securities to the clearing corporation on the pay day in case of physical settlement and make available the required securities in the pool accounts with the depository participants in case of dematerialized securities.	1	
Q14.	**Which feature of an annual Report should one read carefully?**	½	2
Ans:	1) Management Discussion and analysis about the performance and the future prospectus of the company and the industry in which it operates	½	
	2) Auditors report (including annexure and the auditor's report)	½	
	3) Directors report and chairman statement which are related to the current and the future operational performance		
	4) balance sheet	½	
	5) profit and loss account		
Q15.	**What are the participants in the derivative market?**		2
Ans	As with the regular financial markets, derivatives markets have the following participants: Stock Exchange: Where the derivatives are created and traded.	1½	
	1) **Investors:** Investors in derivatives could be retail investors, institutional investors, banks, and corporates. Each investor has different objectives of investing in derivatives.		

2) Regulatory Authorities: They ensure smooth functioning of the markets and ensure fair practices are being followed by all participants. SEBI regulates the equity derivative markets, RBI the interest rate and currency derivative markets and FMC (Forward Markets Commission) the commodity markets. FMC is now merged with SEBI, and hence SEBI overlooks both parts of the derivative markets.		
3) Others: Other participants such as Clearing and settlement agencies, credit rating agencies, investor grievances etc are shared between the financial markets and the 159 derivatives markets.	½	

Q16 **Distinguish between underlying assets and derivatives?**

Ans

	Underlying asset	Derivatives
Time factor	They are the time bound	They are subject to time bound
Ownership right	Equity shareholders gets the rights and privilege holder as a shareholder like dividend and voting rights	Financial derivative holder does not gets the voting rights and dividend
Obligations	The buyer is obligated to buy the asset on the certain stated date	In this, the buyer will have no obligation to buy execute the contract

	Answer any 2 out of the given 3 questions in 30– 50 words each (3 x 2 = 6 marks)		
Q17.	What is the process of cancellation of registration?		3
Ans.	1) In case a trading member / sub-broker intends to cancel the registration as a sub-broker, the sub-broker is required to the following documents: 1. Request letter of the Trading member for surrender of sub-broker registration (on the letter head of TM);	½	
	2) Undertaking from the Trading Member (on the letter head of TM).	½	
	3) Application from Sub-Broker for surrender of registration (Annexure II), if the sub broker is traceable. If the sub broker is non-traceable than a copy of termination notice served to the sub broker along with the proof of delivery by the Trading Member.	½	
	4) Copy of public notification intimating the investors/general public of the surrender of registration of sub broker and not to deal with such sub broker, issued in the local newspaper with wide circulation where the sub broker's place of work is situated	½	
	5) SEBI registration certificate of the Sub-Broker in original. In case the original certificate is lost, FIR copy along with the affidavit must be submitted to SEBI in this regard by the concerned Trading Member and the Sub-Broker separately on stamp paper of Rs.100/- or of appropriate value as defined in the stamp act, duly notarized.	½	
	6) An undertaking from the member that SEBI has not taken/ initiated any action like enquiry proceedings / cancellation / suspension of registration / debarred / administrative warning or prohibited from dealing in securities market / imposed penalty after enquiry / adjudication / prosecution etc. against the sub-broker	½	

	7) PAN card of the sub-broker truly certified by the trading member		
Q18.	**What are the different order books?**		3
Ans.	**1) Pre-open Book** : An order during Pre Open session has to be a Pre Open (PO) order. All the Pre Open orders are stacked in the system till the Pre Open phase. At the end of the Pre Open phase, the matching of Pre Open orders takes place at the Final Opening Price. By default, the Preopen (PO) book appears in the order entry screen when the Normal Market is in Pre Open and the security is eligible for Pre Open Session. Order entry in pre open book type is allowed only during market status is in preopen.	1	
	2) Regular Lot Book : An order that has no special condition associated with it is a Regular Lot order. When a dealer places this order, the system looks for a corresponding Regular Lot order existing in that market (Passive orders). If it does not find a match at the time it enters the system, the order is stacked in the Regular Lot book as a passive order. By default, the Regular Lot book appears in the order entry screen in the normal market. Buyback orders can be placed through the Regular Lot (RL) book in the Normal 90 Market. The member can place a buyback order by specifying _BUYBACKORD'in the Client Account field in the order entry screen. Such company buyback orders will be identified in MBP screen by a _*'(asterisk) indicator against such orders.	1	

	3) **Odd Lot Book**: The Odd Lot book can be selected in the order entry screen in order to trade in the Odd Lot market. Order matching in this market takes place between two orders on the basis of quantity and price. To enter orders in the odd lot market, select the book type as OL.	1	
Q19.	**Explain the process of transaction cycle?**		3
Ans:-	Steps in Transaction Cycle a) A person holding assets (securities/funds), either to meet his liquidity needs or to reshuffle his holdings in response to changes in his perception about risk and return of the assets, decides to buy or sell the securities.	1	
	b) He selects a broker and instructs him to place buy/sell order on an exchange.	½	
	c) The order is converted to a trade as soon as it finds a matching sell/buy order.	½ ½	
	d) At the end of the trade cycle, the trades are netted to determine the obligations of the trading members to deliver securities/funds as per settlement schedule.	½	
	e) Buyer (seller) delivers funds (securities) and receives securities (funds) and acquires ownership of the securities		
	Answer any 3 out of the given 5 questions in 50– 80 words each (4 x 3 = 12 marks)		
Q20.	**What are the reform in Indian security market**		4
Ans:-	1) **Screen Based Trading**: Prior to setting up of NSE, the trading on stock exchanges in India was based on an open outcry system. The system was inefficient and time consuming because of its inability to provide immediate matching or recording of trades. In order to provide efficiency, liquidity and transparency, NSE introduced a nation-wide on-line fully automated screen based trading system (SBTS) on the CM segment on November 3, 1994.	1	

	2) Equity Derivatives Trading: In order to assist market participants in managing risks better through hedging, speculation and arbitrage, SC(R) A was amended in 1995 to lift the ban on options in securities. Trading in derivatives, however, took off in 2000 with index futures after a suitable legal and regulatory framework was put in place. The market presently offers index futures, index options, single stock futures and single stock options	1	
	3) Demutualization: Historically, stock exchanges were owned, controlled and managed by the brokers. In case of disputes, integrity of the stock exchange suffered. NSE, however, was set up with a pure demutualized governance structure, having ownership, management and trading with three different sets of people. Currently, all the stock exchanges in India have a demutualized set up.	1	
	4) Clearing Corporation: The anonymous electronic order book ushered in by the NSE did not permit members to assess credit risk of the counter-party and thus necessitated some innovation in this area. To address this concern, NSE had set up the first clearing corporation, viz. National Securities Clearing Corporation Ltd. (NSCCL), which commenced its operations in April 1996.	1	
Q21.	"Numbering system of ISIN is quite simple. The Numbering system is in compliance with the structure of ISIN adopted by SEBI. ISIN is allotted when security is admitted to NSDL" Justify the above statement		4

Ans:-

ISSUER TYPE	CODE ALLOTTED
Central government	A
State Government	B
Municipal corporation	C
Union territories	D
Company statutory corporation	E
Mutual funds including UTI	F

2

Numbering System of ISIN: The numbering structure for securities in NSDL is of 12 digit alphanumeric string. The first two characters represent country code.

2

The list may be expanded as per need. Maximum issuer types can be 35 (A to Z and 0 to 8. The partly paid up shares are identified by 9). The next 4 characters (fourth to seventh character) represent company identity of which first 3 characters are numeric and fourth character is alpha character. The numbering begins with _001A' and continues till _999A' and proceeds to _001B'. The next two characters (the eighth and ninth characters) represent security type for a given issuer. Both the characters are numeric. The next two characters (the tenth and eleventh characters) are serially issued for each security of the issuer entering the system. Last digit is the check digit.

Q22.	"A spread trading strategy involves taking position in two or more option of the same type that is, two or more calls or two more puts" Explain the above statement with the help of a diagram.		4
Ans:-	There are times when you think the market is going to rise over the next two months, however in the event that the market does not rise, you would like to limit your downside. One way you could do this is by entering into a spread. A spread trading strategy involves taking a position in two or more options of the same type, that is, two or more calls or two or more puts. A spread that is designed to profit if the price goes up is called a	1	
	How does one go about doing this? This is basically done utilizing two call options having the same expiration date, but different exercise prices The buyer of a bull spread buys a call with an exercise price below the current index level and sells a call option with an exercise price above the current index level. The spread is a bull spread because the trader hopes to profit from a rise in the index. The trade is a spread because it involves buying one option and selling a related option.	2	

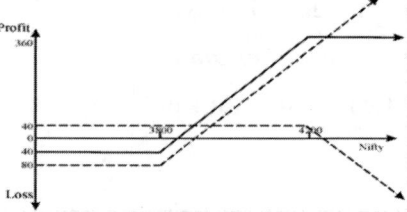

Figure : Payoff for a bull spread created using Call Options

Figure : Payoff for a bull spread
created using Call Options

The figure 6.14 shows the profits/losses for a bull spread. (The index values in this illustration are retrospective) As can be seen, the payoff obtained is the sum of the payoffs of the two calls, one sold at Rs. 40 and the other bought at Rs. 80The cost of setting up the spread is Rs. 40 which is the difference between the call premium paid and the call premium received. The downside on the position is limited to this amount. As the index moves above 3800, the position starts making profits (cutting losses) until the index reaches 4200. Beyond 4200, the profits made on the long call position get offset by the losses made on the short call position and hence the maximum profit on this spread is made if the index on the expiration day closes at 4200. Hence the payoff on this spread lies between -40 to 360Somebody who thinks the index is going to rise, but not above 4200 would buy this spread. Hence, he does not want to buy a call at 3800 and pay a Premium of 80 for an upside he believes will not happen.

Q23.	How the trading System developed over		4
Ans:-	In the past, the trading on stock exchanges in India was based on open outcry system Under the system brokers assemble at a central location usually the exchange trading ring, and trade with each other. This was time consuming, inefficient and imposed limits on trading volumes and trading hours. In order to provide efficiency, liquidity and transparency, NSE introduced a nation-wide on-line, fully-automated screen based trading system (SBTS). Under this system a trading member can punch into the computer, the number of securities and the prices at which he would like to transact. The transaction is executed as soon as it finds a matching sell or buys order from a counterparty.	1	
	Technology has been used to carry the trading platform from the trading hall of stock exchanges to the premises of brokers. NSE carried the trading platform further to the PCs at the residence of investors through the Internet. This made a huge difference in terms of equal access to investors in a geographically vast country like India	1	
	The trading network is depicted in Figure. NSE has a main computer which is connected through Very Small Aperture Terminal (VSAT) installed at NSE office The main computer runs on a fault tolerant STRATUS mainframe computer at the Exchange. Brokers have terminals (identified as the PCs in the Figure 2.1) installed at their premises which are connected through VSATs/leased lines/ modem	1	

		1	
Q24.	**Explain the difference between free float market capitalizations and weighted capitalizations index with formula**		4
Ans:-	1) <u>Free float market capitalizations</u> =Issue size *price*investable weight Factor Index = **(Free float current market capitalizations/free float base market capitalizations)*Base value** Free floor market capitalizations is a method by which the market cap of the underlying index is calculated by multiplying the price with the number of outstanding shares excluding a) government holding in the capacity of strategic investor b) shares held by promoters through ADR/GDR c) strategic take by corporate bodies/individual/HUF d) Investment under FDI category e) equity held by associate/ group companies f)	2	

2) Market capitalizations weighted index:- Each stock in the index affects the index value in proportion to market value of all shares outstanding Index = current market capitalizations / base market capitalizations* base value Where Current market capitalizations equal to sum of(current market price* issue price) of all security in the index Base market capitalizations= sum of (market price* issue price) of all security as on base date	2	

General Instructions:

1) Please read the instruction carefully
2) This question paper consist of 24 question in two section – Section A and Section B
3) Section A has objective type question whereas Section B contains Subjective type question
4) **Out of given (6+18=)24 question, a student has to answer (6+11=)17 question in the allotted time of 3 hours**
5) All questions of a particular section must be attempted in the correct order
6) **SECTION A –OBJECTIVE TYPE QUESTION (30 MARKS)**
   I. This section has 06 question
   II. There is no negative marking
   III. Do as per instruction given
   IV. Marks allotted are mentioned against each question/ part
7) **SECTION B- SUBJECTIVE TYPE QUESTION (30 MARKS)**
   I. This section contain 18 question
   II. A student has to do 11 question
   III. Do as per instruction given
   IV. Marks allotted are mentioned against each question/ part

	SECTION A: OBJECTIVE TYPE QUESTIONS	
Q1.	**Answer any 4 out of the given 6 questions on Employability Skills (1 x 4 = 4 marks)**	
I.	In _____ personality disorder a people feel extremely nervous and got it because he believe that other people do not like him or are trying to harm you a) Anti-Social b) Narcissistic c) Paranoid d) Obsessive	1
II.	How many worksheets are there in one workbook? a) One b) Two c) Three d) None we need to create it	1
III.	Self-motivation is important because— a) It increase individuals energy and activity b) It directs and individual towards specific goal c) It results in initiation and existence of specific activity d) All of the above	1
Iv.	———————— Is the shortcut key to create new spreadsheet a) Ctrl+N b) Alt+N c) Ctrl+shift+N d) Ctrl+Alt+N	1
V.	What is the address of the sale formed by the interaction of third column and fifth row a) A5 b) B3 c) C5 d) E3	1

VI.	----------- Is the opposite of insecure	1
	a) Agreeableness	
	b) Emotional stability	
	c) Extraversion	
	d) Openness to experience	
Q2.	**Answer any 5 out of the given 7 questions (1 x 5 = 5 marks)**	
I.	SEBI has made it mandatory for all the trading members to use — for all clients	1
	a) contract note	
	b) unique client code	
	c) margin requirement	
	d) none of the above	
II.	In current trade scenario—----- facility is not available on trading system on previous trade window	1
	a) Trade cancellation	
	b) IOC	
	c) Trade modification	
	d) Trade and order cancellation	
III.	At 6% annual inflation rate, and atom costing rupees 100 today, would cost rupees— after 2 years	1
	a) 220	
	b) 429	
	c) 440	
	d) 520	
IV.	Derivative can be classified in which of the ways?	1
	a) on the basis of nature of the derivative	
	b) on the basis of underlying asset	
	c) on the basis of place of trading	
	d) all of the above	

V.	———---------- represents the cost of executing a transaction in a given stock, for a specific predefined order size, at any given point of time a) Trading cost b) Ideal cost c) Impact cost d) Actual cost	1
VI.	——-------- Show shows all the activity that have been performed on any order belonging to that user a) message history b) Portfolio c) activity log d) Snap quote	1
VII.	Define UCC	1
Q3.	**Answer any 6 out of the given 7 questions (1 x 6 = 6 marks)**	
I.	——------------ Is an important intermediary between stock broker and client in capital market segment a) Dealer b) Sub-broker c) Exchange d) none of the above	1
II.	All orders which are of regular lot size are multiples thereof traded— a) Odd lot market b) Normal market c) Auction market d) None of the above	1
III.	In activity lock screen—-------- option is not available to users a) Trade modification of option b) Trade cancellation option c) Inquiry option d) Market query option	1

IV.	Define Market capitalization weighted index?	1
V.	In market enquiry screen S indicates—--- and P indicates—------------------------------ a) Sold, Purchase b) Sold, Pre open c) Suspended, Purchase d) Suspended, Pre open	1
VI.	—--------- is to provide need users with a facility to create offline order entry file for selected portfolio a) Trading b) basket trading c) Market capitalization d) Buyback of shares	1
VII.	Define Asset turnover ratio?	1
Q4.	**Answer any 5 out of the given 6 questions (1 x 5 = 5 marks)**	
I.	Define compound interest	1
II.	Acid test ratio is equal to quick asset divided by —--------- -- a) Current assets b) Current liability c) Debtors turnover d) Net fixed asset	1
III.	—--------------- Is the disadvantage of Forward Market a) Lack of centralization of trading b) illiquidity c) Counterparty risk d) All of the above	1
IV.	—------------- Give the buyer the right but not the obligation to buy a given quantity of the underlying asset a) Calls b) Puts c) Forward d) Future	1

V.	What is the PV of rupees 5000 payable 3 years, if the interest rate is 10% per annum (Discrete discounting) a) 3756.57 b) 2365.68 c) 3567 d) None	1
VI.	—----------- Order is not having any special condition associated with it a) Stop loss b) Regular lot c) Pre open d) Odd lot	1
Q5	**Answer any 5 out of the given 6 questions (1 x 5 = 5 marks)**	
I.	—----------- Received end of the day reports for all the dealers under system a) Trading member b) Client c) NSE d) Branch manager	1
II.	—--------- is that period that make close, which uses have enquiry access a) Market close b) Post close market c) SURCON d) No any market period is there	1
III.	—------------- is the main area of focus for a trade in member a) enquiry window b) market watch c) Snap quote d) order window	1

IV.	The expulsion of the trading member Has which of the following consequences ? a) Trading membership rights for forfeited b) rights of the creditors and unimpaired c) Fulfilment of contracts d) all of the above	1
V.	In auction market——---- Party printers order on the same side as of the initiative a) Solicitor b) Competitor c) buyer or seller d) SEBI	1
VI.	Copy of the advertisement shall be submitted to the exchange at least— days in advance before its issues a) 6 days b) one month c) 7 days d) 10 days	1
Q6.	**Answer any 5 out of the given 6 questions (1 x 5 = 5 marks)**	
I.	Define effective Annual return?	1
II.	The main intention of CBOT is to ——--- a) Deal with the credit risk b) To provide centralized location c) Both a and b d) None of the above	1
III.	——---------- are the investors with the present or anticipated exposure to the underlying asset a) Hedgers b) Speculators c) Arbitrator d) All of the above	1

IV.	These are promises to deliver an asset at a predetermined date in a future at a predetermined price	1
	a) Future contract	
	b) Option contracts	
	c) Forward contracts	
	d) Swaps	
V.	Define impact cost	1
VI.	----------- Is an important intermediary between stock broker and client in capital market segment	1
	a) Dealer	
	b) sub broker	
	c) Exchange	
	d) None of the above	
	SECTION B: SUBJECTIVE TYPE QUESTIONS	
	Answer any 3 out of the given 5 questions on Employability Skills (2 x 3 = 6 marks) Answer each question in 20 – 30 words.	
Q7	Write the procedure of Inserting clipart and images in presentation?	2
Q8.	Explain common personality disorder any three	2
Q9.	How will you protect your worksheet or Calc document using the password?	2
Q10.	Explain the components of Calc Screen	2
Q11.	What happens if you write the formula =45/0 in cell A1?	2
	Answer any 3 out of the given 5 questions in 20 – 30 words each (2 x 3 = 6 marks)	
Q12.	What are the desirable attributes of index?	2
Q13.	How will you classify derivatives on the basis of underlying assets?	2
Q14.	Difference between the equity shareholder and preference shareholders?	2

Q15.	What are the special features of marketing inquiry	2
Q16.	What are the benefits of screen based trading?	2
	Answer any 2 out of the given 3 questions in 30– 50 words each (3 x 2 = 6 marks)	
Q17	Explain the difference between industry analysis and financial analysis	3
Q18.	What do you mean by MBP and explain its features	3
Q19.	When did equity derivative trading take place for the first time?	3
	Answer any 3 out of the given 5 questions in 50 – 80 words each (4 x 3 = 12 marks)	
Q20.	If in the market there are two equilibrium prices i.e. where the principle of demand and supply matches. In that case which price will be considered as equilibrium price, if that price also not meet the said criteria?	4
Q21.	What do you mean by secured and unsecured loan? According to you to run the corporate sector, which loan is beneficial for you and why?	4
Q22.	Explain the formula with explanation 1) current ratio 2) Acid test ratio	4
Q23.	Take an example and explain which interest payment will be preferable for you?	4
Q24.	If you want to deal in securities in which securities you want to invest in order to get higher return take risk management as an tool a) listed securities b) Unlisted securities	4

Answer Key

	Section A-Objective Type Questions	
Q1.	**Answer any 4 out of the given 6 questions on Employability Skills (1 x 4 = 4 marks)**	
I.	In ──────── personality disorder a people feel extremely nervous and got it because he believe that other people do not like him or are trying to harm you a) Anti-Social b) Narcissistic **c) Paranoid** d) Obsessive	1
II.	How many worksheets are there in one workbook? a) One b) Two **c) Three** d) None we need to create it	1
III.	Self-motivation is important because— a) It increase individuals energy and activity b) It directs and individual towards specific goal c) It results in initiation andexistence of specific activity **d) All of the above**	1
Iv.	──────── Is the shortcut key to create new spreadsheet a) Ctrl+N b) Alt+N c) Ctrl+shift+N d) Ctrl+Alt+N	1
V.	What is the address of the cell formed by the interaction of third column and fifth row a) A5 b) B3 c) C5 d) E3	1

VI.	----------- Is the opposite of insecure **a) Agreeableness** b) Emotional stability c) Extraversion d) Openness to experience	1
Q2.	**Answer any 5 out of the given 7 questions (1 x 5 = 5 marks)**	
I.	SEBI has made it mandatory for all the trading members to use ------------ for all clients a) contract note **b) unique client code** c) margin requirement d) none of the above	1
II.	In current trade scenario—----- facility is not available on trading system On previous trade window a) Trade cancellation b) IOC **c) Trade modification** d) Trade and order cancellation	1
III.	At 6% annual inflation rate, and atom costing rupees 100 today, would cost rupees—------------------ after 2 years **a) 112.36** b) 112 c) 112.24 d) 112.40	1
IV.	Derivative can be classified in which of the ways? a) on the basis of nature of the derivative b) on the basis of underlying asset c) on the basis of place of trading **d) All of the above**	1

V.	------------ represents the cost of executing a transaction in a given stock, for a specific predefined order size, at any given point of time a) Trading cost b) Ideal cost **c) Impact cost** d) Actual cost	1
VI.	---------- Show shows all the activity that have been performed on any order belonging to that user a) message history b) Portfolio **c) Activity log** d) Snap quote	1
VII. Ans:-	Define UCC SEBI has made it mandatory for all trading members/ brokers to use unique client codes for all clients. Brokers are required to collect and maintain the Permanent Account Number (PAN) allotted by Income Tax Department for all their clients. Brokers should verify the documents with respect to the unique code and retain a copy of the 40 document.	1
Q3.	**Answer any 6 out of the given 7 questions (1 x 6 = 6 marks)**	
I.	-------------- Is an important intermediary between stock broker and client in capital market segment a) Dealer **b) Sub-broker** c) Exchange d) none of the above	1
II.	All orders which are of regular lot size are multiples thereof traded— a) Odd lot market **b) Normal market** c) Auction market d) None of the above	1

III.	In activity lock screen——-------- option is not available to users a) Trade modification of option b) Trade cancellation option **c) Inquiry option** d) Market query option	1
IV. **Ans:-**	Define Market capitalization weighted index? In this type of index calculation, each stock in the index affects the index value in proportion to the market value of all shares outstanding. In this the index would be calculated as per the formulae below: Index = Current market capitalization /Base Market Capitalization × Base Value	1
V.	In market enquiry screen S indicates—--- and P indicates—----------------------------- a) Sold, Purchase b) Sold, Pre open c) Suspended, Purchase **d) Suspended, Pre open**	1
VI.	——-------- is to provide NEAT users with a facility to create offline order entry file for selected portfolio a) Trading **b) Basket trading** c) Market capitalization d) Buyback of shares	1
VII. **Ans:-**	Define Asset turnover ratio? Total Assets turnover ratio measures how efficiently all types of assets are employed. Total Assets turnover ratio = Net Sales Average/ Total Assets	1

Q4.	Answer any 5 out of the given 6 questions (1 x 5 = 5 marks)	
I. Ans:-	Define compound interest Compound interest means that the interest will include interest calculated on interest. The interest accrued on a principal amount is added back to the principal sum, and the whole amount is then treated as new principal, for the calculation of the interest for the next period.	1
II.	Acid test ratio is equal to quick asset divided by ——----- --- a) Current assets **b) Current liability** c) Debtors turnover d) Net fixed asset	1
III.	——-------------- Is the disadvantage of Forward Market a) Lack of centralization of trading b) Illiquidity c) Counterparty risk **d) All of the above**	1
IV.	——------------ Give the buyer the right but not the obligation tobuy a given quantity of the underlying asset a) Calls b) Puts c) Forward d) Future	1
V.	What is the PV of rupees 5000 payable 3 years hens if the interest rate is 10% per annum (Discrete discounting) a) 3756.57 b) 2365.68 c) 3567 d) None	1

VI.	----------- Order is not having any special condition associated with it **a) Stop loss** b) Regular lot c) Pre open d) Odd lot	1
Q5	**Answer any 5 out of the given 6 questions (1 x 5 = 5 marks)**	
I.	----------- Received end of the day reports for all the dealers under system **a) Trading member** b) Client c) NSE d) Branch manager	1
II.	---------- Is that period that make close, which uses have enquiry access a) Market close b) Post close market **c) SURCON** d) No any market period is there	1
III.	------------- Is the main area of focus for a trade in member **a) Enquiry window** b) market watch c) Snap quote d) order window	1
IV.	The expulsion of the trading member Has which of the following consequences? a) Trading membership rights for forfeited b) Rights of the creditors and unimpaired c) Fulfilment of contracts **d) All of the above**	1

V.	In auction market——---- Party enter order on the same side as of the initiative a) Solicitor **b) Competitor** c) buyer or seller d) SEBI	1
VI.	Copy of the advertisement shall be submitted to the exchange at least— days in advance before its issues a) 6 days b) one month **c) 7 days** d) 10 days	1
	Answer any 5 out of the given 6 questions (1 x 5 = 5 marks)	
I.	Define effective Annual return? The effective annual return accounts for intra-year compounding and the stated annual return does not.	1
II.	The main intention of CBOT is to ——--- a) Deal with the credit risk b) To provide centralized location **c) Both a and b** d) None of the above	1
III.	——---------- are the investors with the present or anticipated exposure to the underlying asset **a) Hedgers** b) Speculators c) Arbitrator d) All of the above	1
IV.	These are promises to deliver an asset at a predetermined date in a future at a predetermined price a) Future contract b) Option contracts **c) Forward contracts** d) Swaps	1

V.	Define impact cost	1
Ans:-	Impact cost represents the cost of executing a transaction in a given stock, for a specific predefined order size, at any given point of time.	
VI.	—----------- Is an important intermediary between stock broker and client in capital market segment a) Dealer b) sub broker c) Exchange **d) None of the above**	1
	SECTION B: SUBJECTIVE TYPE QUESTIONS	
	Answer any 3 out of the given 5 questions on Employability Skills (2 x 3 = 6 marks) Answer each question in 20 – 30 words.	
Q6.	Write the procedure of Inserting clipart and images in presentation?	2
Ans:-	Open the slide you want to insert a picture on. On the Insert menu, point at Picture, and then select Photo Browser. In the dialog box that opens, browse to the picture that you want to insert, select that picture, and then drag it onto the slide.	
Q7.	Explain common personality disorder any three?	2
Ans:-	a) Paranoid Feeling extremely nervous and worried because you believe that other people do not like you or are trying to harm you. b) Antisocial Is characterized by a pattern of persistent disregard for and violation of the rights of others. c) Schizoid Is characterized by a lack of interest in social relationships and people tend to be distant, detached and indifferent. d) Borderline Is marked by an ongoing pattern of varying moods, self-image and behavior. These symptoms result in impulsive actions and problems in relationships.	

Q8.	How will you protect your worksheet or Calc document using the password?	2
Ans:-	1. Select Tools menu ➤ Protect document Choose whether to protect Sheet or Document. 2. If you select Sheet, the Protect Sheet dialog box appears If you select Document, the protect Document dialog box 3. Type the password in the Password text box. Again type the password in the Confirm text box. Note that the password is case sensitive. 4. Click the OK button.	

Q9.
Ans:-
	Explain the components of Calc Screen
	
	    a) Title bar: - title bar is located at the top of the tallet window. it display the name of the workbook on which your currently working
	
	    b) Menu bar: - the menu bar is located below the title bar. it has commands like file, Edit etc.
	
	    c) Standard bar:- This bar contains icons to provide quick access to commands such as new open, print, copy and paste
	
	    d) Formula bar:- it contains the name box and long white box, known as input line
		2

Q10. Ans:-	What happens if you write the formula =45/0 in cell A1? If you type the above formula the error message will come like #DIV/0 Because divide parameter cannot be zero	2
	Answer any 3 out of the given 5 questions in 20 – 30 words each (2 x 3 = 6 marks)	
Q12. Ans:-	What are the desirable attributes of index? a) It should capture the behavior of a large variety of different portfolios in the market. b) The stocks included in the index should be highly liquid. It should be professionally maintained.	2

	c) A single stock or a small group of stocks in the index should not move the index significantly. Otherwise, the shifts in other stocks will not be sufficiently captured in the index	
Q13.	How will you classify derivatives on the basis of underlying assets?	2

Type of Derivative	Underlying asset
Equity	Stock / Share
Index	Any broad-spectrum or sectorial index
Interest rate Debt instrument	Loans / asset backed securities
Currency Foreign Exchange Commodities	Any commodity

Q14.	Difference between the equity shareholder and preference shareholders?	2

Equity shareholders are supposed to be the owners of the company, who therefore have a right to get dividend, as declared and right to vote in the Annual General Meeting for passing any resolution.

The act define the preference share as that part of a share capital of the company which enjoy preferential rights as to

a) payment of dividend at fix rate during the lifetime of the company and

b) The return of capital on winding up of the company

But preference shares cannot be traded unlike equity shares and a redeem after a free decided period, also a preference shareholders do not have a voting right

Q15.	What are the special features of marketing inquiry?	2

This screen is not dynamically updated. It displays the security status of the security selected. 'S' indicates that the security is suspended, 'P'indicates that the security is in pre-open (only for normal market) and in absence of the above indicators the security is open for trading.

	The net change indicator for last trade price with respect to the previous day's closing price and the net change percentage for the last trade price with respect to the previous day's closing price are displayed.	
	If the base price is manually changed (due to a corporate action) then the market inquiry will not display the new base price in the closing price field.	
Q16.	Define Future value of money with the example?	2
	Future value is what a sum of money invested today will become over time at the rate of interest. For example the money you invest $1000 in saving account today at the rate ofa 2% annual rate it will be worth 1020 at the end of the one year, the future value is 102	
	Answer any 2 out of the given 3 questions in 30– 50 words each (3 x 2 = 6 marks)	
Q17. **Ans:-**	Explain the difference between industry analysis and financial analysis	3
	Industry analysis: companies producing similar products are a subset of an industry/ sector, for example National hydroelectric power company. National Thermal Power Company Limited. Tata Power Company Limited. belong to the power sector of India. It is very important to see how the industry to which the company belongs is fairing. Specific things like the effect of government policy, future demand of a product etc. Need to be checked. At a time prospects of an industry may change drastically by any alteration in the business environment	
	Financial analysis:- If performance of an industry as well as of the company seems good, then check if at the current price, the share is good to buy. For this look at the financial performance of the company in certain key financial parameters like Earning per share price of the equity future price, Current price of the equity etc. For arriving at an estimated future price. This is termed as a financial analysis	

Q18.	What do you mean by MBP and explain its features	3
Ans:-	The purpose of Market by Price (MBP) is to enable the user to view outstanding orders in the market aggregated at each price and are displayed in order of best prices.	
	Features :-	
	a) Regular lot & special term orders can be viewed in the MBP.	
	The percentage change for last trade price with respect to previous day's closing price, open price (in case of pre-open indicative opening price), high price for a day, low price a day and the average trade price of the security in the given market are the additional fields in the screen.	
	b) No un-triggered stop-loss order will be displayed on the MBP screen.	
	c) Only order details for the best 5 prices information is displayed.	
Q19.	When did equity derivative trading take place for the first time?	3
	Answer any 3 out of the given 5 questions in 50– 80 words each (4 x 3 = 12 marks)	
Q20.	If in the market there are two equilibrium prices i.e. where the principle of demand and supply matches. In that case which price will be considered as equilibrium price, if that price also does not meet the said criteria then which price will be considered as equilibrium price?	4
Ans:-	The opening price is determined based on the principle of demand supply mechanism. The equilibrium price is the price at which the maximum volume is executable. In case more than one price meets the said criteria, the equilibrium price is the price at which there is minimum unmatched order quantity. In case more than one price has same minimum order unmatched quantity, the equilibrium price is the price closest to the previous day's closing price. In case the previous day's closing	

	price is the mid-value pair of prices which are closest to it, then the previous day's closing price itself will be taken as the equilibrium price. In case of corporate action, the previous day's closing price is adjusted to the closing price or the base price. Both limit and market orders 53 are reckoned for computation of equilibrium price. The equilibrium price determined in pre-open session is considered as open price for the day. In case if only market orders exists both in the buy and sell side, then the order is matched at previous days close price or adjusted close price / base price. Previous day's close or adjusted close price / base price is the opening price. In case if no price is discovered in pre-open session, the price of first trade in the normal market is the open price	
Q21.	What do you mean by secured and unsecured loan? According 4 to you to run the corporate sector, which loan is beneficial for you and why? Secured loans are the borrowings against the security i.e. against mortgaging some immovable property or hypothecating/pledging some movable property of the company. This is known as creation of charge, which safeguards creditors in the event of any default on the part of the company. They are in the form of debentures, loans from financial institutions and loans from commercial banks. In case of getting loan the balance should be maintained while taking secured and unsecured loan Secured loan will protect our creditors in case of any default made by the company and on the other hand it will increase our credit rating in market So secured loan will be preferable in case of long term goodwill of the company	
Q22. Ans:-	Explain the formula with explanation 1) current ratio 2) Acid test ratio	

	The current ratio represents the firm's ability to meet the current liabilities from the current assets full stop higher the current ratio higher the firm's ability to meet the short term solvency. current ratio = current assets/current liabilities The acid-test ratio, commonly known as the quick ratio, uses data from a firm's balance sheet to indicate whether it has the means to cover its short-term liabilities. Formula Acid test ratio=Quick assets /quick liabilities Quick assets are defined as a Current assets excluding prepaid expenses Inventories. the quick acid ratio is the measurement of the forms ability to convert the current assets into the cash to meets its current liabilities	4
Q23. **Ans:-**	Take an example and explain which interest payment will be preferable for you Two types of interest rate is there one is simple interest and other is compound interest Simple interest refers to interest will be same on principle and cannot be accumulated and on the other hand the compound interest is interest which is accumulated in principle let's take a example Mr. X borrowed Rs. 5000 from the bank to purchase a household item. He agreed to repay the amount in 2 years, plus simple interest at an interest rate of 10% per annum (year). If he repays the full amount of Rs. 5000 the interest would be: P = Rs. 10,000 r = 0.10 (10% per year) interest rate will be 5000*10%*2 =1000 for two years Compound interest:- For example, if an amount of Rs. 5,000 is invested for two years and the interest rate is 10%, compounded yearly: At the end of the first year the interest would be (Rs. 5,000 * 0.10) or Rs. 500. In the second year the interest rate of 10% will applied not only to Rs. 5,000	4

	but also to the Rs. 500 interest of the first year. Thus, in the second year the interest would be (0.10 * Rs. 5,500) or Rs. 550. Total interest will be charged 500 550 =1050 From the above example it is clear that interest will be more in case of compound interest as compared to simple interest.	
Q24. **Ans:-**	If you want to deal in securities in which securities you want to invest in order to get higher return take risk management as an tool a) listed securities b) Unlisted securities In case of listed securities means these securities are governed by the stock exchange under the guidelines of SEBI In case of unlisted securities he securities are governed by OTC market where there is no any governance of SEBI So if the investor is having complaint under listed securities the investor can go to investor grievance cell to lodge complaints but in case of unlisted securities the customer is not having any type of this facility But under OTC market terms and conditions are settled bilaterally or multilaterally between the parties with the mutual consent. In that case counterparty risk is more	4

General Instructions:

1) Please read the instruction carefully

2) This question paper consist of 24 question in two section – Section A and Section B

3) Section A has objective type question whereas Section B contains Subjective type question

4) **Out of given (6+18=)24 question, a student has to answer (6+11=)17 question in the allotted time of 3 hours**

5) All questions of a particular section must be attempted in the correct order

6) SECTION A –OBJECTIVE TYPE QUESTION (30 MARKS)

I. This section has 06 question

II. There is no negative marking

III. Do as per instruction given

IV. Marks allotted are mentioned against each question/ part

7) SECTION B- SUBJECTIVE TYPE QUESTION (30 MARKS)

1) This section contain 18 question

2) A student has to do 11 question

3) Do as per instruction given

4) Marks allotted are mentioned against each question/ part

	SECTION A: OBJECTIVE TYPE QUESTIONS	
Q1.	Answer any 4 out of the given 6 questions on Employability Skills (1 x 4 = 4 marks)	
I.	It arises because of incentives or external rewards. a) Intrinsic motivation b) Extrinsic motivation c) Realistic Motivation d) Unrealistic Motivation	1
II.	If A1:A4 contains the number 11,13,15,17, the formula =AVERAGE(A1:A4) in cell A5 will display —————————————————————————————— a) 12 b) 14 c) 16 d) 18	1

III.	Personality traits are made up of ————————————— ————————————— characteristics	1
	a) Emotional	
	b) Behavioral	
	c) Mental	
	d) All of the above	
IV.	For protecting the document in MS excel _____ _____ menu from title bar we need to select	1
	a) File	
	b) View	
	c) Data	
	d) Tool	
V.	_____ is the personality disorder characterized by extreme perfectionism, order, and neatness	1
	a) Paranoid	
	b) Narcissistic	
	c) Obsessive	
	d) Paranoid	
VI.	What is the short cut key to close the MS Excel?	1
	a) Ctrl + F4	
	b) Ctrl + W	
	c) Ctrl + E	
	d) Ctrl + X	
Q2.	**Answer any 5 out of the given 7 questions (1 x 5 = 5 marks)**	
I.	_____ segment of NSE commenced its operation in November 1994	1
	a) Capital market segment	
	b) Future and option segment	
	c) Wholesale debt segment	
	d) Currency segment	

II.	To become member of NSE, the deposit requirement should be _ and a) Interest free security deposit and fixed deposit b) Collateral deposit and saving deposit c) Interest free security and collateral deposit d) Interest free security and pledged security	1
III.	Company producing similar products are subset of an sector are coming under a) Industry analysis b) Corporate analysis c) Market analysis d) Financial analysis	1
IV.	Earlier the trading cycle for stocks based on type of securities used to vary between—-------------------- a) T + 2 days b) T + 3 days c) 14 days to 30 days d) T + 5 days	1
V.	____ AD banks can become client member even though they have not follow the prudential requirement with the approval of __ a) Cooperative banks, SEBI b) Commercial banks, NSE c) State Cooperative Banks, RBI d) Union Cooperative Banks, NSCCL	1
VI.	Trading member doing business with an insolvent without obtain the consent of relevant authority, he will be coming under _____ a) Un-business like conduct b) Un-professional like conduct c) Misconduct d) Either a or b	1

VII.	Define Turnover ratio	1
Q3.	**Answer any 6 out of the given 7 questions (1 x 6 = 6 marks)**	
I.	Historically stock managed, owned and controlled by_ _____ a) NSE b) Trading member c) Broker d) SEBI	1
II.	In case more than one price will meet the said criteria the equilibrium price in the opening market will be, where there should be _____ a) Minimum unmatched order quantity b) Maximum matched order quantity c) Minimum matched order quantity d) Either a or b	1
III.	____ is the formal financial statement issued yearly by a corporate a) Balance sheet and profit and loss report b) Directors report c) Financial statement report d) Annual report	1
IV.	A valid combination of user ID, _____ _____ and password needed to access the NEAT system a) Trading member Id b) NSE ID c) Either a or b d) None of the above	1
V.	Define Gross fixed Asset?	1
VI.	—-------- is the part of authorized capital which is offered by the company for being subscribed by the members of the public a) Authorized capital b) Subscribed capital c) Issued capital d) Called up capital	1

VII.	Calculate the value of deposit 2000 made today if interest rate is 5%(Discrete compounding)	1
	a) 2662	
	b) 2316	
	c) 2300	
	d) 2362	
Q4.	**Answer any 5 out of the given 6 questions (1 x 5 = 5 marks)**	
I.	Public listed company making IPO of any security of— have to make IPO only in dematerialization form	1
	a) 10 crores or more	
	b) 50 crores or more	
	c) 20 crores or more	
	d) 25 crores or more	
II.	Trading member doing business with an insolvent without obtain consent of relevant authority, he will be coming under —	1
	a) Un business like conduct	
	b) Unprofessional like conduct	
	c) Misconduct	
	d) Either a or b	
III.	Interest coverage ratio =---------	1
	a) EBIT/interest	
	b) EBT/interest	
	c) EBI/interest	
	d) Earning /interest	
IV.	—------- investors are are with a anticipated and present exposure to the underlying asset which is subject to market risk	1
	a) Hedgers	
	b) Speculators	
	c) Arbitrageurs	
	d) Either a or b	

V.	Define current ratio	1
VI.	---------- is the default password provided by the exchange for the user a) Nse@cm1 b) Nse@12345678 c) Nse@123 d) Neat@123	1
Q5	**Answer any 5 out of the given 6 questions (1 x 5 = 5 marks)**	
I.	---------- future on interest rate were launched on National Stock Exchange a) 31st Aug, 2009 b) 30th Aug, 2000 c) 30th Aug, 2009 d) 31st Aug, 2000	1
II.	------------ displays the information all trades in the system as and when it takes place a) Title bar b) Ticker window c) Toolbar d) Message window	1
III.	---------- refers to ability of a firm to meet its financial obligation a) Debt b) Secured loan c) Liquidity d) Fixed asset	1
IV.	Define simple interest	1
V.	When the user tries to login in with wrong password a message — a) Invalid user b) Invalid password c) Invalid sign d) Client already sign on	1

VI.	A good index is tradeoff between _____ _____ and liquidity a) Diversification b) Price c) Stock d) Profit	1
Q6.	**Answer any 5 out of the given 6 questions (1 x 5 = 5 marks)**	
I.	_____ has an access to an nation-wide facility for equities, derivative, debt/ hybrid a) SEBI b) Trading Member c) NSE d) AP	1
II.	_____ features allow a trading member to get instantaneous market information a) Snap quote b) order/ trade window c) Message window d) Inquiry window	1
III.	Define return on capital employed	1

IV.	_____ index represents the change in the value of set of stocks which constitute the index a) Nifty b) Nifty 100 c) Stock d) Nifty stock	1
V.	_____ order will not be displayed on the MBP Screen a) Stop loss order b) Best 5 price order c) Un-triggered stop loss order d) Total buy or total sell order	1
VI.	A buy order with _____ price gets a higher priority a) Order having equilibrium price b) High price c) Low price d) Where minimum quantity is unmatched	1
	SECTION B: SUBJECTIVE TYPE QUESTIONS	
	Answer any 3 out of the given 5 questions on Employability Skills (2 x 3 = 6 marks) Answer each question in 20 – 30 words	
Q7.	How will you define self-management skill?	2
Q8.	What are the different methods of moving the cell content?	2
Q9.	What are the factors influencing personality?	2
Q10.	Explain the order of evaluation while applying mathematical operations in MS excel?	2
Q11.	What are the steps of sorting the data in ascending and descending order	2
	Answer any 3 out of the given 5 questions in 20 – 30	
	words each (2 x 3 = 6 marks)	
Q12.	Define swaps and explain its types?	2

Q13.	What is stop loss matching?	2
Q14.	What is the online Backup facility	2
Q15.	Explain the Auction market screen	2
Q16.	Explain the previous trade?	2
	Answer any 2 out of the given 3 questions in 30– 50 words each (3 x 2 = 6 marks)	
Q17.	What are the current liabilities and provision and net current Asset in Balance sheet	3
Q18.	What are the basic difference between forward, future and option contract	3
Q19.	What do you mean by MBP explain its features	3
	Answer any 3 out of the given 5 questions in 50– 80 words each (4 x 3 = 12 marks)	
Q20.	NEAT screen is divided into a number of bar and windows. If you want to a) Make the continuous monitoring of the screen b) To see information of all trades in the system as and when it takes place According to you in the above cases which window will help you and how?	4
Q21.	Explain the formula with explanation a) Asset-turnover ratio b) Debt-equity ratio c) Interest coverage ratio	4
Q22.	Explain with the table that membership can be taken individually or in combination	4
Q23.	Explain the matching priority with suitable example	4
Q24.	Mr. Akash needs to be appointed as a trading member, According to you what should be the net worth and other deposit requirement to become a member	4